BEATING THE WHEEL

The System That Has Won Over Six Million Dollars From Las Vegas to Monte Carlo

Biased-Wheel Play, Wheel-Watching Systems,
Electronics, Cheating Methods,
Mathematics, Anecdotes

by Russell T. Barnhart

A Lyle Stuart Book
Published by Carol Publishing Group

A Lyle Stuart Book
Published by Carol Publishing Group
Lyle Stuart is a registered trademark of Carol Communications, Inc.
Editorial Offices: 600 Madison Avenue, New York, NY 10022
Sales & Distribution Offices: 120 Enterprise Avenue, Secaucus, NJ 07094
In Canada: Canadian Manda Group, P.O. Box 920, Station U, Toronto,
Ontario, M8Z 5P9, Canada
Queries regarding rights and permissions should be addressed to:
Carol Publishing Group, 600 Madison Avenue, New York, NY 10022

Manufactured in the United States of America
ISBN 0-8184-0553-8

10 9 8 7 6 5 4 3 2

Carol Publishing Group books are available at special discounts
for bulk purchases, sales promotions, fund raising, or
educational purposes. Special editions can also be created to
specifications. For details contact: Special Sales Department,
Carol Publishing Group, 120 Enterprise Ave., Secaucus, NJ 07094

Contents

Roulette Wheel Parts

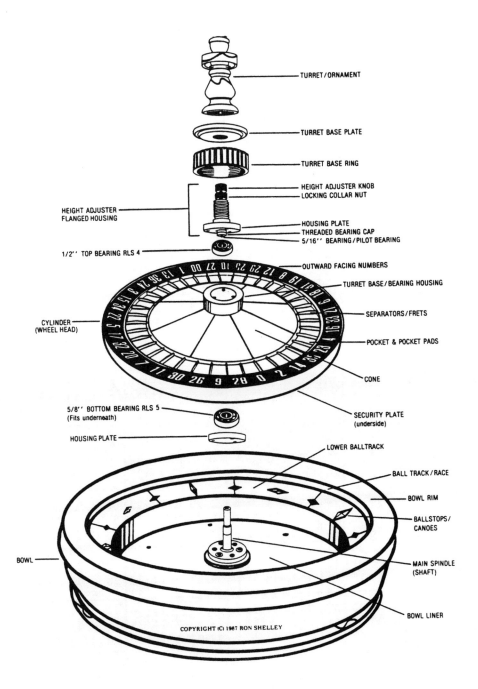

- TURRET/ORNAMENT
- TURRET BASE PLATE
- TURRET BASE RING
- HEIGHT ADJUSTER KNOB
- LOCKING COLLAR NUT
- HEIGHT ADJUSTER FLANGED HOUSING
- HOUSING PLATE
- THREADED BEARING CAP
- 5/16'' BEARING / PILOT BEARING
- 1/2'' TOP BEARING RLS 4
- OUTWARD FACING NUMBERS
- TURRET BASE / BEARING HOUSING
- CYLINDER (WHEEL HEAD)
- SEPARATORS / FRETS
- POCKET & POCKET PADS
- CONE
- 5/8'' BOTTOM BEARING RLS 5 (Fits underneath)
- SECURITY PLATE (underside)
- HOUSING PLATE
- LOWER BALLTRACK
- BALL TRACK / RACE
- BOWL RIM
- BALLSTOPS / CANOES
- BOWL
- MAIN SPINDLE (SHAFT)
- BOWL LINER

TABLE OF NEIGHBORS

Single Zero Wheel									
12	35	3	26	**0**	32	15	19	4	
5	24	16	33	**1**	20	14	31	9	
15	19	4	21	**2**	25	17	34	6	
7	28	12	35	**3**	26	0	32	15	
0	32	15	19	**4**	21	2	25	17	
30	8	23	10	**5**	24	16	33	1	
2	25	17	34	**6**	27	13	36	11	
9	22	18	29	**7**	28	12	35	3	
13	36	11	30	**8**	23	10	5	24	
1	20	14	31	**9**	22	18	29	7	
11	30	8	23	**10**	5	24	16	33	
6	27	13	36	**11**	30	8	23	10	
18	29	7	28	**12**	35	3	26	0	
17	34	6	27	**13**	36	11	30	8	
16	33	1	20	**14**	31	9	22	18	
3	26	0	32	**15**	19	4	21	2	
23	10	5	24	**16**	33	1	20	14	
4	21	2	25	**17**	34	6	27	13	
14	31	9	22	**18**	29	7	28	12	
26	0	32	15	**19**	4	21	2	25	
24	16	33	1	**20**	14	31	9	22	
32	15	19	4	**21**	2	25	17	34	
20	14	31	9	**22**	18	29	7	28	
36	11	30	8	**23**	10	5	24	16	
8	23	10	5	**24**	16	33	1	20	
19	4	21	2	**25**	17	34	6	27	
28	12	35	3	**26**	0	32	15	19	
25	17	34	6	**27**	13	36	11	30	
22	18	29	7	**28**	12	35	3	26	
31	9	22	18	**29**	7	28	12	35	
27	13	36	11	**30**	8	23	10	5	
33	1	20	14	**31**	9	22	18	29	
35	3	26	0	**32**	15	19	4	21	
10	5	24	16	**33**	1	20	14	31	
21	2	25	17	**34**	6	27	13	36	
29	7	28	12	**35**	3	26	0	32	
34	6	27	13	**36**	11	30	8	23	

Double Zero Wheel									
30	26	9	28	**0**	2	14	35	23	
29	25	10	27	**00**	1	13	36	24	
25	10	27	00	**1**	13	36	24	3	
26	9	28	0	**2**	14	35	23	4	
1	13	36	24	**3**	5	34	22	5	
2	14	35	23	**4**	16	33	21	6	
3	15	34	22	**5**	17	32	20	7	
4	16	33	21	**6**	18	31	19	8	
5	17	32	20	**7**	11	30	26	9	
6	18	31	19	**8**	12	29	25	10	
7	11	30	26	**9**	28	0	2	14	
8	12	29	25	**10**	27	00	1	13	
17	32	20	7	**11**	30	26	9	28	
18	31	19	8	**12**	29	25	10	27	
10	27	00	1	**13**	36	24	3	15	
9	28	0	2	**14**	35	23	4	16	
13	36	24	3	**15**	34	22	5	17	
14	35	23	4	**16**	33	21	6	18	
15	34	22	5	**17**	32	20	7	11	
16	33	21	6	**18**	31	19	8	12	
21	6	18	31	**19**	8	12	29	25	
22	5	17	32	**20**	7	11	30	26	
23	4	16	33	**21**	6	18	31	19	
24	3	15	34	**22**	5	17	32	20	
0	2	14	35	**23**	4	16	33	21	
00	1	13	36	**24**	3	15	34	22	
19	8	12	29	**25**	10	27	00	1	
20	7	11	30	**26**	9	28	0	2	
12	29	25	10	**27**	00	1	13	36	
11	30	26	9	**28**	0	2	14	35	
31	19	8	12	**29**	25	10	27	00	
32	20	7	11	**30**	26	9	28	0	
33	21	6	18	**31**	19	8	12	29	
34	22	5	17	**32**	20	7	11	30	
35	23	4	16	**33**	21	6	18	31	
36	24	3	15	**34**	22	5	17	32	
28	0	2	14	**35**	23	4	16	33	
27	00	1	13	**36**	24	3	15	34	

Introduction

Roulette is the third most popular casino table game in the United States and, worldwide, the most popular table game of all. At last count there were 170 roulette wheels in Las Vegas, 155 in Atlantic City, 300 in Great Britain, and 1,500 in Europe.

Can roulette be beaten except by luck? The answer is definitely yes, and in Table 7 (p. 109) I list the Honor Roll of some of the most successful *biased-wheel* system players, who have so far won individually $500,000 in Monte Carlo, $1 million in Las Vegas, and $4 million in Atlantic City.

This is a how-to book, and the biased-wheel system is simple to understand and use. As there is no such thing as a physically perfect roulette wheel, the biased-wheel player may detect mechanical defects by conventionally writing down the numbers as they come up on one ordinary wheel after another until encountering a wheel in which certain numbers keep occurring above average over and over again. This process is called clocking the wheel. Every casino daily uses and discards quantities of dice and cards, but with a roulette wheel costing today as much as an automobile, no casino can afford to discard such an expensive piece of equipment until it has provided years of service— during which period, on a minority of wheels, the unavoidable wear and tear of play will cause significant defects easily exploitable by a player who takes the trouble to look for them. Such, for casinos, is their Achilles heel—the inevitable fatal weaknesses in their equipment—on which the biased-wheel system is based.

The first half of this book is devoted to the crucial experiences of those successful players who have made the Honor Roll of biased-wheel players. Although we all love success stories, that isn't the main purpose of my initial ten chapters, which is to teach the system through a variety of examples: how long these players spent clocking their wheels, whether they bet on one number or on several separated from one another on the wheel or grouped together in a section, whether they adopted a proportional staking system or stuck to flat bets, and—of great importance—how they thwarted secret casino countermeasures such as the casino's rotating the whole roulette bowl a partial turn at the same table; its switching the biased wheel for a random one; its renumbering all the pockets on the biased wheel by rotating the metal, single-ring unit of numbers; and finally its use of the ultimate countermeasure: barring the player simply because he had won too much money too frequently.

The second half of this book explains mainly how to detect a biased number in a sample of clocked roulette spins using only arithmetic. Essentially all we're doing is handicapping a roulette wheel instead of a horse, and to avoid mathematical theory I illustrate my points by using authentic samples of roulette spins: from Monte Carlo a sample of 46,000 spins (three continuous months); from Wiesbaden one of 4,000 spins (two continuous weeks); and from Las Vegas a week each of 3,000 spins from the El Cortez Casino and 5,000 from the Royal Inn Casino.

Casinos don't give away money free, and to beat them we must cultivate knowledge, competence, patience, and leaven our casino experience with a sense of humor.

Russell T. Barnhart

Chapter 1

Criminal Systems

Vladimir Granec

Who is Vladimir Granec, and what has he done?

At first neither Interpol nor the European gaming police (especially those in France and Germany) knew, and accordingly didn't inform the public.

The first persons to realize that something was wrong in the gaming world were certain casino directors themselves, who, so far as roulette was concerned, were beginning to bleed to death. Starting in 1975, complaints began coming in from casino directors as far away as Latin America and Africa, as well as closer by in eastern Europe, in Split and Zagreb, Yugoslavia.

In France inexplicable roulette losses were registered along the Riviera at the Municipal Casino in Cannes, the La Siesta Casino at Antibes, the Juan-les-Pins Casino, the Ruhl Casino at Nice, and the Municipal Casino at Menton. From the French hinterland similar roulette losses were sustained by casinos at Saint-Amand-les-Eaux, La Grande-Motte, Megève, Evian-les-Bains, Vittel, Niederbronn, Sainte-Maxime, and Divonne-les-Bains, the last, near Lake Geneva, the largest casino in France.

As the above places show, one reason the gaming police took years to solve this case was that the roulette mob kept moving not only from

1

casino to casino, in one country after another, but from continent to continent.

In France alone the seriousness of the situation was brought home by Lucien Barrière, director of the Municipal Casino in Cannes and its subsidiary, La Siesta, in nearby Antibes, when on Tuesday, August 10, 1978, he announced at a meeting of shocked shareholders that instead of the expected annual profit a deficit for the year of $3,200,000 existed, an amount lost to a team of mysterious gamblers betting at roulette.

When roulette losses from all the French casinos were brought in and added up, the French gaming police found that the winnings of the mysterious roving band came to more than $6 million, the largest sum lost to roulette in casino history.

Eastward down the Riviera coast the Monte Carlo Casino itself first became aware that defective wheels could be exploited for bias and other peculiarities as early as the sensational raid of an English mechanical engineer named Joseph Jaggers, who in 1873 hired six assistants to note down, for five weeks, the winning numbers at six roulette wheels. At the end of that time, betting on the winning numbers caused by bias, Jaggers played one particular wheel and left Monte Carlo with $325,000—a sum today worth at least ten times that amount.

To detect and exploit biased roulette wheels is, of course, not cheating at all but fair game for gamblers, who rightly assume that it is the casino's responsibility to maintain its paraphernalia in excellent technical condition.

On the other hand, to *cause* a roulette wheel to be biased certainly is cheating, and at the Monte Carlo Casino alone, over many decades, there have been at least three cases of such criminality.

The first incident took place in the late 1890s, but its explanation wasn't revealed to the public or even to the casino until 1926 by the Honorable S. R. Beresford, a longtime Monte Carlo resident and gambler who happened to know one of the conspirators.

"The principals in this ingenious but perverted scheme to rob the Bank," wrote Beresford, "were a well-known habitué and an expert mechanic. The latter, although never in the employ of the [Casino] Administration, managed not only to 'fix' two cylinders but to unfix them when their day's work was done. I do not believe that any [Casino] employee knew anything at all about the matter, nor that there was one amongst them who knew that anything unusual had taken place.

"There is an even more astonishing fact connected with this occurrence—for the authorities themselves had, and to this day have, no knowledge of [how] the trick...was engineered!

"How access to the [roulette] machines was obtained must remain a mystery, but it was stage managed by a long concocted scheme. Upon one cylinder the partitions for three pockets upon either side of number 20 were slightly loosened [thus favoring the seven neighboring numbers 9-31-14-20-1-33-16], upon the other, one whole side of the board was manipulated. All the partitions between the numbers 9 and 34, with 10 as the central number, were loosened sufficiently to soften the impact of the ball [on these 17 neighboring numbers]. The croupiers, whoever's turn it happened to be to spin, did everything in their power to defeat what appeared to them to be an abnormally lucky player. Their efforts to do so only made the results for the player more certain. I must give the reason for this somewhat strange effect.

"In their endeavor to change the luck, or the run of the game, whichever one may please to call it, they whirled the cylinder at an excessively high speed. The consequence was that the ball was compelled to the line of least resistance, for the faster the rotation, the greater became the effect of its contact with the partitions that were firmly fixed. Upon the other hand, contact with the partitions that had been loosened caused little or no rebound, with the result that they provided their intermediate pockets with an easier resting place.

"That a very large sum was won I have no doubt, nor was suspicion in any way aroused, for the whole operation was carried out with keen discretion.... Every cylinder has some distinctive marking, so that there need have been no difficulty in locating the two wheels that had been manipulated.

"It must not be thought that a ball would spend its whole day between the partitions that provided the least resistance; at the same time, its visits would be greatly in excess of normal—sufficient, at least, for the unworthy purpose!

"The operation that I have described provides the most sensational incident ever connected with play at Monte Carlo. The chief conspirator is a member of more than one well-known English club and a very old man now. Should he read these lines by any possible chance, he may rest assured that his secret dies when he himself departs."

The second cheating incident of this type took place a few years later and was reported by Basil Woon, an American writer and habitué of the Monte Carlo Casino.

"Many years ago," wrote Woon in 1929, "some additional tables were [put up] in one of the gaming rooms, and an expert workman employed noted that to give one of the tables the necessary exact aplomb a tiny wedge was necessary. As a rule such wedges, like those on championship billiard tables, are joined into the wood of the base of the table in such a way that they cannot be moved. This workman contrived that the wedge should work loose, and one day, unobserved, quietly removed it.

"He then hired a man to visit the casino every day and take turns with him watching the wheel of this particular table. He wanted to see what influence the removal of the tiny wedge would have. At the end of a week number 19 had come up 42 times more than number 33 on the opposite side of the wheel, and numbers 32, 15, 4, 21, and 0, all neighboring number 19, had also appeared with suspicious frequence.

"He waited a few days more and then, certain of his premises, approached a Russian living in Nice and told him the secret. The Russian tested the man's information, found it correct, and began to play maximums accordingly. He covered 19 and 0 *en plein* [straight up], the second and third columns, which included numbers 15 and 21, the first *carré* [corner bet], covering 4, and the last carré, covering 32.

"Within two hours the bank had been broken twice, the croupiers changed five times, and the director of the games was on hand, watching anxiously.

"When the bank was broken a third time and the Russian was ahead 90,000 francs [$18,000], the director consulted with his assistants, and it was decided to allow the table to continue. Within 20 minutes the bank had been broken a fourth time, and the Russian had won nearly 150,000 francs [$30,000]. He had started with 5,000 francs [$1,000].

"When this happened, the table was covered, and a rule was made that no table could 'go broke' more than thrice in any one evening. It was several days, however, before experts discovered what the matter was, and by this time the Russian and a partner who had come on the second day had accumulated nearly 1,000,000 francs. At that time this was nearly $200,000.

"Years afterward the story came out by the confession of the workman, who had become a property owner in Monte Carlo. Over too much wine he confided in a friend, was overheard, and the next day summoned by the casino management. What steps were taken were not divulged, but the workman left Monte Carlo, never to return. The Russian had long since vanished.

"Since then, elaborate precautions have been taken to prevent any interference with the tables. Every table is tested [by a spirit level] before and after play, and only workmen of proven honorability are permitted in the casino."

Alas, that these last words were always true. As recently as February 1979, a Monte Carlo Casino roulette wheel repairman or mechanic, Giles Charpentier, aided by two illicit assistants, was found to have manipulated two roulette wheels, and all three men were tried, convicted, and jailed for a year in the Principality of Monaco. An elegant adjunct of the Monte Carlo Casino, the International Sporting Club was open in the wintertime on Friday nights for gala dining and gambling, and it was on the Sporting Club's second floor, after the gambling had closed, that Charpentier biased two wheels by surreptitiously inserting thin rubber strips, called *bouncers* in the cheating trade, into the odd-numbered slots, thereby making the ball bounce out of them and into the even numbers.

Given the long tradition, therefore, of biased wheels detected by honest men like Jaggers in 1873, and biased wheels caused by dishonest men like Charpentier in 1979, to solve the gargantuan loss of $6 million by the mysterious roulette team in the late 1970s and early 1980s, the French gaming police carefully examined the wheels in many of the casinos heretofore listed for both bias and bouncers and found absolutely nothing wrong. Meantime, numerous other casinos continued to sustain heavy losses from roulette. Obviously there was a crisis at hand. Perhaps the gaming police were haunted by the words of Albert Einstein, who once remarked, "No one can possibly win at roulette unless he steals money from the table while the croupier isn't looking."

For the gaming police the case was partially broken by an odd stroke of luck that occurred in a London casino. Evidently confident that nobody could possibly hide himself anywhere on the premises before closing time—or break into their casino after closing time—the management never bothered to turn on the security monitors that surveyed both their gaming rooms and equipment. As chance would have it, on a very early morning one of the infrared cameras turned itself on by mistake and, in the dark, filmed a number of unknown men who had removed a roulette cylinder from its wooden bowl and were tampering with its slots.

Given the clue that something might be mechanically wrong with the slots of the losing roulette wheels after all, in 1978, under orders from their Paris director, Roger Saunier (who had personally spent time disconsolately wandering the Riviera's casinos incognito observing various suspects at play), the French gaming police, headed by Deputy Director Roger Lanfranchi, borrowed one of the losing wheels from the La Siesta Casino in Antibes. It was a wheel which had caused its nearby owner, the Municipal Casino in Cannes, to lose $3,200,000 to the mysterious gaming team.

Spinning a ball around the turning wheel for many thousands of spins, the gaming police found that certain slots were indeed favored far more than chance prescribed. Bearing in mind the London break-in, one of the gaming police removed the two small screws that hold fast the metal frets or walls of the winning slots or pockets to the bottom of the wheel head and, under a magnifying glass, compared these tiny screws with those of the losing slots. He found that the threads of the two screws belonging to the winning pockets were slightly thinner than those of the original screws, for which they had been surreptitiously substituted. The result was to loosen and thus favor ever so slightly the frets of these winning pockets, because the ball would bounce away from them with less resilience than from the neighboring losing pockets, whose frets were screwed tight. Lanfranchi concluded that, compared to bouncers, this fraud was the quintessence of subtlety.

But to substitute the illegal for the legal screws on even a single wheel would require considerable time and effort. Were the perpetrators of this fraud hiding people in casinos at night, as had been the case in London? So many casinos had lost money, yet it seemed impossible that all of them could have been broken into from the outside after closing time or had roulette wheel repairmen on the inside who had been bribed. Ultimately the gaming police concluded that it was a combination of the two: some casinos had been broken into, or had been able to hide miscreants until after closing time; others had harbored bribed repairmen.

But was there any other solution?

Through five long years—from 1979 to 1981—the gaming police had been shadowing any players suspected of being members of the international gang.

On October 29, 1981, by Director Roger Saunier's command, the French gaming police arrested in Paris Paul-Henri Thévenin, a 43-year-old man who had been employed for years at a Paris firm specializing in the manufacture of roulette wheels and, for casinos all over Europe, the refurbishment of old ones. The police placed Thévenin in a jail in Nice on a general charge of corruption, which they refused to clarify further, but reports circulated openly that he was directly connected to the international gang of roulette swindlers. The examining magistrate, Jean-Yves Montfort, charged Thévenin specifically in relation to a roulette wheel in the Palm Beach Casino in nearby Cannes, a wheel the gaming police found to contain frets fastened with the nefarious screws with thinner threads. Before showing Thévenin how the Palm Beach wheel was tricked, they asked him to examine it carefully in their presence and disclose if there was anything wrong with it. After the repairman had given the wheel a detailed examination, he declared there was nothing wrong with it. Then the police exposed the trick screws and accused him of lying. In only two years the gang had thereby swindled the Palm Beach Casino alone of more than $4,000,000.

Prior to Thévenin's capture and detention, on January 2, 1978, Judge Montfort had put behind bars in Grasse, the judiciary seat near Cannes, a Czechoslovakian named Boshuslav Pasterjik, a resident of Munich, Germany, whom Montfort accused of complicity in the whole roulette conspiracy. After four months in jail, Pasterjik was released on bail, however, because the police had been able to get out of him little more than that a certain employer had paid him to write down the winning numbers of a roulette wheel in the Municipal Casino in Cannes. And what law was there against that? asked Pasterjik. Don't many roulette players commonly do this preparatory to placing their bets?

Needless to say, before releasing Pasterjik in 1978, who was obviously only small fry, and before releasing Thévenin later on, the gaming police in the privacy of their interrogation rooms on the French Riviera grilled both of these men with the same question: who was their employer, the brains behind the whole conspiracy?

Thus, after years, the gaming police were finally led to a smiling, affable, 200-pound, elegantly dressed gentleman named Vladimir Granec, subsequently nicknamed the King of Roulette and Goldfinger. Like Pasterjik, he was another Czechoslovakian national residing in Munich. Looking into Granec's past, the police found that he had fled Czechoslovakia after World War II, was second in command of the Czechoslovak Department of Radio Free Europe in Munich, was now running a real estate firm, and until 1974 had owned casinos in England and Yugoslavia.

Fully aware of their French colleagues' five years of frustration ending only in the disclosure of the trick screws and a few trivial convictions, the German police shadowed Vladimir Granec carefully in order to gather evidence that would stand up in their own courts.

In March 1980 they made their first overt move, raiding the King of Roulette's villa in Grunwald, a Munich suburb. There they found 260 frets (pocket walls) thinner than the regulation type, glue used around screws, a pair of long tweezers, and two roulette wheels. When asked to explain himself, Granec said that since his past ownership of casinos in England and Yugoslavia he had always maintained an interest in gaming equipment.

In addition, the police found a notebook containing, first, information about four roulette wheels in the Bad Wiessee Casino in Upper Bavaria. (When the director of that casino examined the four wheels in question, he found them to contain a number of thinner frets, whose looseness dulled the rebound of the roulette ball, increasing their win by about 20%, according to the prosecutor at Granec's subsequent trial.) Second, Granec's gaming account from August 1977 to February 1980, showing that opposite a loss, in deutsche marks, of $300,000 was an enormous win of $3,500,000. Third, this mysterious formula: L, $^{2}16^{2}$, 2, 25. (At Granec's trial the prosecutor interpreted the formula to mean that whenever the croupier spun the wheel to the left, signified by L, an accomplice was to bet on the numbers in one section, 25 and 2; and, in the opposite section, number 16 and the two numbers on either side of 16.) Fourth, very detailed notes on a roulette wheel in the Bad Bentheim Casino far to the northwest near the Netherlands. (When the police examined the Bentheim wheel, the frets indicated in the notebook were found to have been loosened and treated with glue.) And fifth, a list of some of Granec's accomplices.

In September 1984 the German police finally arrested the sixty-three-year-old King of Roulette himself and hauled him before the Federal Criminal Court in Munich, accusing him of swindling the Bad Wiessee Casino in Upper Bavaria out of $3,500,000 between 1977 and 1980 from having tampered with the roulette wheels. (For a while Hans Wenta, the 58-year-old German supervisor of gaming equipment at the Bad Wiessee Casino, was also detained. He was accused of having let into the casino after hours either Granec or one of his accomplices to gimmick the wheels, but for lack of evidence Wenta was let go.) After a ten-month trial, however, none of the accusations of fraud held up in court, and Goldfinger was released.

By this time Vladimir Granec had become, in the minds of many roulette players, a folk hero who had beaten *the* system with his *own* system and they hailed the verdict of innocence.

Furious, the German police again brought Vladimir Granec to trial in

Munich in September 1986, but this time the King of Roulette outfoxed the police by magnanimously revealing his roulette system and challenging them to point out wherein lay any fraud.

All he had done at Bad Wiessee, explained the smiling, plump, roulette multimillionaire, was to record by himself—or have recorded by one of his colleagues—the flaws in biased roulette wheels. How did he know which wheels were biased? As soon as a number occurred 10% more frequently than the others, he explained, then he would begin betting on it. And besides, perhaps the wheels *weren't* biased after all. Perhaps he was winning merely by luck. How could they *prove* he hadn't been winning by luck? Listening to Vladimir Granec, the Munich judges were nonplussed. Finding his reasoning ultimately unanswerable, they again threw the case out of court.

Although victorious and more popular than ever with gamblers, Vladimir Granec, the King of Roulette, alias Goldfinger, wasn't really having all that great a time in life. First of all, pending investigations, he had to spend several months in jail. It affected his emotional and physical health, he suffered two heart attacks, and even underwent a coronary bypass operation.

Throwing up their hands, the German police gave up on their case concerning the Bad Wiessee Casino and handed the so-called international gaming conspiracy back to the French gaming police.

In June 1987, marshaling their own body of evidence, the French judges in Grasse came grimly to the very opposite verdict of their German counterparts.

First, the French judges issued innumerable international arrest warrants—a somewhat impotent gesture, inasmuch as the roving team of roulette players had long ago decamped from France and were now nowhere to be found.

Second, the French judges summarized the ingenious workings of Vladimir Granec's organized system of plunder. First, somehow or other, a roulette wheel was always secretly got at and gimmicked. Second, a few accomplishes would sit at that roulette wheel and, over an adequate period of time, note the numbers appearing more frequently than prescribed by the law of averages. Third, still another team of accomplices would replace the first group and begin betting, with money supplied by Granec, on the indicated numbers. And finally a last team, who were trusted bagmen, would collect the bettors' winnings and spirit it back to the King of Roulette outside Munich.

Then the judges issued their verdict for those members of the roulette team who, though convicted, were absent from court. Among these accomplices were Richard Aeschacch, Herbert Hollriegel, Ivan Kersnic, Milan Kubes, Adolf Kypena, Fritz Mielnikowiez, and Boshuslav Pasterjik (the latter the small fry jailed in Grasse in 1978). How seriously the French judges considered the Granec case is indicated by the severity of their sentence for one of Granec's most trusted lieutenants, Richard Aeschacch: three years in prison and a fine, in francs, equal to $165,000. For each of the other six accomplices the judges pronounced a sentence of three years in prison and a fine of $85,000.

Then the judges turned to the only three members of the nefarious roulette team whom the French gaming police had been able to locate, arrest, and bring into court to stand trial in Grasse. These three individuals were Mr. and Mrs. Stepanek Schonrock, resident in Düsseldorf, Germany, and Madame Mannah Wieczorek, a Polish national resident in Switzerland.

Before the judges the prisoners' defense had been simple. All three admitted readily to playing not only for Vladimir Granec but with his money in exchange for from 2% to 20% of their winnings, but they knew nothing whatever about the roulette wheels being gimmicked. They had sincerely believed, they emphasized, that Vladimir Granec had finally discovered a miraculous roulette system whose workings he understandably wanted to keep secret. The judges disbelieved them and sentenced Mr. and Mrs. Schonrock to three years in prison (thirty months of which were suspended) and, on each, levied a suspended fine of $50,000. To Mannah Wieczorek they gave a suspended sentence of one year in jail and a fine of $85,000.

But in the end, what of the absent Vladimir Granec himself? What of the mastermind—of Goldfinger, the King of Roulette? For him the French judges pronounced the harshest sentence of all: five years in jail and a fine of $500,000.

Today, however, ensconced in his comfortable villa outside Munich, the King of Roulette knows that, with his gross international winnings estimated at over $10 million, he has the dubious distinction of going down in gambling history as the largest winner at roulette on record.

Chapter 2

Wheel Watchers

William Nelson Darnborough, Edward O. Thorp and Claude Shannon, Thomas A. Bass and James Doyne Farmer, and Laurance Scott

One of the most spectacular and popular gamblers at Monte Carlo was a handsome young American named William Nelson Darnborough from Bloomington, Illinois. How he beat roulette at Monte Carlo from 1904 to 1911 has always been a well-kept secret.

For a description of Darnborough's extraordinary accomplishment we turn again to the memoirs of the Honorable S. R. Beresford, who was a personal acquaintance.

"An American named Darnborough," wrote Beresford, "enriched himself to the extent of 83,000 pounds [$415,000] from the Monte Carlo Casino alone....He undoubtedly broke all records for continuous gain, for every shilling of his money was won upon the numbers at roulette.

"Mr. Darnborough was probably the most remarkable man, so far as gambling is concerned, that ever passed into the casino at Monte Carlo. Never before or since have such masses of gold and notes been heaped upon a roulette table. The most astonishing feature of his operations was the lightning speed with which he placed his stakes. He would commence to stake his money when the croupier commenced to spin,

11

continuing to dab the board with piles of money.... His masses in reserve encroached on the board itself.

"It was truly wonderful to watch him ambidextrously at work; one hand would have been altogether insufficient for his purpose so both hands were engaged at lightning speed in shoveling from the reserves to the section of operation.

"When Darnborough was playing, it was rare indeed to see another stake upon his side of the table; he invariably...monopolized the board.... Since it would have been obviously impossible for him to have counted out the correct amount for every maximum stake, the confusion at times was very real. After every spin, whether it might have been successful or otherwise, there were always many stakes that had to be readjusted; the time taken up by this readjustment may easily be imagined!

"A table at which this king of all roulette players was playing would rarely exceed 10 or 12 spins an hour; the inconvenience to others was therefore, of course, intense; at the same time the majority were well content to sit and watch an expert demonstration of how to play roulette in maximums.

"There were many intense and dramatic moments when this high play was on. Upon one occasion the ivory ball rode round and round the ledge, as it sometimes will do, strangely refusing to drop into any of the partitioned spaces. It is a rule of play that if the cylinder should cease rotation, or in other words come to a standstill whilst the ball is on this ledge, that the spin shall be annulled: it is left to the gaming supervisor to decide the moment at which the cylinder actually comes to rest. The croupier who has put the ball into motion will then cry out, 'All bets are off'; at the same time picking up the ball and replacing it in the numbered pocket into which it last fell.

"It was upon the occasion of one of Darnborough's heaviest bets that the ball took it into its head to loll upon the ledge above the numbered pockets. Now the cylinder upon such occasions revolves for some time at a speed greater than the ball itself, one reason being that the ball frequently contracts a slight wobble; there is also a more scientific explanation.

"Upon the occasion in question the section containing Darnborough's winning number passed and repassed the ivory ball constantly. At times it appeared as though the ball must become dislodged; each time, however, that it approached the brink it managed to recover itself, and the crazy performance was continued.

"A great number of players from all parts of the casino, hearing the shouts and laughter of those already witnessing an unusual excitement, were rushing to see what had occurred, when—plonk!—the little ball fell into 29! At the moment of falling, the ball was traveling faster than the fast-moving cylinder; it was in fact chasing the one number that Darnborough most desired!

"The strain of playing upon this immense scale was undoubtedly very great. Mr. Darnborough occasionally, therefore, spent a few days of rest at the La Turbie Hotel [in the French Alps overlooking Monte Carlo]. Of many sensational players he was beyond comparison the most sensational.

"It may be added that Mr. Darnborough left the game when at his zenith as a winner and has never returned to the scenes of his amazing triumphs. Modest and unassuming, he left a host of friends when he retired from Monte Carlo in order to return to the [English] country life he loved."

So much for William Nelson Darnborough's period of play at Monte Carlo from 1904 to 1911. Although the young American was not the only gambler who has exploited the secret system in question, he was undoubtedly its most spectacular exponent and received the most publicity. To quote a Reuter's dispatch for December 14, 1910, in both the London *Daily Express* and the London *Evening Telegraph*: "Mr. Darnborough leaves Monte Carlo for London today with winnings of 64,000 pounds [$320,000] from one month's stay. He began with a capital of 1,200 pounds [$6,000]. He won up to 93,000 pounds at his peak. He won from 12,000 to 16,000 pounds a day. He left feeling his luck was at an end."

But, of course, as a few observers of the time suspected, luck had nothing to do with Darnborough's success—or the success of other players who have independently conceived of the same system and put it into quieter, more prudent operation. This method is called the *wheel-watcher* system.

One of the few people who ever succeeded in finding out how the wheel-watcher system works was a French civil engineer, writer, and lecturer named Gaston Vessillier. Whether Vessillier ever witnessed Darnborough actually gamble I don't know, but the civil engineer was so obsessed with uncovering Darnborough's secret that, in his spare time, in Paris and Monte Carlo, he frequented the haunts of gamblers, quietly buttonholing casino habitués and plying them with questions. It took him years, because the few cognoscenti naturally didn't want their successful system made public.

So after years of research this is what Vessillier discovered:

"This system," he wrote in 1924, "is based on the bettor's glancing, sufficiently ahead of time, at the speeds of the rotating ball and wheel relative to each other, and at the relative position of the ball to the target numbers on the moving wheel. The practitioners of the wheel-watcher system claim that, after first determining these mechanical conditions, they may then calculate the mean or average of the points of fall of the ball into the numbers just as artillerymen calculate the trajectory of a shell onto a designated surface.

"As soon as the wheel watchers finish their calculations, they bet immediately not only on the individual target numbers themselves but also on the corresponding even chances, all of which represent the artilleryman's designated surface, and the bettors naturally hope that the ball will fall into one of the predicted pockets.

"According to the practitioners of the system, although they lose more frequently than they win, when they do win, their gains outweigh their losses.

"When I asked various wheel watchers precisely how they glance at and assimilate the mechanical conditions of the roulette wheel, each claimed his own personal approach.

"In general they adopt a reference point past which both the ball circles going one way and the wheel circles going the other. Then, during the time of only one, two, or three spins, they calculate from the differences of the two revolutions, or even from the coincidence of their revolutions, the precise moment when the relative speeds of the two objects in motion will give an accurate indication of the target sector into which, on average, the ball will fall among the 37 different numbers.

"As soon as their appraising glance at the two objects in motion has provided them with the necessary information, the bettors hurriedly make their bets on the layout, for they have at most only two, three, or four seconds between the last spin when they made their calculation and the moment when the croupier calls 'No more bets.'

"Because of this paucity of time, users of the system must have one or more confederates make the actual bets—confederates to whom the wheel watchers give a covert, prearranged signal as soon as their calculations are made.

"In addition, it should be noted that, because the relative positions of the circling wheel and ball will not always fulfill the conditions necessary to an accurate prediction, the wheel watchers and their confederates may not play every spin."

The secret of Darnborough's success—and that of any wheel

watcher—is contained in Vessillier's penultimate paragraph: "...users of the system must have one or more confederates make the actual bets— confederates to whom the wheel watchers give a covert, prearranged signal as soon as their calculations are made."

Obviously Darnborough was the overt confederate making the bets to whom the secret partner, the wheel watcher, was making the covert, prearranged signal. In order to reach all 37 numbers while, with both hands, he rapidly shoveled his many wagers out onto the layout, Darnborough always stood in the middle of the long side of the table, with his left shoulder toward the roulette wheel.

But where was the wheel watcher himself, the silent partner who was to make the signal? No one today knows this man's name, but he would station himself unobtrusively among the crowd of gasping onlookers and pretend to share their enthusiasm for Darnborough's success. This partner always stood on the other side of the table from Darnborough but never exactly opposite. Instead he would stand innocently near the wheel behind the croupiers, glance down at the spinning ball and inversely rotating wheel, and make his calculations as to which quarter of the wheel the ball would probably fall into. Then just before the croupier intoned "No more bets," Darnborough would covertly and quickly glance diagonally leftward across the roulette wheel to perceive the signal (which involved the position of his partner's hands) and place his largest bets onto those numbers in the indicated quarter.

Such was the sensational application of the wheel-watcher system from 1904 to 1911 by a young American from Bloomington, Illinois, whose accumulated win of $415,000 was a fortune worth at least ten times that amount today.

Another American from Illinois, this time Chicago, is Edward O. Thorp, author of the celebrated blackjack book, *Beat the Dealer* (1962), who as early as 1956 conceived the goal of beating roulette through an application of theories of physics and mathematics, in both of which he holds degrees.

In December 1958 he first visited casinos in Las Vegas and studied regulation roulette wheels in operation there. It wasn't until two years later, while a mathematics instructor at Massachusetts Institute of Technology, however, that Thorp convinced his colleague, Professor Claude Shannon, a senior mathematician and founder of information theory, that a scientific prediction of roulette spins might be feasible.

Having purchased a regulation roulette wheel from Reno, Nevada, the two mathematicians set it up on a billiard table in Shannon's basement laboratory, a gadgeteer's paradise of hundreds of electric and electronic devices like tools, switches, pulleys, motors, transformers, condensers, and transistors.

Did the two mathematicians discover that roulette is scientifically predictable? Here is what Thorp wrote in an academic paper on the subject:

"Using algorithms, it was possible by eye judgments alone to estimate the ball's final position three to four revolutions before exit (perhaps five to seven seconds before exit, which was ample time in which to bet) well enough to have a plus 15% expectation on each of the five most favored numbers. A cigarette pack-sized transistorized computer, which we designed and built, was able to predict up to eight revolutions in advance. The expectation in tests was plus 44%."

Perhaps the best description of what Thorp and Shannon went through in their quest is that of the science writer Thomas A. Bass, who in his book, *The Eudaemonic Pie* (1985), about his own roulette adventures, wrote:

"Around the wheel they stationed a strobe light, a clock, a movie camera, and the switches needed to coordinate the strobe and clock while filming the ball in motion. Their research...concluded that roulette is a highly predictable game.

"Thorp and Shannon then set to work to build a computer. They came up with a transistorized analog device the size of a cigarette pack. It received data via four push buttons, which were compressed on successive revolutions of the rotor [wheel] and ball in front of a fixed point....

"Claude and Betty Shannon, Edward and Vivian Thorp, and their computer checked into the Riviera Hotel and Casino on the Las Vegas Strip in 1962. Thorp was already well known in Nevada, having made a big splash the previous year publicizing his card-counting strategy...[so] Thorp was not a welcome sight to the casino owners of Nevada. Later he was barred from play and took to wearing disguises; he grew a beard, donned wraparound sunglasses, and traveled always in the company of friends. But at this stage of his notoriety he still had access to most of the clubs, and none of them suspected that he was out to beat them at a game other than blackjack.

"The Thorps and Shannons spent a week at the Riviera. They took in some shows, lounged around the pool, played diversionary blackjack, and did their best to beat roulette. For security reasons they had developed a two-person system, with a radio transmitter built into their 'cigarette pack' computer. The radio informed the bettor of the winning octant by means of a do-re-mi scale whose tempo was calibrated to the ball-wheel configuration it was meant to be mimicking. These radio signals were picked up by a hearing aid and 'a little bitty loudspeaker with flesh-colored wire attached to it, which we shoved into our ear canal. The trouble,' said Thorp, 'is that the wires kept breaking. So we shopped around and got steel wires about the size of a hair, but even these were fairly fragile.

" 'Sometimes I was the bettor, and sometimes I was the data taker [wheel watcher]. We traded off. But it would take us a while to get wired up in our hotel room and get in there. It was a real hassle putting it all together. It's a long, tedious project, even though it's conceptually very simple.'

" 'Difficulty with read-out devices' is Thorp's modest confession in print as to why he and Shannon gave up on their roulette computer after three or four sessions. During a recent conversation in his office at the University of California at Irvine, Thorp was more graphic in describing a general snafu of broken wires, gibbering beeps, shocks, and other electronic failures. He and Shannon tried sporadically over a number of years to debug their system, until they finally abandoned it as a bright idea whose implementation had eluded them.

"Their computer ended up in Shannon's basement, 'where it's gathering dust,' said Thorp. 'If I were doing the whole thing over today, I'd use digital technology, a microprocessor. It's really the way to go. You don't have to use linear approximations or the other kinds of approximations that analog computers like. You could solve the equations and put in the right curves.'"

Turning in his book to his own team of a half dozen mathematicians and physicists who in the late 1970s and early 1980s did indeed go the route of the microprocessor to conquer roulette, Thomas A. Bass explains that they fitted this receiving computer into the soles and heels of his oxford leather shoes so that, when he stood innocently betting at various Las Vegas roulette tables, he felt tickles on his feet at three different places and frequencies—signals as to which numbers he should bet sent by the wheel watcher lounging inconspicuously near the wheel. The latter, an astrophysicist named James Doyne Farmer, disguised as a New Mexico plainsman, would himself be making casual bets on the red or black while actually concentrating on clocking and correlating the inverse revolutions of the ball and wheel and then, from his own shoes, radioing to Bass the predicted octant of numbers by pressing his big toes on two microswitches.

Although Bass and his team of men and women scientists, technicians, and players did win some money in both Las Vegas and Reno, in the end they too were defeated primarily by the same problems that frustrated Thorp and Shannon: the time, expense, and difficulties in refining and perfecting modern electronic technology. This is a pity, for the electronic sending and receiving devices of both teams yielded an advantage of 44% over the bank at every spin compared to the 15% of the old-fashioned hand signals used by William Nelson Darnborough and later wheel watchers like him.

During 1991 an electronic variation of the wheel-watcher system was applied intermittently by two anonymous gamblers from Freiburg, Germany. Openly wearing a wrist calculator (like a wristwatch) and sitting next to the wheel as the wheel watcher, "Rupert B..." would press a button on his calculator after the spinning ball had made two rotations. By the time the ball had circled the track four times the calculator's read-out could predict the optimal single number on which the team should bet. Eschewing secret signals like William Nelson Darnborough and his followers, Mr. B. would openly announce this optimal number to his partner standing near the croupier at the end of the table. Then the partner would immediately bet a unit chip on that number plus its three neighbors on either side (on the wheel)—for a total of seven numbers.

How did the team do? First they visited the Valkenburg Casino in southern Holland and won there 100,000 guilders ($55,250), leaving the casino perturbed and astonished.

Then they shifted back to Germany, where at the Travemünde Casino, northeast of Hamburg, they suffered nothing but losses. At Baden Baden, in the southwest, their wheel-watcher variation was at first fairly successful, but after a few such days the casino unfortunately instituted their countermeasure of refusing any bets made after the croupier had begun to spin the ball. As this countermeasure foils any wheel-watcher system, the pair of gamblers had to halt play.

Next they shifted to the Bregenz Casino, at the western tip of Austria, where for the first few days they were again quite successful. Then the casino administration ordered its croupiers always to spin the ball at high velocity: this foiled the successful use of the electronic calculator.

Next the pair of gamblers returned to Germany, where in various casinos in the Bavarian Alps they alternately won and lost.

And finally Mr. B and his parter returned to Holland, where all the casinos threatened them with permanent barring.

Such was the peripatetic year of two doughty German gamblers. After it was all over, Mr. B. declared that, although profitable, the whole electronic wheel-watcher venture had been so arduous and stressful that he decided to return to more conventional methods of roulette play.

In the end, however, the final blow to the use of electronic devices to beat roulette (or any casino game) may have been dealt by the law courts as well as by casino policy. In Nevada the possession or use by a player of an electronic device to aid his play in any game is now a felony (SB #467 of July 1, 1985). In Atlantic City, casinos may also take legal countermeasures to thwart players. In places such as the Caribbean, England, and Europe, players caught using such electronic devices may be fined and permanently barred from casino play. Whether these measures unfavorable to players will be ever changed or mitigated only time will tell.

On the other hand, it should be borne in mind that, to date, there are no specific laws against using electronic devices for advantage roulette play on either the many cruise ships leaving American ocean ports or on the rising number of Mississippi River river boats offering casino games.

In this matter of the legality or illegality of the use of electronic devices to beat roulette, prudence is obviously the watchword.

On the perfectly legal *non-electronic* wheel-watcher front, however, all is not lost. A successful American gambler, Laurance Scott, has produced an excellent book, *How to Beat Roulette* (Dona Ana, 1989/1990), combined with a practice video of a roulette wheel and its ball in action. Together these items depict in detail the one-man wheel-watcher method as well as, to a lesser extent, the two-man version used so successfully by William Nelson Darnborough at Monte Carlo and outlined by Gaston Vessillier in his French book in 1924. Although I myself consider it as difficult to be a competent non-electronic wheel watcher as an expert blackjack counter, those interested in Laurance Scott's book/video package should write for purchasing details to Laurance Scott, Dept. W-1, P.O. Drawer V, Dona Ana, New Mexico 88032.

In addition, also obtainable through the above address is Laurance Scott's nine-page technical pamphlet entitled *Biased Wheel Report* (Dona Ana, 1991), which every serious biased-wheel player should read.

Chapter 3

Can the Croupier Control the Ball?

Alois Szabo, S. R. Beresford, Stephen Kimmel, and Edward O. Thorp

Alois Szabo, Hungarian journalist and author, was an old friend of mine who haunted the casinos of Europe from 1914 to 1968, especially those along the French Riviera. On a sultry afternoon in July, 1961, I was pleased to introduce him to that volatile, eccentric enthusiast of the gaming world, Henri Daniel, founder in 1927 of the French gaming magazine *Hasard et Jeu*. We used to sit around Daniel's modest office in Nice at 12 rue d'Angleterre and think up ways of breaking the bank at Monte Carlo.

There was one point on which we all agreed. No croupier can ever *consciously* influence, even in the slightest degree, the ultimate destination of the ball as it circles the roulette wheel. Indeed, no croupier can get it into even a predesignated *half* of the wheel, let alone into 1, 2, or 3 favored numbers.

Here are Szabo's words on this significant subject from *The Pitfalls of Gambling and How to Avoid Them* (1954):

"In theory it seems not impossible that an adroit croupier with tremendous experience might succeed in directing the ball according to his wish, but he could do so only if he could spin as he wanted and if there were no obstacles to divert the ball on the border of the roulette machine.

"During the thirty-odd years that I frequented the casinos I naturally had a number of occasions to be in contact with the employees, and among them several croupiers. (One of them was my landlord for years.) They were unanimously agreed that it was ridiculous even to speak of directing the ball on the roulette wheel.

"To this someone might answer, 'You don't think those people would be foolish enough to give away the secrets of their trade!'

"Yes, but you cannot suppose that croupiers who had been discharged for one reason or another had any scruples of loyalty towards the [Monte Carlo] Casino. And yet even these assured me that it is a vain proposition to try to tinker with the ball. One of them told me that in the Roulette School he and his colleagues tried countless times not to spin but simply to drop the ball into a certain number, and even in this they succeeded very rarely.

"The oldest croupiers, after a lifetime of practice, agreed that only under the following conditions could one possibly succeed in spinning the ball into a predetermined section of the wheel:

"1. If the spinner could throw from a fixed point in every instance.

"2. If, each time he does so, the wheel were turning in the same direction as the ball.

"3. If the wheel were always turning at the same speed.

"4. If he could always spin with the same hand.

"5. If, and this is most important, there were no obstacles [canoes or ball stops] on the machine.

"But the facts are: 1. There is no fixed point from which to throw the ball, because the croupiers must spin from the number where the ball stopped. 2. The wheel always turns in the opposite direction from that of the ball. 3. At a speed determined by the *chef* [table chief]. 4. The croupier is obliged to spin with the hand nearest the machine (that is, if the croupier sits on the right of the wheel, he is naturally obliged to spin with his left hand). 5. There are *several obstacles* on the border [lower ball track] which always make the ball jump.

"Under these conditions it can be safely said that technically it is absolutely impossible to direct the ball into a predetermined number or section.

"But if the contrary were the case and there were magician-spinners who could drop the ball into a given number, there can be no doubt that, instead of rendering a service to the casinos, such spinners would bring about their ruin.

"You couldn't expect a croupier in possession of such a talent not to try to use it first for his own benefit. Nothing and nobody could stop him from working with an accomplice, who would play the numbers into which he spun the ball, and they could soon be millionaires at the expense of the casino."

In Monte Carlo, between Rampoldi's Restaurant and the outside entrance to the Salle Privée of the casino, there used to be a pathway through the casino gardens. One summer evening, seated there under a gnarled olive tree, I chatted with one of the croupiers who had come out to take some air on his break. Finally I casually asked the age-old question: "Can you make the roulette ball go into any predetermined numbers?" To which he replied, "If I could, would I be working in the casino?"

And we mustn't forget S. R. Beresford, whom Henri Daniel met in Monte Carlo in 1924, who for more than 25 years knew an old Monte Carlo croupier named Edouard.

"Edouard told me frankly," wrote Beresford, "that in his opinion no man could control the ball sufficiently to make even one half of the board [wheel] to have a better chance than the other half. He also told me that he has sat for hours at a time endeavoring to spin a ball so that it would fall into a given half of the board *whilst the wheel was stationary.* With the wheel revolving, no matter how experienced the spinner, every section has an equal chance with any other. The myth that some spinners could control the game died out with the advent of the fourteen obstacles; no reasonable person can any longer attribute results to the influence of any human agency."

So much for the question of whether a croupier can *consciously* influence the ultimate destination of the ball around the roulette wheel.

But does a croupier, whose tedious job seems often to turn him into a bored automaton, inadvertently influence the destination of the ball on an *unconscious* basis? Does the croupier, hour after hour, himself understandably become a machine whose coordinated arm, wrist, and finger motions habitually propel the ball a *particularly frequent number of pockets away from its last position* and therefore into a predictable section?

Perhaps the clearest proponent of this traditional position—for it isn't an original one—is Stephen Kimmel, who has dubbed it the *dealer's signature.* Kimmel claims that each roulette dealer's signature is highly personal, differing characteristically from that of every other dealer, and that this characteristic may be first clocked, second evaluated, and then played to one's advantage.

Kimmel gives the the following simple, theoretical illustration. Suppose we sit down at a Las Vegas roulette wheel and record the first five numbers as follows: 19-9-36-21-7. He points out that their distinctive feature is not that they're red or black, high or low, but that, *on the wheel,* counting clockwise, each one is 14 pockets away from its predecessor.

In practice, of course, this signature of *exactly* 14 pockets would never obtain. In practice, between the first and second numbers the difference might be, say, 11 pockets, between the second and third numbers 14 pockets, between the third and fourth numbers 12 pockets, and between the fourth and fifth numbers 14 pockets again. As 14 is the difference that occurs most frequently (in my absurdly short, theoretical sample of only 4 spins), it constitutes the dealer's signature.

How many spins do we need to clock or track a dealer's signature? Kimmel says at least 50 spins are necessary, but in Las Vegas he himself played 199 in order in to get a clear signature, and I myself suggest that many more would usually be required.

Here is how we obtain the dealer's signature. First we go to a casino and *clock* the roulette wheel, *writing down* all 199 or whatever numbers just as they occur in sequence. Then we go home and, on a large sheet of paper, write down a column of numbers from 0 to 18 on the left side of the page and from 19 to 37 (for a 38-slot wheel) in the middle of the page. As we know, most European and larger American casinos provide roulette players with printed diagrams of roulette wheels (on the reverse of score cards). Using one of these diagrams as our guide, and always moving clockwise, we count the number of pockets occurring on the wheel between the first and second numbers, which were, say, 0 and 30. As there are four such pockets (for numbers 28-9-26-30), we put a dot on our sheet next to number 4. Next we count the number of pockets on the wheel between the second and third numbers, which would be 30 and (say) 1. As there are 14 such pockets, we put a dot on our sheet next to number 14. Similarly we proceed through the entire list of spins for the session, marking a dot to record the difference between each of the occurring numbers. (The total of dots will always be one less than that of the spins.)

What happens if the ball circles the wheel several times and plops into the same number again? (By regulation in America the ball must circle

TABLE 1

A Particular Dealer's Signature in 199 Spins

1	2	1	2
4	0	2	19
6	1	1	20
5	2	5	21
7	3	10	22
8	4	8	23
4	5	10	24
6	6	7	25
2	7	10	26
4	8	10	27
3	9	13	28
1	10	7	29
4	11	9	30
1	12	5	31
5	13	3	32
3	14	5	33
3	15	3	34
5	16	3	35
5	17	5	36
2	18	4	37
		198	

Column 1: The number of spins in which a specific difference in pockets (between the last two winning numbers) was thrown.

Column 2: The 38 specific differences in pockets.

the wheel at least four times and in Europe at least seven.) With no difference here in the number of pockets between the last two numbers that occurred, we put our dot next to the 0 at the top of the column, which is column 2 in Table 1 above.

Similarly, if the ball circles the wheel and lands just before the pocket that it was in last, as this is the maximum number of pockets between numbers, we put our dot next to the 37 at the bottom of our column— again column 2 in Table 1 above.

These details had to be explained, because Kimmel never clarifies them.

Drawing on the graph of the data which Kimmel obtained from his most lucrative session in Las Vegas, the one of 199 spins, I've listed two columns of numbers in Table 1 (p. 24). Focusing on column 1, we see that Kimmel would have put four dots opposite 0 (*i.e.*, during the 199 spins there were four spins when the ball circled the wheel and plopped right back into the last winning number, the one whence it started), six dots opposite 1 (representing the six spins when the ball ended up in the next pocket *after* the last winning number) and...four dots opposite 37 (representing the four spins when the ball journeyed the maximum number of pockets or distance, landing in the pocket just *before* the last number that occurred).

As we observe from column 1, 13 is the largest number, signifying the most *frequently* occurring difference in pockets between any two numbers. Hence for this session in Las Vegas the number *opposite* 13—which is 28—is the dealer's signature. (In other words, in 199 spins thirteen of them showed a difference of 28 pockets between sequential winning numbers.)

So much for the method of first clocking and then discovering the dealer's signature—here 28. How do we use it?

Let's say that, instead of Kimmel, we're sitting at the roulette wheel. Suppose the last number that came up was 7. As soon as the dealer indicates this, we take our diagram of the wheel and count clockwise 28 pockets from number 7, arriving at 23, which is the next number we play. And for the rest of the 199 spins we follow the same process, always betting on the number that lies exactly 28 pockets away from the last winning number. That's all there is to it.

(Here's a suggestion. When the dealer's signature is a number larger than 18—which will happen in half the sessions—to lessen the tedium of counting, lay the pen across the diagram of the wheel. As the number directly across the way always signifies 18 in our total, we may start counting [clockwise] from there rather than from 1 itself. Alternatively, if we don't mind subtraction, we may subtract the dealer's signature number from 38 and count counterclockwise from the last winning number.)

Rather than use the dealer's signature—here 28—to try to hit on the head a target number that is always exactly 28 pockets clockwise from the last winning number, Kimmel chose to play a whole *sector* of 10 *neighboring* numbers surrounding the target number.

The obvious advantage of this is that, instead of having only 1 chance out of 38 to win, we have 10 chances out of 38 to win. But the obvious disadvantage is that, even when we do win, we necessarily lose 9 chips or units of money at the same time that the dealer is pushing over our gross win of 35 units. So our net win is always just $35 - 9 = 26$ units. And, of course, when we don't win at all, we lose all 10 units. Just the same, I believe that most people who will play the dealer's-signature system will want to play a sector of neighboring numbers—say, anywhere from about 5 to 12 numbers.

Here is how Kimmel played a sector of neighboring numbers. We note in column 1 of Table 1 (p. 24) that the *double*-digit (best) frequencies for this particular dealer occur opposite (in column 2) the 10 pocket-difference numbers of 21 through 30—so these were the 10 pocket-differences that Kimmel played on every turn of the wheel. Why did he do so?

This would be his reasoning. If we add up the frequencies for the pocket differences of 21 through 30, we have $5 + 10 + 8 \ldots 9 = 89$, and $(89/198) = .449 \ldots$, in other words, almost *half* the time the dealer will inadvertently spin the ball into the target sector beginning 21 pockets away from the last winning number. This contrasts happily to only about a *quarter* of the time, which we deserve from the standpoint of ordinary probability $(10/38) = .263$.

Here is an example of 10-bet sector play, i.e., on each spin putting a 1-unit wager on each of 10 neighboring numbers. Suppose the last occurring number was 4. Before the dealer can spin the wheel again, we quickly count clockwise, around the diagram of the wheel, 21 pockets and arrive at number 36, so we next play *this* number *plus* the next 9 numbers (situated at pockets 22 through 30 away), which are 13-1-00-27-10-25-29-12-8. It's that simple.

Here is what Kimmel has to say about his successful foray in Las Vegas with this system:

"We collected data on five dealers at an average of 150 spins each. Then we selected three dealers with the strongest signatures. That offered the best profitability ratio. Our worst dealer proved to have a signature slightly different from the one we had estimated. We made only $100 after play for two hours. The other two proved more profitable. On the dealer [represented by Table 1] we averaged over $150 an hour at a 50-cent table."

Such is the system called the dealer's signature, based on the supposition that a dealer may *unconsciously* influence the destination of the ball, through habit propelling it a particularly frequent number of pockets away from its last position.

Does the dealer's signature-system work?

Not according to the competent gambler and mathematician Edward O. Thorp, who responded this way:

"Stephen Kimmel asserted that a dealer who works eight hours a day, 50 weeks a year, tends to spin the ball and rotor [wheel] in a habitual, regular way. This would make possible accurate prediction—a bet on 10 pockets, Kimmel contended, would have a 50% chance of success.....

"I don't believe Kimmel's approach works..... Here's why: there are three important conditions that must remain roughly constant throughout play for the player to take advantage of the dealer or, as Kimmel calls it, the dealer's signature. These conditions are (1) the rotor velocity should be approximately the same each time the ball is spun, (2) the spinning ball should make approximately the same number of revolutions each time, and (3) the initial position of the rotor when the dealer launches the ball should be approximately the same each time. This third condition, which is not mentioned [by] Kimmel, is crucial." (Compare Thorp's and Szabo's conditions for similarities.)

Then Thorp elaborates on why he believes Kimmel's system won't work because of (3) above, and states, "Because Kimmel did not discuss variations in the point of release, I do not believe in his method.

"There is a better approach to this statistical analysis of roulette. Watch a dealer and count the number of revolutions the ball makes on the stator [motionless roulette bowl] from the time of release until it crosses onto the rotor [wheel]. Note how constant that number of revolutions is. The results of your observations can be statistically stated as some average number of revolutions plus an error term.

"Next, count the number of revolutions the rotor makes during the time the ball is on the stator. This will give you another average for the number of rotor revolutions, plus a second error term. Finally, count how far the ball travels on the rotor after it has crossed the divider between the rotor and stator. You can summarize these results as some average number of revolutions or pockets plus an error term.

"In order for this approach to work, it is necessary that the square root of the sums of the squares of the error terms be less than 17 pockets."

In other words, the root mean square error must *always* be *less* than 17 pockets (17 is a constant that never changes), and Thorp summarizes various root mean square errors in his accompanying table—17 is where the value changes from the minus fluctuation in our favor to the plus one in our disfavor, for the minus fluctuation indicates an error less than 17 pockets.

This is all very well, but as Thorp points out, in practice at a real roulette table with a real dealer and his real signature, this root mean square error is unfortunately *almost always larger* than the (minus) fluctuation of fewer than 17 pockets required for our winning.

Just the same, Thorp explains what we should do on those few occasions when we find winning feasible: "In the unlikely event that the root mean square error is less than 17 pockets, then—and only then— you have a chance to win. The key lies in using the position of the rotor, when the ball is launched, as your starting point for predicting where the ball will fall out on the wheel. For example, suppose you find that for a certain dealer the ball travels 8 revolutions with a root mean square error of 5 pockets. Suppose also that during this time the rotor travels 4 revolutions, with a root mean square error of 6 pockets. And suppose still further that once the ball is on the rotor it travels 13 pockets, with a root mean square error of 8 pockets. Given these suppositions, you can predict that the ball will travel 8 revolutions plus 4 revolutions plus 13 pockets from the launch point, or 13 pockets beyond that point. The root mean square error is the square root of 5 squared plus 6 squared plus 8 squared. This turns out to be 11.2 pockets, well within the required error of less than 17 pockets. In this case the prediction system would work.

"However, I think you will find that when you collect this data, the errors at each stage are several times as large as I have used in this example. My own observation [in actual casinos] is that the dealer error in the number of revolutions for the ball spin is about 20 pockets for the more consistent dealers; it is much larger with a less consistent one. I also noticed that the rotor velocity is not nearly as constant as Kimmel....would like. That is because the dealer gives it an extra kick every few spins to rebuild its velocity.

"It is also true that the deflecting vanes [obstacles or canoes] on the sides of the rotor [lower ball track] add considerable randomness to the outcome, as do the frets or spacers between the pockets. The upshot is that I don't believe that any dealer is predictable enough to cause a root mean square error of less than 17 pockets. I'm willing to examine proof to the contrary, but I would be very surprised if anyone could ever produce it."

So there we are—what's wrong with the Kimmel system is that, far too frequently for us to make an average profit, the ball comes to rest either way beyond our sector of 10 neighboring numbers or way before it, and in Thorp's own observation of dealers in actual casinos the error fluctuation is as large as 20 pockets for even the dealer whose signature is the most favorable to us.

This topic reminds me of a trip I recently made to Las Vegas. One evening I was standing at the roulette pit downtown at the Golden Nugget Casino, conversing with the pit boss, Stirling Hawkins, a noted authority on roulette in all its facets, along with my friend, Professor Louis Simonoff, who teaches mathematics at the University of Nevada at Las Vegas. Stirling Hawkins had just pointed out to us that of the Nugget's two operating roulette wheels—at that moment both mobbed by gamblers—one was made in 1987 by John Huxley Ltd. of London, with the new-style, low-profile frets or pocket walls that hopefully (for the house) produce a more randomizing, scatter effect with the ball, and the other in 1952 by Hans Benteler & Sons of Chicago, with the old-fashioned, American, higher frets that, according to some, tend slightly to trap the ball too soon after its fall, thereby fostering successful prediction by a few observant sector players or wheel watchers.

While we watched the ball circle the Hans Benteler wheel, at which there was particularly heavy betting, I exclaimed to my two conversationalists, "I will now demonstrate my latest wheel-watcher ability. I predict that the ball is going to fall into any pocket *except* the double zero."

We all watched the ball suspensefully circle the wheel three more times, and you guessed it—naturally the ball fell into double zero.

"Well," commented Professor Simonoff, "so much for the root mean square error."

Chapter 4

Early Biased-Wheel Players: Monte Carlo and Ostend

Joseph Jaggers, The Italian Syndicate, and Victor Bethell

The horizontal gaming wheel was invented around 1720 by an anonymous Londoner for his new game that he called *roly poly*. When Parliament outlawed it in 1745, the legal text referred to it specifically as "a certain pernicious game called roulet [sic] or roly poly."

Roly poly offered no numbers on which to wager. Instead a player bet that the circling ivory ball would fall into either a white or black pocket or slot, and the banker's advantage consisted of one white and one black so-called bar slot, which two slots were reserved for himself. In the 1720s another anonymous Londoner, exploiting the popularity of such card games as faro, painted playing cards on the slots, which customarily totaled anywhere from 25 to 31, and thus created long-odds bets. He called his game *ace of hearts*.

To circumvent a 1739 anti-gambling law, in the resort of Tunbridge Wells an Englishman named Cook invented a third game, which he called Even Odd or EO. Retaining the two bar slots in the total of 40 slots, Cook changed the alternating white and black slots of the roly poly wheel to 20 even and 20 odd slots, but in the 1745 law EO was also outlawed. Although illegal, it remained a popular game.

By at least 1788, and probably many years earlier, this *even-chance* game, which the French called *roulette*, was being played in a few low-class Paris gambling dens, and it likewise had two bar slots in the total of 20 red and 20 black alternating slots—but as yet had no numbers. Thus in France roulette *without numbers* was a game imported entirely from England.

Around 1648 Louis XIV's prime minister, Cardinal Mazarin, an ardent gambler from Italy, introduced to the French an Italian game called *hoca*, with a layout of 30 numbers but no even-chance bets. The croupier held a soft, leather sack containing 30 unmarked balls, each containing a folded piece of parchment on which was written a number from 1 to 30. After shaking the sack, the croupier would remove a ball at random, take out and unfold the parchment, and announce the lucky number.

Slightly later a second and similar Italian game arrived in Paris, called *biribisso* by the Italians and *biribi* by the French, gradually replacing hoca, but both were extremely popular. In the eighteenth century biribi was Voltaire's favorite game.

There were two layouts for biribi.

One layout was a large square containing 70 numbers plus the even-chance bets of red, odd, and high bordering the right side of the layout, and black, even, and low bordering the left side. The banker's advantage lay in his giving short odds, e.g., instead of paying off at the mathematically fair 69 to 1 on a single number, he paid out only 63 to 1.

The other layout for biribi was a popular street version, regularly confiscated by the Paris police. This one had only 36 numbers plus the even-chance bets of odd and even, and high and low. (There was no room for red and black on the smaller street layout, which was sometimes folded up like a map and kept hidden from the police in the operator's pocket.)

In Paris during the 1790s five leading gaming clubs grew up on the second floor of that fashionable tourist mecca, the Palais Royal, with its enormous courtyard of cafés and restaurants and 180 shops under the surrounding lamp-lit arcades. Besides the most popular dice and card games, these five clubs also featured the large, 70-number biribi. Until about 1796, even-chance roulette was found in only one or two low gaming dens in the basement of the Palais Royal and in some other second-rate locations around the city.

Then about 1796, roulette exactly as we know it today, with its 36 numbers and zero and double zero, suddenly appeared in the second-floor gaming clubs of the Palais Royal and became the rage of Paris— and very quickly that of the rest of the gaming world. And so it has remained to this day.

How had roulette evolved? Here is my own theory. Recognizing, on the one hand, the great popularity of the street version of biribi, with its 36 numbers and 2 even chances (but with its clumsy bag of balls), and on the other hand, the efficiency of the roulette wheel, with its 2 bar slots and alternating reds and blacks, an inspired anonymous gaming supervisor in one of the upstairs clubs took a roulette wheel from one of the basement dens and transferred the 36 biribi numbers to the alternating red-and-black slots. Then he renamed the 2 bar slots zero and double zero. And finally the Frenchman placed the English wheel at the head of the Italian layout: at that moment the world's most famous and elegant gambling game was invented.

At roulette's inception around 1796, thousands of illegal gambling dens existed in Paris, including the five clubs in the Palais Royal. To bring this situation under control, in 1806 Napoleon legalized only these five clubs, plus six others in the general vicinity, and those at a handful of mountain resorts like Spa, Aix-la-Chapelle, and Aix-les-Bains.

By the time of Waterloo in 1815, legal gambling had spread to a few German resorts as well. Especially after the closing down under Louis Philippe of the gambling at the Palais Royal in 1838, legal casinos thrived at the principal watering places of Wiesbaden, Ems, Kissengen, and Baden-Baden, featuring roulette with its 2 zeros and 36 numbers. (The only other game offered was trente-et-quarante.)

One of the favorite casinos of these German gambling resorts became that at the little town of Bad Homburg, ten miles north of Frankfurt on the Main, a casino founded in 1841 by a Frenchman, François Blanc, born ironically in 1806, the very year Napoleon legalized the game of roulette that was to make his fortune. At Bad Homburg Blanc used some of the French supervisors and croupiers who had worked at the Palais Royal before it closed in 1838.

Here is what that amiable English journalist, George Augustus Sala, found at the Homburg roulette table on his trip with two friends to gamble there in the winter of 1866:

"The gaming salons, if not inconveniently crowded, had their full complement of players. There were the same calculating old fogies, the same supercilious-looking young men, the same young girls and full-blown women, with a nervous quivering about the lips, the same old sinners of both sexes whom one has known at these places the last ten or fifteen years, busily engaged at trente-et-quarante.

"At the roulette table, too, one had no difficulty in recognizing the old familiar set. The handsome-looking young Russian noble who 'spots the board' with gold coins—the fat bejeweled-fingered Jew who seeks to emulate the Muscovite lord with silver florins—the Englishman and his wife, evidently residents, who play against each other, quite unconsciously, at opposite ends of the table—the youthful, yet 'used up' little French marquis, who dresses in the English fashion, and brings with him his own private pocket rake, that he may hook in his golden winnings the more readily—the elegantly dressed, shriveled, hag-faced woman who plays for the run on the colors—the nervous, care-worn young Englishman, who plays heavily against the see-saw, with other nervous fellow-countrymen staking their gold on the first, second, or last dozen numbers—professional gamblers, well and ill-dressed, with sharply defined Mephistophelean features, quick, restless eyes, and villainously compressed lips, who, after trying all systems, generally get landed croupiers or swindlers in the end—seedy-looking Poles of the last emigration, who prudently place their florins on two, three, or four numbers alone, and deep-calculating Germans, who make ventures with painful hesitation, and after long intervals of abstention, and, as a matter of course, almost invariably lose; prostitutes—French, German, English, Polish, Italian, and Jewish—of every nationality—most of them young— so young in fact that the world well may be called their mother, robed like princesses, and becoiffured, bejeweled, and begloved as only prostitutes ever seem to be, and who lay down their gold with charming indifference, though with a decided partiality for zero and the first four numbers.

"These, with watchful old women and Germans of hang-dog look that beset every public gaming table, waiting for a chance to pounce upon the stakes of the more unsuspecting players, are some of the characters whom we recognized around the roulette table that night, when the play ran high and the players were more than usually eager."

Such were the cosmopolitan gamblers who haunted the German casinos in the 1860s, and when, owing to pressure from Prussia, all of them closed down in 1872, many of their habitués took the train down to the Monte Carlo Casino, which in 1863 François Blanc had opened in the small principality of Monaco, east of Nice.

The big gamblers from Homburg François Blanc recognized immediately.

There was, for example, the senile Countess Sophie Kisseleff, whom Fyodor Dostoyevesky had immortalized in his novel, *The Gambler* (1867). At Homburg Countess Kisseleff had lost more than $4,000,000 at roulette over ten years, and the grateful town had named a street after her. As soon as she arrived in Monte Carlo, the Russian aristocrat managed to mislay a purse containing $5,000.

Then there was Vincenzo Bugeja, a Maltese merchant who at the trente-et-quarante table in Homburg had always played with $1,000,000 available to him. There in 1872 the Maltese had quickly won $220,000, lost back $60,000, and left with a profit of $160,000. Indeed, when the Maltese arrived in Monte Carlo in October, 1873, François Blanc became so worried that he quickly wired a Paris bank for an additional $60,000 to bolster the casino's local cash reserves of $400,000. But this time luck favored the bank. After winning $14,000, Bugeja left in October, having lost back all his profits plus $20,000.

But the ups and downs of such wealthy gamblers were due entirely to luck, and François Blanc knew that even if a gambler such as the Maltese won a huge amount, he would almost always return and lose it back.

What Blanc was not prepared for in 1873 was a gambler who won legitimately but not by luck, and such a one was an Englishman named Joseph Jaggers, who that winter proceeded to figure out a way of winning an enormous sum of money.

This method is still practiced, is perfectly honest and legal, and since 1873 it has won, in casinos throughout the world, from Europe to Latin America to the United States, more than $6,000,000 in the well-publicized ventures alone. How much the strategy has won for gamblers who have won only moderate amounts, especially on a regular basis, and not talked about their successes, God only knows. The strategy rightly haunts every casino proprietor.

In the winter of 1873 a Yorkshire engineer and mechanic, Joseph Jaggers decided to desert the fog of Lancashire cotton mills and vacation in Monte Carlo. Although more than 186,000 other people visited the principality of Monaco in the same year, neither François Blanc nor any of his casino attendants recognized Jaggers as one of the big gamblers who keep casino proprietors awake at night. The reason was simple: Jaggers had never been to a casino before.

The monumental Beaux-Arts Monte Carlo Casino of today is not at all the modest, two-story building it was in 1873 when Jaggers walked up its steps. In those days the casino looked like a kind of white, elongated villa in a simple, classical style. Standing in its vestibule, the large, cheerful, rubicund Englishman glimpsed to his right a small reading room occupied by a few croupiers, duennas, and broke gamblers perusing the newspapers and magazines of Europe. Before him was an unpretentious, one-story hall dignified by only a half-dozen people lounging on leather wall sofas, quietly talking, smoking or pondering their gambling systems on scorecards. Across the way stragglers were passing through doors to a modest afternoon concert in the ballroom. Jaggers turned left into the ticket bureau, where he showed his passport and received a free entry ticket to the gaming rooms, open all year from 11:00 A.M. to 11:00 P.M. Now he turned left and walked down a short corridor toward a liveried flunky, who swept him through some swinging doors into the first of the two gaming rooms.

The engineer found himself in the modest Renaissance Room where gamblers surrounded two double-ended roulette tables. Each table seated 16 gamblers and was served by a staff of eight. Two pairs of croupiers sat facing one another across the center roulette wheel, and two supervisors on higher chairs separated each pair. At each end of the table sat a croupier, whose job it was to push with his rake the losing wagers toward the center croupiers, who then paid off the winners. Standing around each roulette table were as many as 50 men and women struggling to place their wagers between the arms of those lucky enough to have obtained chairs.

Jaggers glanced at a small sign hanging over the nearest table, stating that the capital of the table was 60,000 francs ($12,000).

Another liveried flunky bowed Jaggers into the second gaming room, the large, skylighted Moorish Room, built only the year before. It contained four double-ended roulette tables and, in the rear, two trente-et-quarante tables.

Crowds pressed around each gaming table, and the scene was much like that painted at Homburg by George Augustus Sala, but Jaggers wasn't interested in his colorful fellow gamblers. As his business in England was the manufacture of spindles for Lancashire cotton mills, he became fascinated by the roulette machines themselves, which in theory are perfectly balanced and therefore produce purely random results. But Jaggers began to wonder about their accuracy, and within the next few days hired six clerks to sit all day long at all six tables in the casino and take down the numbers, as they came up, of each roulette wheel. To his clerks he didn't explain his purpose; but inasmuch as innumerable gamblers, both then and now, record numbers as they come up on each roulette wheel, this activity of wheel clocking was neither illicit nor unconventional.

For the next week Jaggers spent most of every day in his hotel room, digesting the statistical results delivered in the evening by his six clerks. In those days, just as now, a Monte Carlo roulette wheel produced about 55 spins an hour. If a clerk recorded numbers for 8 hours a day, his employer would accordingly receive the results of 440 spins a day, or roughly 3,000 spins a week.

At the end of a week the Yorkshire engineer emerged from his hotel room ready to do battle. What had been his activity? He had constructed statistical profiles of all six roulette wheels and found that the sixth—the last one in the Moorish Room—was definitely biased toward certain numbers, numbers which occurred far more frequently than their theoretical average.

Jaggers returned to the casino, showed his entry card to the flunkies, and walked quietly to the sixth wheel in the Moorish Room, where he began betting on nine biased numbers. As he won, he gradually increased his stakes. By the time the engineer had won $10,000 he was being watched by two worried inspectors, and by the time he'd won $50,000 he was being watched by three. Naturally, they tried to identify his system. The inspectors even thought that he might be cheating. By 11:00 P.M., when the casino closed, the Englishman had won as much as $70,000.

On the following day Jaggers returned to the Moorish Room and at the sixth wheel began wagering on the same nine biased numbers, which were:

7-8-9-17-18-19-22-28-29

and it's helpful to reorder these nine biased numbers just as they're located around the wheel itself, for the following six of these numbers...

9-22-18-29-7-28

are all actually adjacent to one another on the wheel, i.e., they're immediate neighbors; whereas we should note that the remaining three numbers...

8-17-18

are scattered about singly.

Thus fully two-thirds of the biased numbers obliged Jaggers to play a sector of the wheel.

In order to throw off the three inspectors who kept studying his mysterious system, Jaggers played simultaneously a variety of random numbers along with the nine biased ones, but after four more days this no longer fooled the casino, for the engineer had won an incredible $300,000. Worse, every time Jaggers placed a wager on the layout, scores of enthusiastic onlookers followed suit with their own bets and together won almost as much. The casino was desperate.

Finally noticing that the engineer always played at the same roulette wheel, one inspector came to suspect that it might indeed be defective in some way—subtly off balance or the like—so one night after closing, the casino shuffled all six roulette wheels from one table to another.

When Jaggers sat down the next day to play, the casino watched carefully to see if he would detect their subterfuge. The Englishman fell into the trap, and gambling heavily at the sixth table—but at the wrong wheel—he lost a whopping $200,000 before realizing what had happened. An engineer with a good memory and acute vision, Jaggers recalled a slight scratch on the bowl of the biased wheel and began nonchalantly roaming the casino looking for it. After ten minutes he found it—at the first table—where he sat down and where, over the next three weeks, with conservative play he accumulated an astounding $350,000. This brought his total net gain to $450,000, against which the lucky win of $160,000 by the Maltese was paltry.

To solve this new crisis the Monte Carlo Casino dispatched a courier by train to their Paris roulette-wheel manufacturer, who realized that the defect in the sixth wheel was perhaps due to the type of frets or metal walls or partitions that separated one pocket or slot from another. Heretofore the manufacturer's roulette wheels had been assembled with totally immovable frets, but he realized that, if these frets were replaced by movable ones, then any night after closing, a biased roulette wheel could be readjusted to accuracy by a casino mechanic's merely interchanging its frets at random among the 37 numbers. Thus, by the casino's ability to change on a daily basis the physical conditions of a roulette wheel, any system dependent on bias would be destroyed.

Such was the method whereby the Monte Carlo Casino ultimately prevailed over Joseph Jaggers and his ingenious roulette system, which had nearly ruined them. The courier immediately returned to Monte Carlo with a whole case of the new movable frets, and within a few days, on all six roulette wheels in the casino, these new partitions had replaced the old immovable ones.

Naturally, all this was kept secret from Jaggers, and the casino waited eagerly to see how he would react to their second countermeasure. In particular, would he now lose back to them the fortune which they considered rightfully theirs?

Jaggers returned to the casino and as customary looked for the wheel with the scratch on it. When he found it, he sat down to play. By the end of two days he had lost $75,000. At this juncture he suddenly stopped, for he realized that for a second time the casino had somehow altered playing conditions. Having won, however, a total of $325,000 (worth more than ten times that amount today), the English engineer decided to call it quits. Picking up his huge winnings, he bade farewell to the casino staff and returned to the Lancashire cotton mills and the world of spindles. He never returned to Monte Carlo again.

For seven more years the Monte Carlo Casino remained secure behind its assumption that movable frets or partitions would protect its roulette wheels from bias. The trouble is that the assumption is false, because each movable fret is secured to the large, underlying disc or security plate of the wheel head by two small, perpendicular screws. If these screws become loose, the fret too becomes loose, less rigid, vibrating imperceptibly, and therefore is less able to bounce the ball away from that particular pocket or slot. As that slot receives more than its fair share of balls, its number has become biased.

In 1880 this weakness of movable frets was discovered by 18 Italians, who formed themselves into a syndicate to exploit the frailty. In 1878 Charles Garnier, architect of the recently built Paris Opera House, was commissioned by the Monte Carlo Casino. Garnier tore down the simple public hall and replaced it with the present two-story atrium, replaced the ballroom with a small opera house, and then in 1880 built a third elegant, muraled gaming room onto the end of the Moorish Room.

The construction of the Garnier Room, as the casino named it, raised to ten the number of roulette tables on the casino floor. As soon as the Garnier Room was finished in the fall of 1880, the 18 Italians, which included the wives of the male gamblers, went to work. Over a period of several weeks they unobtrusively clocked all ten roulette wheels by taking down the numbers on the conventional scorecards handed out by the casino flunkys. So that they could maintain their seats they made modest wagers on a few single numbers, the even chances, and the dozens.

Like Joseph Jaggers, the 18 Italians found only one defective wheel, but one biased wheel is all that's ever needed. The Italians, however, had one enormous advantage over Jaggers. As soon as the Englishman began winning large sums, he became the cynosure of official attention, and this situation continued until the day the engineer left the casino forever. By contrast, the Italians were too numerous ever to be completely identified, and the fact that some of them were women initially threw off suspicion. In addition, although Jaggers won much more money, he made it during a relatively short visit, whereas the Italians could avert suspicion by not only wagering modestly but by also spreading their winnings among 18 people over a period of two whole months.

Here are the nine biased numbers of the defective wheel on which the Italian syndicate played:

0-8-12-14-15-17-24-28-31

and reading clockwise, their order on the European wheel is:

0-15-17-8-24-14-31-28-12

We recall that by coincidence Jaggers also played nine numbers, of which six were neighbors on the wheel, obliging sector play. This is not true of the Italians, however, although among the nine biased numbers there are indeed two pairs, for numbers 14 and 31 are located side by side, as are numbers 28 and 12.

Jaggers always bet separately on each number, i.e., *en plein*, or straight up, whereas the Italians ingeniously spread out their wagers on the layout *à cheval*, or split, across numbers 12 and 15, numbers 14 and 17, and numbers 28 and 31, while simultaneously playing straight up numbers 0, 8, and 24.

But even if as many as 18 players are betting in shifts of three or four at a time from 11:00 A.M. to 11:00 P.M. on only nine numbers at one particular wheel, their success can't be hidden forever, because the profit of the table as a whole keeps dropping, and the casino accountants keep track of such matters on a daily basis.

The English journalist William Le Queux later interviewed Antoine Martin, director of surveillance of the Monte Carlo Casino, and gave this account of the Italians, who...

"...played incessantly from the opening of the rooms till their close, only absenting themselves 10 minutes a day in order to get a drink of lemonade and eat a sandwich....[They] became the center of attraction. Their winnings were so phenomenal that the table was now given

200,000 francs [$40,000] a day instead of 70,000 [$14,000] in order that the bank should not be so frequently broken. Sometimes, of course, they had a short run of ill-fortune, but it quickly passed....

"Yet another week passed, and the report spreading of these wonderful winnings caused the casino to be crowded to excess. Around the table, day after day, an excited mob stood watching every [spin] and applauding as each *coup* was made....An account had been kept of their gains, and the Administration were appalled to find that already they had placed nearly 900,000 francs [$180,000] into their pockets.

"At last it was decided to try the same system as that [which the gamblers themselves] worked, so one night after the casino was closed, a dozen of the chief officials..., including the director, went to the table and commenced playing on zero and...8 and 24.

"In an hour they had won approximately over 30,000 francs [$6,000]! From that, all were confident that at last [the secret of] the system had been discovered."

So after two frustrating months the casino finally realized once more what had happened a second time. With Jaggers they had first moved the defective wheel to another table in the hope that he wouldn't find it. When that didn't work, they reconstructed its frets. In the case of the Italians, after two months the casino removed the wheel entirely, a move the Italians quickly perceived. This wheel was never put back into play on the casino floor.

On the subject of the Italian raid the French gaming writer Martin Gall commented in 1883:

"In recent times a syndicate of Italians succeeded in winning substantial sums at the Monte Carlo Casino by playing a defective roulette wheel....Assuming that the casino was so negligent of its own interests that it didn't bother to verify the accuracy of its own paraphernalia, the success of the Italians isn't the least bit surprising. The casino must know that its income, accruing from its regular advantage of zero over the players, depends on the perfect, mathematical equilibrium of the various chances, and it's strange indeed that, even after the irregularity of the results had been going on for so long a time, the casino waited so long to replace the defective roulette wheel. In imitation of the Italians other syndicates have since been founded, but, alas, they haven't succeeded. All the newcomers tried to follow the same path—to exploit an instrument of chance that can never be perfect, but they unfortunately set about their goal after the casino itself realized what had happened and had taken corrective measures."

How much did the Italian syndicate win from the Monte Carlo Casino? They won an astounding $160,000, but although Jaggers left with all his winnings intact, it must be sadly related that the Italians, having become addicted to the excitement of the gaming halls, returned and tried to conquer the perfectly well-adjusted roulette wheels that produce nothing more than random results. So, alas, they all lost back individually what they had won collectively.

There have always been unexplained mysteries concerning the profits—and losses—of roulette tables, and one may only conjecture as to their causes.

In 1935, for example, the historian Charles Graves reported the following:

"Life is a funny business. Six times I have been to Monte Carlo, and on each occasion I tried hard to get in touch with René Léon [the noted managing director of the Monte Carlo Casino]. And each time he proved too elusive for me. Then [here in London itself] within twenty-four hours I achieved this seven-year-old ambition of meeting the redoubtable René face to face, and better still, of persuading him to talk about Monte Carlo....

"[He told me that] a roulette table can easily lose a million francs [$40,000] a day (a charming little statistic)....This subject of the rate at which tables win and lose is fascinating. According to René Léon, each of the sixty-five roulette tables [of which at most twenty have ever been on the casino floor at one time] has a pedigree like a racehorse, giving the total profit or loss for each preceding year. And the joyous thing is that, despite the use of a spirit level three times a day, which has to be accurate to within a millimeter, there are six tables which show a loss to the casino year after year. All the croupiers want to roll the ball there, because naturally they [receive more tips from winning than losing gamblers].

"What are the lucky tables' numbers? René Léon refused to tell me in London but promised to point them out to me for my own private information and necessary action on my next visit to Monte Carlo. These tables lose as much as 600,000 francs [$24,000] a year compared with an average profit of a million francs [$40,000] a year shown by the others. One particular table, which used to stand in the reading room, lost over a million francs [$40,000] every year for three years until it was removed.

"Why does the casino not remove the other six? The answer is that in every steak, kidney, and oyster pudding there is always one oyster, if you can find it. In this case, as I say, there are six. Nobody is able to explain the mystery. The spirit level report has to be signed three times a day by three responsible officials to say that the drop of liquid is exactly in the center. If it is not at first, thanks to atmospheric changes, then the table legs are altered by hydraulic pumps until they are exactly level. But still those six tables lose. I can tell you this, however, they are all in the 'kitchen' [the first and largest gaming room, formerly called the Moorish Room], as opposed to the *salles privées* [the so-called private rooms always open to the public] and the Sporting Club [the semi-private gaming club].

" 'Let me say at once,' said René Léon, 'that it is impossible for a croupier to roll the ball into any particular hole. The metal lozenges and the rebounding make this impossible.'...

" 'The reason why Monte Carlo has such a reputation for breaking people is that so many are broke before they arrive, except for 500 [$20] or 600 francs with which they make their final desperate fling.

" 'In my long experience, by the way, I recall only one case of a man who arrived in this condition and who was successful. He was an Italian duke. He arrived with a thousand francs [$200]. He turned it into a million [$200,000] and left within a week. That was when francs were worth twenty-five to the pound. The extraordinary thing was that he never once had a losing throw [spin]...'

"In reply to another question Monsieur Léon said that the record sequence for a color is held by black, which turned up two summers ago [in 1933] twenty-two times running. Red's record is nineteen times. He did not know the record for an individual number, but three times is not at all unusual."

So much, among other interesting facts, for the mystery of six continuously losing roulette wheels in the Monte Carlo Casino, and according to Walter Tyminski, editor of *Rouge et Noir News,* a parallel mystery occurred more recently in Las Vegas:

"The Las Vegas Strip Roulette Mystery:

"The six largest Las Vegas Strip casinos, those who win $60 million or more a year, reported a total drop of $6,928,870 at their roulette tables during October, 1984. [*Drop* signifies the dollar sum of the roulette chips bought by the gamblers.] The drop figure was not unusual, but the reported win (loss) was. The group reported a loss of $9,323,856 for the month.

"What happened? We haven't been able to find out. Big wins or losses are usually the talk of the Strip, but we haven't been able to find anyone who knows how a $12 million swing took place on the Strip during

October. (A win of approximately $5 million was expected for the month.)

"Roulette can be beaten by clocking the wheel, and properly designed and utilized covert computers can give the player a significant advantage over the house. However, we find it hard to believe that any casino let players they did not know beat them for anywhere near $12 million. If high rollers utilized the services of advisers [wheel watchers] equipped with covert computers, a $12 million win, or thereabouts, is still hard to believe."

Given that the enormous wins of Joseph Jaggers and the Italian syndicate represent the most notable successes of biased-wheel play at the Monte Carlo Casino in the 1870s and 1880s, how many gamblers in contrast were playing this system on a modest, inconspicuous basis in order not to attract notice from the casinos? Because such players seldom leave any record of their gains, for they understandably don't want to alert the casinos and become barred, we have no way of knowing, but there was at least one, the Honorable Victor Bethell, who reported his success in 1901.

Victor Bethell was a delightful, well-known character around Monte Carlo from the 1880s into the 1920s, and he was a friend, not surprisingly, of S. R. Beresford. Both did their fair share of gambling and were a fund of anecdotes about the Riviera gaming world. In his editorial office I once asked Henri Daniel if he'd ever met Bethell, as he had Beresford, and he sighed and said that unfortunately he never had.

Bethell was the representative of Smith's Bank in its corner of the Galerie Charles III opposite the casino (later replaced there by the Banque Nationale de Paris) and did much to help fellow British gamblers limp back to London with dignity. During this period Smith's also operated a branch on the seashore at Ostend, Belgium, where roulette was played chiefly during the packed summer season, when Bethell would temporarily forsake the then off-season Monte Carlo to operate the Ostend branch—and play roulette at the casino.

Because everything Bethell says about biased-wheel play is important from the standpoint of the effort one must put into clocking wheels, the statistical problem of assessing winners, and the required amount of capital, I am quoting his words in their entirety:

"At one of the Belgian establishments," he wrote in 1901, "[I] found that the wheels were never moved from table to table, and from an analysis of the results, acquired by marking the numbers at the same table two hours every day for a month [at 55 spins an hour, about 3,400 spins], it was apparent that certain numbers invariably turned up oftener than others. As some numbers were continually increasing their lead, and others daily falling more and more behind, it was evident that the cylinders were never adjusted. The result of about two hours' play every day for twelve days [totaling 1,300 spins] was a win of seventy-five louis [$300]; then [my] victorious career was brought to an end by the table being closed at the end of the summer season.

"The difficulty, however, is to frame a system of staking which will survive a run of adverse luck. The advantage the player obtains from his observations of the vagaries of the table is so small that a win is only assured by having a large capital and playing a large number of coups.

"Although there may be half a dozen 'good' numbers and six 'bad' ones, there will always be a group of about twenty-four numbers whose score remains about the normal figure. Although the 'bad' numbers may not come out oftener than usual, there may be at any time such a long succession of the normal ones that the backer of the 'good' ones may at a given moment be largely out of pocket. The only way to avoid this is to take half the normal numbers on your side and back about eighteen numbers every spin of the wheel, i.e., six 'good' ones and twelve normal. This insures the player against any very long run of bad luck, and armed with four hundred units he ought to be able to beat the bank at every sitting.

"The player must be able to select a wheel with a distinguishable mark on it before attempting this system, and he must, moreover, keep a careful analysis of the table every day in order to perceive at once if the Administration have tampered with the cylinder during the night."

I have one important criticism of Bethell's biased-wheel strategy. I think it was a serious mistake for him to play *any* of the 24 random numbers—those he calls normal—just so he could play on 6 biased ones as well as on 12 random ones for a total of 18 numbers on every spin of the wheel. He was just lucky that the 12 random ones didn't lose and thereby destroy all his profit of $300 from his 6 biased numbers, to which he should have devoted his betting *entirely*. In this respect, look what happened to the 18 Italians when, subsequent to their biased-wheel play, as individuals they began wagering on random numbers—they lost all their winnings. The strategy of exactly how we should bet on biased numbers is extremely important and will be discussed later.

As Bethell left no record of how he sorted out, on a piece of paper, the statistical data of his successful biased-wheel play at Ostend, I have arranged the results of a similar number of spins clocked at a Monte

Carlo wheel by one of his contemporaries, a fellow Britisher, W. Duppa-Crotch, who made a brief foray to the Riviera in February 1891.

The two gamblers make an interesting contrast. Victor Bethell was modest and friendly and definitely willing to devote the time necessary to clock a roulette wheel in order to win money. By contrast, W. Duppa-Crotch was superficial and vain. In addition, like most gamblers, he was totally unaware of the strategy of biased-wheel play as evidenced by the fact that he thought that the fluctuations of all 37 numbers in his roulette sample were entirely random, when in fact they all were *except* for the biggest winner, number 1, which is very strongly biased. His only comment on the very high frequency of number 1 was the naive one that it would undoubtedly soon "even up" and perform normally like all the others.

This is an important point: a small fortune was staring Duppa-Crotch in the face, but as he simply wasn't aware of it, he therefore didn't bet and, unlike Bethell, didn't win anything.

After spending two days in the Monte Carlo Casino, writing down a sample of exactly 1,000 spins from one particular roulette wheel, W. Duppa-Crotch returned to London from his vacation and there, with sparse comment, published his result in a popular magazine. And that was that.

I have taken the raw numbers from Duppa-Crotch's trip and in Table 2 (p. 46) arranged them in a way that clearly and immediately points up why number 1 is such an outstanding winner and why all the 36 other numbers are totally random, banal, and worthless to any gambler. The format of Table 2 is the way I myself arrange all my own roulette samples, whether I've played them or not. The procedures of arranging the winners in descending order of frequency is simple and easy and always tells us, by our merely glancing at the tops of columns 1 and 2, whether there is or is not a number that's worth playing. (And, as in the case of Jaggers and the Italians, for example, there is often more than one number that's worth playing.)

As a whole, this is a normal sample to the point of banality. First let's calculate the simple average frequency and then, as a preliminary example, the probability of one random, *unbiased* number. Then we'll be able to recognize easily why number 1 is so *biased*.

Duppa-Crotch's sample or game consists of 1,000 spins, and so we know that each number should occur in theory on average $pn = (1/37)(1000) = 27.02$, or 27 times. From column 2 we see that three numbers (13, 16, and 23 in column 1) occur exactly the average 27 times. Not only

TABLE 2

Frequency table of 1,000 spins played in 1891 at Monte Carlo by W. Duppa-Crotch. In 48 occurrences the leader (the most frequent), which happens to be number 1, gives a strongly biased frequency of 1/20.8.

1	2	3	1	2	3
1	48	1/20.8	3	26	
10	34	1/29.4	18	26	
29	34	1/29.4	30	26	
24	33	1/30.3	32	26	
31	33	1/30.3	4	25	
2	32	1/31.3	12	25	
34	31	1/32.3	15	25	
0	30	1/33.3	9	24	
8	30	1/33.3	17	24	
14	30	1/33.3	21	24	
36	30	1/33.3	33	24	
28	29	1/34.5	5	23	
19	28	1/35.7	20	23	
22	28		35	23	
25	28		6	21	
13	27<		27	21	
16	27		7	20	
23	27		11	20	
			26	15	1/66.7

in this sample but in all samples, regardless of the number of spins, about half of the numbers will occur above average and half below. In this sample 15 numbers happen to occur above 27 and 19 numbers occur below 27.

We can see that the 15 numbers above average are spread out quite normally, with no large gaps between them. From column 2 we note that three numbers (19, 22, and 25) occur 28 times; one number (the next above) 29 times; four numbers 30 times; one number 31 times; and so on upward in frequency until there is a large jump or gap between number 10, which occurs 34 times, and number 1, which occurs an incredible 48 times.

We note that number 10 is the second best winner here, occurring 34 times. As there is no significant gap between its frequency and those of numbers 29, 24, 31, and so on down, we suspect that its frequency is entirely ordinary. By means of the normal approximation to the binomial distribution, we may calculate this frequency.

Here is the question we ask. At the end of 1,000 spins, what is the probability that a specific number—say 10—occurs 34 times (or more)? The answer is that the probability of this is .1061416 or about 1/9.42. In other words, number 10 has as much as one chance in 9.42 (quite frequent) of occurring 34 times (or more). Put another way, in 9.42 such samples or games it will occur once on average. If we do the same calculation for the 13 numbers occurring between 34 times and the average 27 times, we'll find that their probabilities are equally high and thus entirely normal.

With the foregoing as background, we may appreciate why Duppa-Crotch passed up a small fortune by *not* staying at Monte Carlo and betting on number 1 as long as the casino would let him. And as long as he had bet modestly, why would they have even noticed him among all the random winners? Victor Bethell wouldn't have allowed a golden opportunity like this to slip through his fingers!

We now ask the same question as we did with number 10. At the end of 1,000 spins, what is the probability that the most frequent number—say 1—occurs 48 times (or more)? The answer is that the probability of this is as small as .00125 or exactly 1/800. So that's how we know that number 1 is not just biased or strongly biased but *very strongly biased*, for the probability of only one chance out of 800 is certainly very, very small. We would have to go through as many as 800 samples or games of 1,000 spins each before finding, on average, only one in which the best winner occurs *as often as 48 times* (or more). If number 1 had occurred, say, even 38 rather than 34 times, that wouldn't have been particularly unusual. But *in only 1,000* spins a high frequency of 48 times is absolutely extraordinary.

For practical gambling purposes, do we have to perform this mathematical calculation to detect a biased number? The answer fortunately is no. I did the binomial calculations for numbers 10 (normal) and 1 (abnormal) only to illustrate their significant difference.

Fortunately, columns 2 and 3 show how we may obtain an equally useful answer with only one simple calculation.

Beginning with the second best winner, number 10, we notice that the values in column 2 decrease from 34 to 27 smoothly, without gaps or differences, and the same is true for the values in column 3, which decreases from 29.4 smoothly, without gaps or differences, to 35.7, the average.

In contrast, however, let's take the two entries opposite the best winner, number 1 (which we happen to know is very defective). If we subtract (in column 2) 34 from 43, we get a large gap or difference of 9, and the same is true of the corresponding relative frequencies at the top of column 3: 29.4 − 20.8 = 8.6, an enormous absolute difference compared to the differences in the frequencies below it.

Column 2 gives the *absolute frequency* of a roulette number, and it's obtained merely by counting up the total number of times a number occurs in a given sample of spins. It's an interesting value and must be obtained to calculate the relative frequency.

Column 3 yields the *relative frequency* of a particular number, and it's obtained by multiplying the number of spins of a sample or game by the total number of times a particular number occurs. Thus in Duppa-Crotch's sample or game of 1,000 spins the biased number 1 occurs 48 times, yielding a relative frequency of (1000) (1/48) = 20.8.

Now here is my important point. For any gambler wanting to detect a biased number, obviously in preparation for playing it, the *relative frequency* is the value or number he must obtain, and as we've just seen, it's an answer very easy to calculate.

Why does the relative frequency of 1/20.8 indicate that Duppa-Crotch was unfortunate not to have stayed at Monte Carlo and gambled on number 1? Because, as we know, number 1 should occur only once every 37 spins on average, but the frequency of 1/20.8 or roughly 1/20 signifies that on average, based on a game of 1,000 spins, this best winner was actually occurring as often as *once every 20 spins*, and every time the number hit, he would have won not just the mathematically fair 19 to 1 but the bank's actual 35 to 1. Accordingly, on each spin he would have averaged a huge 80% advantage over the bank, which on its part regularly conquers almost all gamblers with its mere 2.70% advantage on a single-zero wheel and 5.26% on a double-zero one.

So in the manner of Joseph Jaggers and the Italian syndicate, Duppa-Crotch could have also easily won money *had he only recognized* the highly favorable profit potential, because that's how even *one* very strongly biased number may benefit the knowledgeable gambler who's on the lookout for it and eager to exploit it.

In assessing the gambling value of raw roulette samples like that of Table 2 (p. 46) the reader should be aware that no mathematical calculations are usually necessary. He will find that, after only a little practice, playable biased numbers will easily spring to his attention.

Chapter 5

Modern Biased-Wheel Players: Reno and Las Vegas

Albert R. Hibbs and Dr. Roy Walford

Reno: 1947

Any gambler who is considering a specific system, whether a biased-wheel strategy or not, naturally wants to know how that system works on a day-to-day basis in a real casino, at a real moment in time, with real gamblers. Theory is all very well, but what happened when the system was actually used?

That is why the successful biased-wheel play, first in Reno, then in Las Vegas, of Albert R. Hibbs and Dr. Roy Walford is so important, because their narrative illustrates gamblers grappling on a daily basis with the following significant and inevitable questions:

How long must we clock a wheel to discover a biased number? How much capital will we need to play that number? How should we apportion our wagers—on one biased number or simultaneously on several that are neighbors? Given a specific length of time, what is the frequency of the longest losing run between occurrences of our biased number? Should we stay with the winner that we've already clocked, or should we switch to another number that has emerged as more promising? If we win, will we be harassed by the casino? Will they eventually bar us?

In November 1947, Albert R. Hibbs, 25, of Chillicothe, Ohio, and Roy Walford, 23, of San Diego, California, two University of Chicago graduate students in (respectively) mathematics and medicine, drove a Model A Ford to Reno, Nevada, with a combined capital of $300. Hibbs, already with a master's degree in mathematics, had previously bought a toy roulette wheel in Chicago and had convinced Walford that real casino roulette wheels would probably also have biases.

To assess the performance of these two students we should keep the following in mind. Although at Monte Carlo the hourly average, both today and yesterday, is about 55 spins per wheel, in Reno, Las Vegas, and Atlantic City the hourly rate is double that, i.e., 110 spins an hour, and as Hibbs and Walford decided to play uninterruptedly in alternating shifts, that gave them about 2,600 spins in each 24-hour playing cycle.

In Reno the first casino they saw was the Palace Club, where they settled in for four days of making minimal wages while quietly clocking several roulette wheels. Finally they discovered that a particular wheel indeed had one biased number. (We're naturally reminded of the sole biased number on the wheel clocked by W. Duppa-Crotch. The crucial difference, of course, is that Hibbs and Walford knew about the system and were seeking biased numbers for play.)

Betting at each spin first a cautious half dollar and then a dollar on their biased number, the two students parlayed their humble $300 capital into an amazing $5,000 in only 40 hours.

How did the Palace Club react to these two young men's multiplying their capital almost 17-fold in such a short time?

Allan Wilson is a California mathematician and himself a successful biased-wheel player in Reno of an enormous 80,000 spins, and in his book, *The Casino Gambler's Guide* (1965), Wilson described how the house reacted:

"During this period of time, the house attempted to break up their winning streak by numerous hostile actions. The speed of the wheel was varied from fast to slow, and a large and a small ball were frequently interchanged. Dealers were changed more quickly than usual. At one point, when the boys were doing quite well, the boss came over to watch. When their number came again, he angrily waved the dealer out and took over himself. Leaning back with an air of 'Now everything is under control,' he spun the ball. Around and around it whirled, and then, plunk—right into their number once more. When their winnings reached the $5,000 level, the house changed the wheel. The Palace Club had had enough!"

To thwart winning players by varying the speed of either the roulette wheel or the ball has been a casino countermeasure for a long time. Here, for example, is the complaint of an English gambler in 1895 about the Monte Carlo Casino:

"And the skill of the croupiers adds another element of disadvantage to the system player in the rapidity of play. In my one week of 4,012 spins at Monte Carlo the average number of coups per day was 573, or about fifty-two an hour, or nearly one a minute.

"Fast as that play is, the croupiers can go faster, and if they happen to detect players betting on systems in which calculations are necessary, they can hit up the pace to seventy coups an hour if there are not too many players at the table.

"And so, if the system player seems to be a dangerous customer, or if the croupiers wish to make him think they are afraid of him, they can make the rate of play such that simply for want of time to work out the exact amount to be staked on the following coup the player misses a whirl of the wheel, and his play is balked. Especially is this so if the player has reached high figures."

In Las Vegas I know a pit boss at a large Strip casino, and when I asked him recently about this countermeasure of casinos varying the speed of play, he replied: "We call that 'the short spin.' If a system player's been winning too much or too long, the dealer spins the ball slowly so that it drops off the ball track and into the numbers after only a few spins. This doubles the number of spins per hour and so quickens the player's loss."

It might be mentioned here that, for some time, in many German casinos a gambler has been allowed to choose the speed of play that pleases him. Thus, although in a casino most roulette tables continue to function at the traditional, moderate pace, a few other tables in the same casino are called (in English) Quick Tables, where the speed is accordingly much faster. Most system players prefer the traditional, slower tables.

Thus, to sum up about this important matter of speed: If a gambler is using an ordinary staking system, a dealer may speed up the game and thus the bank's profit by decreasing the *ball's* revolutions. But if a player seems to be winning—as in the case of Hibbs and Walford in Reno, Nevada—owing to a possible bias somewhere in the wheel itself, the dealer may speed up the *wheel's* rotation in order to try to cancel out or lessen any possible physical dysfunction—by the ball's being strongly bounced about and dropping more or less directly into some random slot rather than being misguided, to the casino's disadvantage, by a slower descent over possibly defective frets or a warped lower ball track.

So having tried to thwart Hibbs and Walford by varying the speed of both wheel and ball, as well as by alternating the size of the ball, the Palace Club finally turned to their only remaining countermeasure—the ultimate one, we recall, invoked by the Monte Carlo Casino against Joseph Jaggers and against the Italian syndicate: they removed the wheel.

No sooner had the Palace Club taken away the roulette wheel than Hibbs and Walford calmly rose, gathered up their $5,000 winnings, and marched across the back alley and through the rear of the more famous Harolds Club, fronting Reno's main thoroughfare, Virginia Street.

At Harolds Club the two youths followed the same procedure as at the Palace Club—before playing, they clocked a wheel, but whereas they had spent *four* days clocking wheels at the Palace Club before finding their biased gem, at Harolds they spent only *one* hasty day at one wheel, and as I shall explain presently, I think this was their grave error.

At Harolds Club the day's clocking indicated red number 9 would be their ticket to fortune. Once more the two youths decided to spell each other in eight-hour shifts. Hibbs was dark and Walford blondish with thinning hair. Both students were tall, gaunt, wore formal coats and ties, and soberly sipped milk. Under the watchful eye of three women dealers, the two gamblers gradually increased their wager on number 9 as they won.

How did they do? In only 48 hours they won an amazing $6,000, and in 60 hours this sum flew up to $14,500. Walford played from 2 to 13 chips a spin, with a top bet of $19, so that at 35 to 1 he would win $655 on every occurrence of red number 9. During each 24-hour playing cycle, or roughly 2,600 spins, both students wagered only on number 9. In other words, unlike Joseph Jaggers, they didn't try to camouflage their play from the casino with diversionary bets on random numbers too. Although they didn't whisper a word to either the casino or to any of the onlookers about biased-wheel play, neither student was the least bit secretive and openly kept a black notebook into which he recorded every roulette number, winning or otherwise, as it occurred.

Talk of the students' amazing success spread like wildfire, first locally in Reno, then nationally on radio and in newspapers, which tracked their daily wins and losses. For Harolds Club such publicity was priceless, and Raymond Smith, Sr., the elder proprietor of Harolds Club, quite aware that the rival Palace Club to their rear had, in their exasperation, finally removed their roulette wheel, announced to the press that at Harolds Club the particular winning wheel would stay put "even if it costs me a million bucks."

From Virginia Street crowds poured into Harolds Club to watch the two students place their wagers, methodically chart the wheel, and rake in their winnings. The press of onlookers around their table—including the gamblers eagerly imitating them with their own wagers—was considerable. Around the Reno casinos other gamblers began clocking wheels and recording results in their own little black notebooks, hoping the system could be successfully imitated.

Then, after 60 hours of play the system began to founder. Losing *streaks* began to set in, for the magic number 9 didn't occur as frequently as before. Then long losing *runs* arrived when it didn't occur even a single time.

The first serious losing run took place on one of Hibbs's daytime shifts: number 9 didn't occur for as long as 176 spins. The second serious losing run took place on one of Walford's nighttime shifts, when number 9 didn't occur for as long as 300 spins. That alone caused a loss of ($19) (300) = \$5,700, which dropped their win from \$14,500 to \$8,800. From that point it kept going down and down, and when it reached \$6,500, the avuncular Raymond Smith, Sr., drew the students aside. He reminded them of that traditional gambling adage—quit while you're ahead. Wisely, Hibbs and Walford took his advice. Thus, on Thursday morning, November 20, the two young men threw in the towel, and at 6:00 A.M. fell exhausted into their hotel beds, clutching their final win of \$6,500.

Any two gamblers who begin with a small capital of \$300 and end with a win of \$6,500 may only be called resoundingly successful. But of this sum Hibbs and Walford won as much as \$5,000 at the Palace Club and only \$1,500 at Harolds Club.

So what went wrong with the system at Harolds Club?

Here is the mistake that I believe these two successful gamblers made. At the Palace Club they spent an adequate *four* days clocking the wheels, whereas at Harolds Club they spent only *one* such day. In four days at the Palace Club they found a truly biased number and won by it, but at Harolds Club, after only a single day of clocking, the two youths deluded themselves into thinking that a *random* winning number—the chosen number 9—was a *biased* winning number. From our study of Victor

Bethell's game at Ostend we recall that roughly half of every sample of spins will always be random winning numbers—there are always plenty of them to bewitch us and seduce us into wagering on them, alas—and as I say, that's the trap into which I believe Hibbs and Walford fell at Harolds Club. Had they spent more than only one day clocking the Harolds Club wheel, they would have found that their favorite red number 9 was indeed exactly what it turned out to be—just another fickle, fluctuating, random winner that almost invariably incurred a long losing streak.

A brief analysis of the frequency of losing runs will help us avoid making the same mistake as that made by Hibbs and Walford.

Table 3 opposite is based on a sample of 46,080 consecutive roulette numbers—an entire three months—recorded from one table in Monte Carlo in 1933 by Dr. Hans Hartman. I divided this sample into 45 sessions, each 1,024 spins long. Arbitrarily selecting zero as my designated number, I counted through each 1,024-spin session, noting the *length* of the *longest losing run* that occurred at *any* time during that session—for it's the longest losing run that usually bankrupts us, not the shorter ones, which we can survive. By *length* I mean the number of losing spins between winning occurrences of zero (for Hibbs and Walford it was red number 9).

As we observe from Table 3 opposite, the longest losing run during the first session was 159 spins, the longest losing run during the second session was 153 spins...and the longest during the 45th and last session was 122 spins.

How long did Hibbs and Walford play the Harolds Club wheel? For 60 hours or at most *three days* or $(3)(2,600) = 7,800$ spins, and their longest losing run was an extraordinary 300 spins. How long is the Hartman sample? It constitutes *three months* or 46,080 spins, and yet it doesn't contain a single losing run as long as 300 spins. (The longest is 268 spins in the 17th session.)

I believe the foregoing supports my opinion that at Harolds Club Hibbs and Walford were in actuality playing a fickle random number.

So much for an actual sample of long losing runs over a long period. How about theory? What is the theoretical frequency of a losing run of 300 (or more) spins on a 38-slot American wheel? (It should be mentioned that on a 37-slot European wheel the result would be little different.) The answer is that such a long losing run will occur on average only once every 113,340 spins. Given that a Harolds Club (or any Nevada) roulette wheel produces on average 2,600 spins in every 24-

TABLE 3

The *longest* losing run of a single number (zero) during each of the 1,024-spin sessions (45 of them) in a three-month sample of 46,080 roulette spins (Average length: 147.87 spins)

1	159	17	268	33	125
2	153	18	136	34	98
3	185	19	135	35	140
4	131	20	160	36	130
5	100	21	168	37	145
6	85	22	202	38	106
7	232	23	85	39	115
8	134	24	172	40	104
9	134	25	116	41	136
10	71	26	194	42	171
11	149	27	223	43	170
12	128	28	117	44	182
13	192	29	149	45	122
14	120	30	106		
15	260	31	259		
16	94	32	101		

hour period, then a losing run of 300 (or more) spins will require an average of as many as $(113,340/2,600) = 44$ days—not just three days.

The foregoing calculations are based, of course, on the frequency of a number's occurring normally once every 38 spins. It is said that Hibbs and Walford thought that at Harolds Club the relative frequency of their so-called biased number was as large and advantageous as $p = 1/30$. If this frequency had indeed been true, then a losing run of 300 (or more) spins would occur on average only once every 784,314 spins or require an average of as many as $(784,314/2,600) = 302$ days—again not just three days.

Accordingly my opinion is that Hibbs and Walford won $5,000 at the Palace Club through playing a *biased number* and won $1,500 at Harolds Club through *luck* (and lost there $14,500 − $6,500 = $8,000 through *ill luck*).

So verily we must celebrate the victory of Hibbs and Walford for the gambling achievement that it was. Indeed, from a trifling capital of only $300 to a win of $5,000 was a marvel which had nothing to do with luck.

It deserves our applause for intellectual calculation, shrewdness, and endurance. But such an achievement contains a most important lesson for the rest of us. Had Hibbs and Walford clocked the Harolds Club wheel for, instead of just one day, the adequate four days that they clocked the Palace Club wheels, perhaps they would have carried away a good deal more than $5,000.

The lesson is obvious. Whether we be Victor Bethell or Albert R. Hibbs and Roy Walford, we must take great care to *avoid* random numbers.

Those we leave to the ordinary players.

Las Vegas: 1948

Having enjoyed such success in Reno in the fall of 1947, Albert R. Hibbs and Dr. Roy Walford (by now an M.D.) decided, not surprisingly, to taste again the fruits of biased-wheel play. Their $5,000 winnings from Reno they had gratifyingly used to help pay off graduate-school expenses at the University of Chicago.

So in the spring of 1948, when they sat down at the center roulette table of the Golden Nugget Casino in downtown Las Vegas, as soon as their identity became known, America's two nationally celebrated roulette players drew a capacity crowd as they began cautiously wagering just 50 cents on every spin of the wheel.

But what's going on here? Didn't the two youths clock the Golden Nugget wheel at all? Were they going to repeat their serious Harolds Club error? This important point we'll clear up anon.

As any gambler considering biased-wheel play may face many aspects of what happened to Albert Hibbs and Roy Walford in Las Vegas—the problem of sufficient capital, the length of losing runs, the ratio of one's bets to gains and losses, the fatigue from gambling long hours—the information gained from their venture in Las Vegas is absolutely invaluable, because it provides a chronicle of what occurred on a *day-to-day* basis. Such data is rare. Indeed, I know of no other such record.

The marathon play of these two young men required a whole month and took place essentially at two casinos in downtown Las Vegas.

On Thursday, April 15, 1948, Hibbs and Walford started their play at the Golden Nugget, spelling each other in six-hour relays. Although friendly as ever to the gallery, they would not divulge their starting capital. While jotting down all the occurring numbers in their little black notebooks, they cautiously bet 50 cents on red number 9 (only by coincidence the same number bet at Reno).

On Friday morning, April 16, after twelve hours of cautious play, the youths raised their bet to $1 a spin. Their winnings ballooned by noon to $500 and by midnight to as much as $1,200.

On Saturday, April 17, although their winnings remained flat, they decided, nonetheless, to increase their wager from $1 to $2.50 a spin. The two gamblers were experiencing typical fluctuations of a roulette number, their red 9 not occurring for a whole half hour and then occurring as many as three times in four minutes.

After 53 hours of play, however, a losing streak set in, and their winnings shrank to $700. For Hibbs there was a long losing run of 146 spins, and for Walford a long one of 192 spins, but as we note from Table 3 (p. 55), these lengths are quite within the normal range of every session of roughly 1,000 spins.

Even late at night there was always a crowd of people who enjoyed watching the two young men tempt fortune. At one point Dr. Walford was talking to a spectator and failed to place a wager on number 9. It came up, so he lost a bet of ($2.50) (35) = $87.50. The young physician laughed at his misfortune but quickly stopped talking and concentrated on his game. When asked by the press why they hadn't come to Las Vegas straight from their Reno victory, Hibbs replied, "Oh, we fully intended to drive right down to Las Vegas, but we both had to return to our university classes in Chicago." In answer to how long they intended to stay in Las Vegas, both youths pointed with smiles to the beards they were growing for Helldorado, the annual, three-day, wild West celebration and parade, which would begin on Thursday, May 13. In the parade many male participants sport beards. At any rate, on Saturday at 11:30 P.M. both gamblers called a temporary halt to their game and fell gratefully into bed.

On Sunday, April 18, Hibbs and Walford started at noon again at the center roulette table at the Golden Nugget but finally gave up wagering on their celebrated number 9 for a split one-dollar bet between number 1 and zero—numbers which are adjacent on the American wheel. At first their pile of chips grew to $300, then shrank back to the $210 with which they had started. Just the same, through these plus-and-minus fluctuations they kept to their $1 split bet on numbers 1 and zero, drawing along with them numerous wagers from the crowd of enthusiastic onlookers who came and went throughout the day.

On Monday, April 19, around 5:00 A.M., the two youthful gamblers took stock of their winnings, which after four days of round-the-clock play hadn't progressed as much as they'd hoped. After a conference they decided on a radical departure from their previous strategy. Instead of playing on just one or at most two numbers, they decided to play on as many as *nine* numbers, and this involved sector play.

Accordingly they began betting just five cents on each of the following nine numbers: three chips on zero, 1, and 13 (all three neighbors on the wheel); four chips on 2, double zero, 28, and 9 (again all four neighbors on the wheel); plus two chips on 26 and 29 (roughly opposite each other on the wheel).

But as this strategy showed only a slight gain, by 8:15 A.M. the two gamblers decided to cash in all their chips, which came to $250. This netted them only $40 since their resumption of gambling on Sunday noon the day before.

All told, they had now spent 73 and a half hours—slightly more than three days—in almost continuous gambling at the Golden Nugget. "Well, we did okay," announced the two young men rather bleakly to the press. After playing a little blackjack for fun, they disappeared to bed.

According to the Golden Nugget Casino, since the youths had started gambling the previous Thursday evening, their net winnings came to $740.

Just the same, because they hadn't yet found a wheel with a *sufficiently* significant bias, the two youths felt quite discouraged, so during the next three days—Tuesday, Wednesday, and Thursday—they decided to case wheels in other Las Vegas casinos. First they clocked wheels in both the downtown Pioneer Club and Las Vegas Club. Then they did the same in the plusher casinos out on the Strip.

Returning at night exhausted to their modest downtown hotel room, the two young men tried to keep their eyes open long enough to read the mail stemming from their national and international publicity as winning roulette players. One letter was from a man in Russian-occupied Germany who asked if they wouldn't mind sending him $650 so he could pay off a debt. Another was from a mother on the East Coast who suggested solicitously that they forward her money so she could put her "little girl" through college.

The two young gamblers laughed. Neither of them was the least bit wealthy, and they themselves were risking their own capital in an attempt to win enough to buy, in Chicago, a small sailboat enabling them to pursue research in tropical medicine in the Caribbean. Such was the avowed purpose of their gambling trip to Las Vegas.

On Thursday, April 29, having failed to find any playable wheels in the Strip, the youths finally decided on a wheel at the Pioneer Club at the corner of First and Fremont Streets. There they sat down hopefully at 10:00 P.M.

On Friday, April 30, by 2:00 A.M. they had gradually accumulated an additional $300 by wagering just 75 cents a spin, again on only one number. They had abandoned partial sector play as counterproductive. This time the single magic number that they picked was zero, which during one stretch occurred as often as three times in only two minutes. But unfortunately that was its height. From that moment on, zero disappeared almost completely, and Dr. Walford, whose shift it was, lost back to the Pioneer Club not only their $300 profit but also $300 from their $740 win from the nearby Golden Nugget Casino. Thus by 10:00 A.M. Friday morning their total net profit had shrunk to only $440.

Discouraged, the two young men switched from roulette to playing some blackjack but lost at that too. Now quite disconsolate, they retired to their downtown hotel room. "But we will try again," exclaimed Dr. Walford bravely.

At this point, dumbfounding the press and surprising everyone across the country, the two young men disappeared from the Las Vegas gambling scene for three whole days. Then...

On Tuesday, May 4, they calmly reappeared to the enthusiasm of everybody in Las Vegas and of the national press. Where had they been? They laughed and wouldn't say, but they denied that they had gone broke at the Pioneer Club. "We're still ahead," they announced.

Then they sat down at the tables in both the Golden Nugget and the Eldorado Club, not actually to gamble at roulette, but to clock the wheels again. Studiously they wrote down all the numbers that occurred, while the public watched them curiously.

On Wednesday, May 5, the two young gamblers finally chose the Golden Nugget again over the Eldorado. Working around the clock in six-hour shifts, they managed to lose $180.

By noon on Thursday, May 6, they were terribly discouraged. They had reached a loss of $200. As their total net win was now down to only $240, they decided despondently to call off the gambling ventures once and for all. "We're through for good. You can't win," they declared to the press.

"We're terribly tired," explained Dr. Walford. He claimed that they both had dots before their eyes from writing down numbers in their little black books. After getting some sleep, the physician declared, they planned to leave Las Vegas and return to Chicago to concentrate their efforts on buying the sailboat for their cherished trip in the Caribbean to do research in tropical medicine. "At least we should get E for effort," he concluded, sadly plucking at the beard that he'd been growing for the Helldorado parade in which they would now never march. The two youths bade goodbye to the roulette wheel of the Golden Nugget Casino and returned to their hotel room.

As soon as they awoke from a long sound sleep, however, Hibbs and Walford found on their doorstep Ralph Paige and Tudor Scherer, managers of the Pioneer Club, who proposed to grubstake the two young men for $500 if they'd only return to the wheels at the Pioneer Club. Grubstaking is an American Western tradition in which the staker risks his money in exchange for something of value—if not business profits, then the publicity that the Pioneer Club was openly hoping the young men might bring to their gambling hall.

Realizing that the research sailboat in Chicago might still be within their grasp, Hibbs and Walford agreed to the grubstake proposition and somewhat doubtfully returned to the scene of their recent downfall, the Pioneer Club. There they sedulously clocked the wheels for three more days—Friday, Saturday, and Sunday. Then...

At this point the second part of their marathon play began.

On Monday, May 10, the team sat down in the morning to gamble at a particular roulette wheel in the Pioneer Club. Their $500 grubstake provided them with a thousand 50-cent wagers.

I use the word team, because a third and most important party had now openly joined them. This was Jack Cortez, 32, a friend from New York who heretofore had worked behind the scenes clocking wheels for Hibbs and Walford all over Las Vegas ever since their first appearance at dusk at the Golden Nugget on Thursday, April 15.

This is a most important point, because we now realize that the two youths indeed hadn't repeated the serious error that they'd made at Harolds Club in Reno. Now we see that before Hibbs and Walford had even stepped into the Golden Nugget on April 15, their friend, Jack Cortez, had been clocking the wheels there for them.

In addition, having Cortez on the betting team itself was a great help to Hibbs and Walford, because now, instead of the more arduous six-hour stretch, a player could just take a four-hour shift at the wheel.

The first player was Jack Cortez, who sat down on Friday morning at 2:00 A.M. After playing only 50-cent chips on numbers 5, 22, and 31 (22 and 31 are neighbors, and 31 is roughly opposite), the New Yorker finally narrowed these prospects down to black 22, which before noon had occurred five times in only a half hour. Didn't Cortez, asked an onlooker, think he could raise his bet a little higher? "No," he replied, "we're going to keep playing only 50 cents until we're positive that that's the number we'll stay on."

By noon on Tuesday, May 11 their constant stake was still a cautious 50 cents, but zero had been substituted for unremunerative black 22. Trying to exceed their topmost win of $740 at the Golden Nugget, the three young men, after only 30 hours of play, managed to push their profit up to $700. Onlookers pressed around their table to watch them on their seesaw. What happened, a reporter asked them, to numbers 5, 22, and 31? "Oh, we gave those up," replied Cortez. "We plan to stick with zero—at least for a while."

By late afternoon Wednesday, May 12, the team finally allowed their stake per spin to inch up from 50 cents to $1.25, because winnings had increased from $700 to as much as $1,500.

By now the three young men had been gambling strenuously in Las Vegas for almost a whole month.

In their appropriate way the first thing the three youths did was pay off their $500 grubstake obligation to the two managers of the Pioneer Club, Ralph Paige and Tudor Scherer.

Word of the team's win attracted a throng of spectators, who crowded four and five deep around their table, offering silent encouragement. Zero was still the magic number on which the team was wagering, and whenever it came up, the Pioneer Club dealers themselves were delighted to pay it off. What would the young men do with their winnings? asked the press. "Our goal," insisted Dr. Walford, "is still to win enough money to finance our yachting trip in the Caribbean and conduct research in tropical medicine."

On Thursday, May 13, the first day of the Helldorado celebration, which featured the parade of bearded Westerners and their calico-dressed females, Hibbs and Walford disappeared to join the jubilation, leaving Jack Cortez gambling at the chosen roulette wheel in the Pioneer Club. As their magic number, zero, hadn't occurred for a disappointingly long time, at one point an idea occurred to the bored Cortez. He pleasantly asked the dealer if he, Cortez, might spin the ball once round the wheel. At Monte Carlo, of course, such informality would never be countenanced, but this was relaxed Las Vegas, and the dealer agreed. So the wheel turned, Cortez spun the ball, and...bingo!—or rather, zero— the ball dropped right into the lucky number! The spectators laughed and applauded. This so appealed to Cortez that later on in the evening he suggested the venture a second time—and again zero repeated! Naturally this brought a second wave of applause and laughter from the crowd, and when the bearded Hibbs and Walford returned from the Helldorado celebration, they had to admit the omen was a great way to end the team's fourth gambling day at the Pioneer Club.

On Friday, May 14, at noon the team allowed their bet to inch up from $1.25 to $1.50 per spin, because their winnings had increased from $1,500 to $1,700.

In addition, they at last gave up putting their hopes on zero and switched to its nearest neighbor, red number one.

On Saturday, May 15, in the small hours of the morning, the team allowed their bet on number 1 to rise from $1.50 to $2.25. In the daytime they re-raised their wager from $2.25 to $3.00, and on Saturday night from $3 to a big $5 as their winnings soared from $1,700 to $3,000 and finally to $5,000.

Here we must point out another important aspect of the team's successful strategy: they were keeping their bank-to-bet or winnings-to-bet ratio at a prudent proportion of 1,000 to 1 in order to be able to last through a long losing run. (See Table 3, p. 55.)

Of the trio of gamblers, the biggest winner during the last 14 hours had by chance been Jack Cortez, but on this sixth day of the second part of their marathon all three of the players received applause and warm encouragement from the crowd, and as they counted their stacks of chips, several score Helldorado celebrants jammed round their table at the Pioneer Club, including Albert Hibbs's father, and his sister and brother-in-law, Mr. and Mrs. Bart Jones of Chicago.

On Sunday, May 16, by midnight the trio were wagering as much as $10 a spin, and their winnings had hit $12,300.

On Monday, May 17, by 8:00 A.M. they were betting $22 a spin, and winnings had climbed to $20,000. By noon the wager reached $25 and winnings $23,000 (as much as $7,000 above their top Reno win of $14,500 at Harolds Club before it slipped back to the final $6,500).

Although at first the Pioneer Club was pleased with all the national publicity it was reaping from the young trio's rising win, a grave drawback to the casino was the crowd of onlookers, two of whom were likewise betting every spin on red number one, and so far they'd won respectively $1,800 and $2,000. With as much as $40 riding on every spin, the Pioneer Club was losing a small fortune.

On Tuesday, May 18, after eight days and nights of their second marathon roulette game, Albert R. Hibbs, Dr. Roy Walford, and Jack Cortez, the Rover Boys of the roulette wheel, as the press had dubbed them, hit the enormous cumulative win of $36,000. Then it slipped back $6,000 to $30,000, where the three bettors halted.

Why did the three biased-roulette-wheel gamblers stop at $30,000? Why didn't they go on? The reason was that at this sum Ralph Paige and Tudor Scherer of the Pioneer Club threw up their hands and told the players to halt. In exchange for publicity the Pioneer Club was simply losing too much, and they couldn't afford it! So at this point the two managers invoked the traditional rule of the grubstake, which obliged them to pay off only half the win of $30,000. Accordingly, the team's final win came to $15,000, or more than double the $6,500 Hibbs and Walford had won from their biased-wheel venture in Reno.

On Tuesday morning, May 18, each of the three team players cordially shook hands with Ralph Paige and Tudor Scherer, waved goodbye to the applauding crowd, and proudly walked out of the Pioneer Club into the bright Las Vegas sunshine, each with a pocketed win of $5,000.

Let's assess as a whole the two biased-wheel forays of Albert R. Hibbs and Dr. Roy Walford.

In their trip to Reno in November 1947, they won $6,500, whereas in the one to Las Vegas in April 1948, they won more than twice that, or $15,000 (and if we put aside the grubstake-loan condition of the gambling hall's paying off only half of what they won, that would have been $30,000).

Why did they win so much more in Las Vegas than in Reno? Was it just luck? Of course not, because we must always keep one thing strictly in mind: Biased-wheel play is *not* a matter of luck. We're not gambling. We're not playing roulette. We're playing a particular *wheel*.

In Reno the youths began by winning and ended up by losing, but stopped with a good profit of $6,500. In Las Vegas it was the reverse—they began by losing (along the way understandably becoming quite discouraged) and ended up by winning $15,000. But as every gambler knows, both cycles are entirely normal, and any biased-wheel player should expect them.

Then why did Hibbs and Walford win so much more in Las Vegas?

In Table 4 (p. 64) I've summarized the data of their biased-wheel trip to Las Vegas, and it's evident that these figures contain the answer: in Las Vegas they applied successfully the lessons learned the hard way in Reno.

Our own first and paramount lesson to be learned from their thirty-day gambling venture is that *every biased-wheel player must do a sufficient amount of clocking.* As we note from the bottom of Table 4 below, Hibbs and Walford (and ultimately Cortez) spent 14 days sedulously clocking wheels and 13 days actually gambling—an almost even ratio. In this way they avoided the Reno pitfall of betting on random numbers.

TABLE 4

Summary of the Hibbs/Walford biased-wheel play in Las Vegas, 1948

1 Days	2 Spins	3 Activity	4 Cumulative win
		Golden Nugget	
3	8,000	*playing*	$740
10		clocking	
		Pioneer Club	
.5	1,300	*playing*	$440
3		disappeared	
1		clocking	
		Golden Nugget	
1.5	3,300	*playing*	$240
(19)	(12,600)		
		Pioneer Club	
3		clocking	
8	20,800	*playing*	$15,000
30	33,400		$15,000

Actual days *playing:* 13   Final win: $15,000 ($30,000, if paid off in full)
Actual days clocking 14

Our second lesson from their foray is that the team was willing to try playing more than one biased number, i.e., sector play. Thus on Monday, April 19, at 5:00 A.M., Hibbs and Walford at the Golden Nugget decided to bet only 5 cents on each of as many as nine numbers, of which three and four numbers were two sets of neighbors. But as by 8:15 A.M. this strategy had shown only a slight gain, they stopped playing it and returned to only a single biased number. Here is the important lesson they learned about sector play: if it works, fine, but if it doesn't pay off, *drop it*. It's all very well to say that with nine numbers we're covering as much as $(9/37) = $ one fourth of the wheel, but the ball can drop into only *one* of those numbers, so even when we win, we lose 8 units—a considerable drain on our resources.

Our third lesson from their venture is that, to stay in the game and not lose a fortune, the biased-wheel player must consistently bet only the *minimum* wager (whether on a single number or otherwise) until he begins winning—*only then* may he safely raise his wager. If we look at column 4 of Table 4, we note that this proportional betting strategy enabled Hibbs and Walford to stay in the game during the first dismal 19 days when their cumulative win was dropping steadily from $740 to $440 to finally a depressing $240. By the same token, beginning Wednesday, May 12, at the Pioneer Club, during the last six marathon days, the team gradually and *proportionately* increased their wager on their single number (red number one) from the minimal 50 cents to as high as a huge $25 per spin, because all the while they were maintaining their bank-to-bet ratio to a constant and conservative 1,000 to 1.

Such are some of the crucial reasons why, in their overall Reno and Las Vegas gambling ventures, Albert R. Hibbs and Dr. Roy Walford won a total of $6,500 + $15,000 = $21,500.

It wasn't luck.

And it certainly wasn't irresponsible biased-wheel play.

It was the careful application of the basic principles that make biased-wheel play work.

It took considerable thought and ultimately courage.

Accordingly, shouldn't we congratulate these two gamblers?

Chapter 6

Modern Biased-Wheel Players: Reno and Las Vegas

Allan N. Wilson and Robert Bowers; also The Jones Boys

"My own entry into the roulette business was triggered by the flood of publicity on the coup at the Pioneer Club [in Las Vegas]. Inspiring accounts of the success of Hibbs and Walford were printed in the West Coast newspapers, and I followed them with rapt attention. At the time, I was a student in physics at the University of California at Berkeley. Between classes in atomic particles and quantum statistics, I was constantly distracted by the thought of applying my knowledge of math and physics to the roulette. Then fate threw me in with Bob Bowers, another physicist who had witnessed Hibbs and Walford in action at Harolds Club [in Reno].... And after their sensational run in Las Vegas, my classmate and I could hardly wait for the spring semester to end...."

Such is the opening paragraph describing his own biased-roulette play by Allan N. Wilson in *The Casino Gambler's Guide* (1965), from which I quoted in the previous chapter. The book is perhaps the best popular exposition of casino games in general.

From our study of the forays of Joseph Jaggers, the Italian syndicate, and Hibbs and Walford, we know that large sums may be won from such play. But that isn't why we read Wilson, who made only a small sum. We read him not only because he's a good storyteller but because he assesses his experience from a scientific standpoint.

Allan Wilson and Robert Bowers reached Harolds Club in late June 1948.

Naturally, their first order of business was to locate a biased wheel. But how does anyone find this most desirable of gaming objects?

"We believed that the mechanical defects of a wheel are of a sufficiently subtle nature that one would rarely be able to find a 'hot' wheel just by looking at it," wrote Wilson. "Anything that would stare you in the face would obviously have been repaired by the club a long time ago. Accordingly, we selected a wheel solely on the basis of comfort."

After clocking and playing this wheel for a whole month or 80,000 continuous spins, however, the two young men concluded that that particular wheel was hot but not hot enough. The best number was red 19, but as it came in at a relative frequency of only 1 in 35 spins (compared to the estimated 1 in 30 spins for Hibbs and Walford), Wilson and Bowers didn't consider it profitable enough. Their very small starting capital of $50 (compared to Hibbs's and Walford's $300) had increased to a profit of only $300, hardly a fortune.

"At this point," concluded Wilson after a month of playing the first wheel, "we decided to reexamine some of our basic assumptions. Perhaps a really worn-out, beat-up wheel would present much better possibilities for a biased number. With this in mind, we gave some of the other wheels [in Harolds Club] a once-over, and on the first floor we found a choice-looking specimen, which looked as though it was on the verge of retirement. Paint was chipping off in numerous places, and the pockets were so badly worn that the fibered structure of the wood was readily apparent. We soon concluded that it would be highly unscientific to leave town without acquiring a more balanced experience."

After one week's play or 20,000 spins, however, the youths had lost back to Harolds Club about $100 of their $300 profit, so they gave up also on the second, antiquated wheel, about which "the biggest surprise was that black 10 was running only slightly above average. It had a tremendously worn pocket, and just looking at the wheel, one would guess that it would catch the ball more often than the others."

Such are Allan Wilson's comments on trying to locate a sufficiently biased wheel in Harolds Club. The youths tried twice there, picking the first wheel simply because it was situated in the casino in a comfortable location, and the second because it was "a really worn-out, beat-up wheel." In neither choice were the two gamblers successful.

What had Wilson and Bowers done wrong in finding a biased wheel?

In my opinion they didn't do anything wrong. They proceeded intelligently. The fact that they didn't succeed in finding a significantly biased wheel in Harolds Club means nothing. In such a search nothing is guaranteed, for in any casino most wheels are probably unbiased or at least insufficiently so for advantage play.

The problem of first finding a biased wheel is undoubtedly the most difficult and frustrating aspect of the whole system. I've given considerable thought to the matter, discussed it with roulette wheel experts in Las Vegas, Reno, and Atlantic City, and have done my share of wheel clocking not only there but in Havana, San Juan, Haiti, St. Martin, London, Constance, Lindau, Estoril, Ostend, Spa, Homburg, Wiesbaden, Baden-Baden, Bregenz, Garmisch, Divonne-les-Bains, Aix-les-Bains, Cannes, Nice, Monte Carlo, Menton, San Remo, Marrakech, and elsewhere.

Referring to Wilson's comments on the two wheels that Bowers and he played in Harolds Club, I have found that a roulette wheel that looks to be in excellent condition, and therefore an unpropitious candidate for play, may be found to be biased as often as another which looks old and beat-up, and accordingly a great prospect, is found to be unbiased.

Recently, for example, I walked into Harolds Club to find, on the first floor, a bored dealer, his arms folded, waiting for customers at a roulette table that had once been electronically wired so that, when the ball dropped into a slot, this closed an electric, seeing-eye-type circuit that lit up only those areas of the layout pertinent to the winning number. Accordingly, if the ball fell into 17, under the layout lights would go on simultaneously under only number 17, black, odd, the middle dozen, and the middle column.

"I last saw an electronic table like this a few years ago operating at the Landmark Casino in Las Vegas," I said to him. "Why isn't yours working?"

"Because the circuits kept breaking down, so the lights would go on the blink, and it cost $45 an hour to have a qualified electrician come in and fix it," the dealer replied amiably. "So now we use it just as a regular roulette table. To hell with the lights."

I glanced into the 38 pockets of the wheel. In the bottom of each pocket was a hole almost an eighth of an inch in diameter. When the table is operating electronically, a light shines through each hole of the spinning cylinder or wheel head until the falling ball closes the seeing-eye circuit that illuminates, under the layout, only those squares or rectangles pertinent to the winning number. Unless these holes had been drilled with exceptional precision, which I doubt, then the diameters of certain holes would necessarily favor their particular numbers over those of others. In addition, the condition of the roulette wheel was deplorable—worn pocket pads, chipped chrome frets, an uneven upper ball track.

So this recent wheel in Harolds Club *looked* like the most propitious candidate for biased-wheel play in the world. Yet there is always the other side of the coin. Take the wheel clocked in the Monte Carlo Casino in 1891 by W. Duppa-Crotch. We recall that from the standpoint of probability there was only 1 chance in 800 that the lead winning number (number 1) would occur, instead of the average 27 times, as often as 48 times in only 1,000 spins. In other words, that number was unquestionably biased. Yet I'm willing to bet that W. Duppa-Crotch's wheel *looked* just as normal and in as good condition as all the other wheels in the Monte Carlo Casino.

Which brings me to my conclusion: just as we can't tell a book by its cover, so we can't tell a biased-roulette wheel simply by looking at it. Assuming that all else is equal, however, we might as well play first that wheel which *looks* to be in the poorest condition.

In respect to Wilson and Bowers clocking and playing only one wheel for as long as four weeks or 80,000 spins, I confess thinking that Hibbs and Walford were far more successful because they were willing to abandon any wheel that wouldn't produce winners in a reasonable length of time—say in at most a few days. As we note from column 1 of Table 4 (p. 64), with the help of Jack Cortez they were willing to scout wheels for 11 whole days not only in downtown Las Vegas but out on the Strip until fate awarded them the wheel in the Pioneer Club that paid off the big $15,000. In other words, their profit arose from a willingness to be versatile—to switch flexibly from wheel to wheel rather than from just number to number on the same wheel like Wilson and Bowers.

I believe Wilson's interesting description of their marathon play on just one wheel supports my conclusion:

"After several days at the [first] table [in Harolds Club] we began to adjust to the weird routine of four- or six-hour shifts at the wheel. By the fifth day, red 19 was leading the field. With 13,700 trials [spins] on record, 19 had won 412 times, compared with an average of 360 for all numbers on the wheel. Those extra 55 wins had given number 19 an average of once in 33 spins. We cautiously began betting a 10-cent chip straight up on number 19. It continued to prosper, so a day later we boosted the ante to a quarter. After another 24 hours, we raised our bet to 50 cents per spin. We rocked up and down for a couple of days, and then quit betting for a while—scarcely any richer than we had started. Since our initial playing capital was around $50, this meant we had gone as high as $150 and then back down. At bets of a half dollar, a modest losing run like 200 [spins] in a row would force us to quit playing, even on a number that was a winner in its long-term average. This was especially true when we accumulated capital on smaller bets and lost it on larger ones.

"As our data rolled on up past 20,000 trials, we kept looking for other numbers that might 'qualify.' Several times we made runs ranging from 10 cents to 50 cents on different numbers such as red 36, black 24, and black 35. On this play we broke approximately even. Then 19 came surging along again, and after three weeks of sampling for a total of around 60,000 plays, we hopped onto the favorite again. With bets gradually rising from 50 cents to $1.25, we parlayed our $50 up to $600 in a couple of days. But no sooner did we reach this figure than we encountered a cold streak, and we were knocked down to $300. At this point we quit on 19. We were forced to conclude that [this first] wheel was 'hot,' but not hot enough! After four solid weeks, we had rolled up a record of 80,000 continuous plays, which even to this day [in 1965] far exceeds anything this author has ever heard of....Number 19 had maintained an overall average of 1 in 35 for a whole month."

But profits, not an endurance record, should properly be a gambler's goal. Wouldn't Wilson and Bowers have fared far better in trying, say, five wheels, each for 16,000 spins, rather than sticking to one profitless wheel for 80,000 spins? (And after an interval at a second wheel they returned to play the first one for an additional profitless 20,000 spins.) In the same circumstances Hibbs, Walford, and Cortez would have never been so hidebound, and in Las Vegas their flexibility paid off for the substantial sum of $15,000. In Reno these three would have assuredly tested numerous other gaming halls.

Speaking of endurance records, we should attend carefully to Wilson's opinion about the necessity for round-the-clock play:

"The reader may wonder why [Bowers and I] decided on a continuous 24-hour play. Couldn't one play intermittently and thereby enjoy a sensible schedule? The answer is, of course, that we had to keep our eye on the wheel every moment of the day. Since we were hoping to detect some significant mechanical imperfection, we could not afford the risk of anything happening to the wheel in our absence."

What Wilson means, of course, is that they feared that, while the two youths slept, the wily casino would switch roulette wheels on them.

I myself don't believe in the necessity of round-the-clock play, and here is my explanation. Except in Nevada, every casino in the world, whether those at Monte Carlo or Atlantic City, has what today is called *down time*, when they're closed overnight, and that's when the casinos customarily switch roulette wheels which they fear may have become biased in favor of some players. As we recall, that's what the Monte Carlo Casino did to Joseph Jaggers and later to the Italian syndicate. They have done the same to others. That's what Atlantic City now customarily does too.

As Nevada has round-the-clock play, however, no casino there has down time. So when do they switch wheels on the players? The answer is—*whenever they want to*—and on a later trip to Reno in 1951 that's exactly what Harolds Club did to Allan Wilson and Robert Bowers when these two young men threatened to win substantially due to a very biased number 3 on their wheel.

As Wilson describes the dramatic scene:

"At this point the pit boss unexpectedly sent a mechanic in to test the wheel. First he laid a carpenter's level across the rim. The bubble didn't show a true horizontal, so he cranked up the feet of the table until he was better satisfied. Actually, we didn't care a hoot about that because we didn't believe that a slight tilt could affect the success of any number very much. But then he began feeling the metal slots between the numbers. When he came to [our hot] number 3, he got very excited, and went running off to tell his boss.

"Meanwhile, we commenced playing at $4 per spin instead of the quarters we had played previously....We played for about an hour with the new stakes, rocking up and down, when suddenly the owner himself appeared on the scene. He stopped the action immediately. Then he picked up the ivory ball and conducted his own little test on the wheel. He held the ball against the metal slots, spun the wheel very fast, and listened to the noise that the ball made upon the slots as it went around, 'Klunk-klunk-klunk-ping—klunk-klunk-klunk-ping.' That was enough for him, and he growled that the mechanic who was responsible for that wheel should be fired. He ordered a new wheel!

"Everybody was stunned, for this was the first time in the history of [Harolds Club] that the management had ever changed a wheel on any roulette player. It was supposed to be the biggest and most generous club in Nevada.... Everyone was astonished: the players, the spectators, the dealers, and even the pit bosses. We were utterly crushed, of course, for all our data-taking became useless."

Hence if in Nevada a casino not only may but does change a wheel on a player, there is absolutely no necessity for any exhausting, round-the-clock marathon, because a player's physical presence at the table doesn't prevent the management from changing the wheel in front of him anyway.

This policy actually favors the player, because it allows him to adopt a reasonable schedule and get some sleep.

But on our return, is there any way we may detect whether the wheel that we were clocking or playing was changed in the interval by the wily casino?

Yes, thank heavens, there is—the same one used by Joseph Jaggers when the Monte Carlo Casino switched wheels on him and the next day he noticed that the scratch, which he had noted on the outside of the bowl, was missing.

Every roulette wheel has a physical individuality which in the roulette-wheel trade is called its *signature*. Although each roulette wheel has any number of individual characteristics which are easily identifiable, such as whether the cone is brass or nickel-plated or whether the ornament is inscribed with the manufacturer's surname, the most popular signature has always been the grain somewhere on the wood. If we have memorized a distinctive patch of grain on, say, the lower ball track and on our return the next day the patch has vanished, however, we must remember that on down time the casino's mechanic may regularly give the bowl a quarter turn to redistribute any possible bias or disequilibrium. In Atlantic City, for example, for this same purpose some casinos move every single roulette wheel to another table once a month, so that, if there are twelve tables, every single wheel takes an entire year to circle the gaming room.

When S. R. Beresford lived at Monte Carlo, for the purpose of identifying bias he kept a file on the individual characteristics of every single roulette wheel in the casino:

"When at times I missed an old friend among the cylinders [on the casino floor], I used to enquire of the croupiers what had become of it. The usual joking answer was, 'It's sick.' At one time I rather fancy that I knew nearly every cylinder in use by sight. I have an index...where twenty of them have their 'dossiers' pigeon-holed....

"...many of the [old-fashioned roulette] machines had serious defects.

There was one I used to allude to as 'Monsieur Deux' [Mr. Two] on account of the fact that the number 2 appeared to come out more frequently than its rightful average. Going up to the table in which Monsieur Deux was working, I would ask the table outfit if it had yet appeared. It was never necessary to give the number. 'Has it turned up?' was quite sufficient. Some one or other of the croupiers or Chef de Partie [table chief] would answer yes or no, another would have his little joke with some whimsical answer, such as a laconic 'sick,' meaning it had not been able to come out. 'Not yet, monsieur, it's been waiting for you,' was another reply that I am able to recall....

"[At any rate] it is by the grain in the wood upon which these numbers are painted that one recognizes a cylinder. [Red] one, three, five, seven, or nine are the easiest numbers upon which to notice any peculiarity of grain."

As I mentioned, today the grain in the wood is still the conventional way biased-wheel gamblers identify and relocate a particular roulette wheel that has been moved. Many of them prefer using the grain on the slanting lower ball track (on which the metal obstacles or canoes are affixed) of the motionless bowl to the grain on the whirling numbers, which are consequently much more frustrating to read.

When a casino moves a wheel from one table to another, it is to redistribute any bias or disequilibrium. Their action is not a subterfuge to delude players, for they're quite aware that *knowing* players can't be fooled: a wheel's signature can't be disguised.

On their third and last trip to Reno, in 1955, Allan Wilson and Robert Bowers again experienced countermeasures by the casino—this time the well-known Nevada Club—and as they're all still applicable today, it's of practical importance that we know what these countermeasures entailed:

"One evening, having played some blackjack here and there, we sauntered into the Nevada Cub [on Virginia Street]. Our attention was immediately attracted to the roulette layout, which contained no less than three single-zero wheels in a row. To our utter amazement, over one of these wheels was a gigantic scoreboard. It had 37 mechanical registers, displaying the number of wins for each number on the wheel.

"The records showed more than 26,000 trials. [actually 26,113]. Number 33 was way out in front with 866 wins versus a normal 705. It was averaging [a relative frequency of] 1/30, a veritable Hibbs-type number! Also, numbers 0 and 2 were rated at 1/32. Considering the size of the sample, *all* these numbers were hotter than any we had ever seen before. We stared at each other in numb disbelief, and then asked what we were waiting for!

"My partner Bob took the night shift, and bet 75 cents on 33 and 0 each time. All night long our two numbers came roaring in, and we rolled up more than $300. When Bob's wife came to relieve him for breakfast, however, the nonchalant attitude of the operators changed. They realized a 'syndicate' was in operation, and promptly reversed the usual directions of rotation of ball and wheel. Then, later in the day when I took over, the boss ordered *alternate* rotations of ball and wheel, à la Monte Carlo. My bank rocked up and down on $1 bets, but the downs took over, and by 6 P.M. I had lost back all but $125 of our previous night's winnings. We quit, reasonably convinced that the management would not allow a big win on scientific play.

"Subsequently I struck up a conversation with one of the habitués of the club, whose gambling activity was dictated by the signs of the zodiac. He realized the point of bias play and said that many people had been playing dominant numbers on single-zero wheels in this club over a period of several years. Some, in fact, had been successful, but the club had installed the registers for its own protection and generally discouraged such players—first by alternate rotation, then by changing wheels. One man was held to $2 bet on any number, whereas the usual limit was $25.

"Our informant knew of three times that the club had switched wheels, and of two occasions when others had done so since our own misadventure [at Harolds Club in 1951]. All this tended to confirm the conclusion we had reached three years earlier: Even though it might land them some juicy publicity, most club owners were in no mood to lose big hunks of money on imperfect roulette wheels."

On their third trip to Reno, therefore, owing entirely to casino countermeasures, Wilson and Bowers were prevented from winning more than $125 in about 24 hours or 2,600 spins of biased-wheel play.

But if on their first trip in 1948 the relative frequency of their winning number (red 19) was a rather unprofitable, low 1/35 during their four-weeks' marathon of 80,000 spins, in contrast on this third trip in 1955 the relative frequency of their winning number (black 33) was a strongly biased, advantageous, high 1/30.2—a veritable Hibbs-type number, as Wilson crowed enthusiastically. Thanks to the convenience of the gambling hall's overhead mechanical register summing the 26,113 previous spins, with the best winning number (black 33) as occurring 866 times at the high frequency of 1/30.2, the two gamblers had been relieved of $(26,113/2,600) = 10.043...$ or about ten days of tedious, round-the-clock wheel clocking. Thus all they had to do was wager

TABLE 5

Ranked by Best Frequency (Column 5)

	1 Place	2 Date	3 Spins	4 No.	5 Best	6 (Worst)
1	Monte Carlo	1882	2,738	18	25.8	50.7
2	Monte Carlo	1901	5,370	12	29.8	46.7
3	Monte Carlo	1896	4,015	30	30.0	47.8
4	Reno	1955	**26,113**	33	30.2	44.1
5	Monte Carlo	1923	4,763	28	30.5	48.6
6	Monte Carlo	1933	3,862	16	31.0	45.4
7	Las Vegas	1979	5,860	1	31.0	48.0
8	Lindau	1975	7,465	28	32.7	42.4
9	Homburg	1960	12,327	3	33.1	40.6
10	Baden-Baden	1962	12,164	7	33.8	42.2
11	Macao	1970	20,080	2	33.8	42.4
12	Reno	1951	48,608	3	33.8	41.8
13	Wiesbaden	1970	87,222	2	33.8	38.8
14	Baden-Baden	1962	133,131	17	34.4	40.3
15	Reno	1948	79,800	19	34.9	41.7
16	Homburg	1960	145,026	24	35.4	38.6
			598,544			

Note: The two Homburg entries (9 and 16) are from the same sample, as are the two Baden-Baden entries (10 and 14).

consistently on black 33 (and also on zero), which they proceeded to do—to win $125. We must remember that this sum was not won by luck.

Table 5 (above) reveals why Wilson and Bowers were so justifiably enthusiastic about betting on black 33.

By comparing Table 5 to Table 2 (p.46), it's easy to understand. Table 2 illustrates the game or sample of 1,000 spins of W. Duppa-Crotch. Once more I recommend to biased-wheel players this convenient format. For our purpose none of these frequencies was of interest except the best winner (number 1), because that was the one we would have bet on. In order to calculate the best frequency—always the gambler's guide—we merely divided the total of the sample—1,000 spins—by the number of absolute occurrences of the best winner—48 for number 1—which yielded an extraordinarily high relative frequency of $(1,000/48) = 20.8$, or $1/20.8$.

Following this procedure, I've taken 16 other games or samples and listed them in Table 5 (p. 75). As indicated at the bottom of column 3, the sum of the spins of these 16 games comes to a very large 598,544, or almost 600,000 spins.

Although we might list the results of Table 5 from the standpoint of various criteria (such as by chronology of date in column 2), I've ranked the results on the basis of column 5, the relative frequency of the *best winner* in each of the 16 games. (For the record we also find in column 6 the relative frequency of the worst loser in each game. These figures correspond to the worst loser in W. Duppa-Crotch's game, which was the final entry in Table 2, p. 46. Number 26 occurred only 15 times in 1,000 spins for a low frequency of 1/66.7.)

As we observe, there is a direct correlation between the figures in column 5 and those in column 3, which signify the total spins in each game, from a low of 2,738 in game 1 to a high of 145,026 spins in game 16. What we observe, of course, is that the best frequencies on average increase *in proportion to* the number of spins. This follows the law of large numbers and is what we should expect to find.

Why were Allan Wilson and Robert Bowers so enthusiastic about playing the single-zero game at the Nevada Club in Reno in 1955?

The results of their game (summed overhead in the casino's mechanical register) I have listed as game 4. The reason for their enthusiasm wasn't simply the high best frequency of number 33 (see column 4), which was 1/30.2 (see column 5). The reason was that these two mathematicians realized that this high frequency of 1/30.2 *doesn't normally belong* to a sample as enormous as 26,113 spins. In column 3 we notice how 26,113 spins breaks the continuity in the average increase of spins. Such a large, five-digit number of spins would ordinarily fit between games 11 and 12. We note how this five-digit number sticks out among all the ordinary four-digit numbers which precede and follow it. Games 3 and 5 also have a high frequency of roughly 1/30—*but* their sample size of respectively 4,015 spins and 4,763 spins are appropriate to this high frequency: in other words, for a *small* sample of 4,000 or 5,000 spins a relative frequency of 1/30 probably indicates nothing more than a random number (and as gamblers we don't want to have anything to do with fickle, random numbers), whereas for a *large* sample of 26,113 spins a relative frequency of 1/30 unquestionably indicates a strongly biased number—that gem we're always looking for.

Mathematicians as well as gamblers, Allan Wilson and Robert Bowers knew all this and accordingly couldn't wait to bet on black 33.

But as the non-mathematical gambler might commit the error of thinking that a high relative frequency of 1/30—*without regard to the number of spins*—indicates necessarily a great biased number on which to play, Table 5 is most instructive.

The problem of distinguishing between random and biased numbers (to which we'll return) is not at all easy even for the most sophisticated. We have only to recall how Albert R. Hibbs, with his master's degree in mathematics and consequent knowledge of such techniques as the Poisson approximation and the Chi Square test, had to pursue for his first 19 days or 12,600 spins in Las Vegas numerous hopeful candidates for bias before, in the Pioneer Club, hitting the truly biased red number 1, whereby he won his share of the $15,000. (See Table 4, p. 64).

So much for the extraordinary three trips to Reno by Allan N. Wilson and Robert Bowers to play biased roulette wheels.

Wilson's report on two other biased-wheel gamblers, who won even more than Hibbs and Walford, is equally interesting and of considerable practical value:

"In the summer of 1957 two University of Nevada students, called the 'Jones Boys,' allegedly won a large sum on a biased wheel at a Reno club. Eventually the wheel was changed. Then in the summer of 1958 the same pair turned up in Las Vegas and engaged in two remarkable coups. Both operations were witnessed, so there is no doubt that they occurred.

"At the time of their arrival in Las Vegas, the students had attained the same entrepreneurial status as Al Hibbs, hiring others to do preliminary clocking. Their agents sampled round-the-clock clocking for eight days at a downtown club, placing 5-cent bets to hold their place at the table. Then the masters marched in and immediately wagered $10 per spin on each of eight adjacent numbers. Thus they played a 'sector' of the wheel. It was the busy Fourth of July weekend, and the Jones Boys were then unknown in Las Vegas. Consequently, their play attracted little attention at first, especially since they had an initial downward fluctuation of $3,000. Playing in 6-hour shifts round the clock, however, they soon recovered the loss and forged ahead at the end of 24 hours. As time progressed, the management became increasingly concerned, and gradually introduced countermeasures in the form of varying the speed of the wheel and ball. When this proved to be of no avail, they finally changed the wheel at the end of 40 hours of play. Thereupon the players cashed in their chips, some $12,000 ahead, and departed.

"This might have been considered a satisfactory end to their Las Vegas operations, but there was a bigger coup to come. Although the students temporarily left town, their 'casers' did not. To the sharp observer, the casers could be seen busily circulating from club to club in search of another suitably biased wheel. These precursors, incidentally, never appeared to write anything down; nor, for that matter, neither did their mentors. Unquestionably this modus operandi tended to conceal their objectives. The hired hands evidently found a wheel that met their specifications at another casino, and they played for six days with 5-cent chips. During the first week of August [in 1958] they selected a sector, but this time with some gaps between the numbers played; they bet on five numbers altogether. Instead of staking a fixed $10 wager, as they had at the other club, they played a silly little cycle of $5, $10, and $15. This was clearly intended as camouflage, but it is doubtful that any such purpose was accomplished.

"Amazingly, they were allowed to play for 72 consecutive hours, during which they won $20,000. It appeared that the pit bosses and other management personnel firmly believed that it was all due to luck and that the standard roulette wheel simply *could not* possess enough bias for a player to win consistently. Nonetheless, somebody's patience finally wore thin. At the end of the three cycles of 24-hour, night-and-day play, the players were approached by the management and told to leave.

"It is easy to make a rough estimate of the advantage that appeared to be working for the players during the second visit to Las Vegas. They played for 72 hours, at a rate of somewhere around 100 decisions [spins] per hour, for a total of around 7,000 decisions. They won $20,000, or about $3 per decision. They bet an average of $10 per spin, on each of five numbers, or $50 per decision. The profit was thus $3 per $50 investment, or 6 percent, on the average. Allowing for fluctuations, the percentage on the numbers that they were playing was between 4 and 8 percent."

In order to estimate such matters as how much capital he will need to live through the severity of downdrafts or how long a losing streak will be (or its worst manifestation, a losing run—Table 3, p. 55), every biased-wheel player should know first the relative frequency that he's playing and second the percent advantage he has over the casino. Fortunately, if we know one, we may know the other, and in Table 6 opposite I have calculated what I consider the 21 most useful answers.

For instance, if we're playing a regular, 38-slot American *unbiased* wheel (its numbers being accordingly random), what is the casino's advantage over us? Opposite entry 1 we observe that, given a frequency of 38 (slots), the casino's advantage *over us* is 5.26% per spin.

TABLE 6

Player's percent advantage on any biased wheel, whether European or American, at payoff of 35 to 1.

	1 Frequency	2 Percent Advantage	
1	38	− 5.26%	(*unbiased* double-zero wheel).
2	37	− 2.70%	(*unbiased* single-zero wheel)
3	36	0.00%	
4	35.5	1.41%	(*biased* wheel—European or American)
5	35	2.86%	
6	34.5	4.35%	
7	34	5.88%	
8	33.5	7.46%	
9	33	9.09%	
10	32.5	10.77%	
11	32	12.50%	
12	31	16.13%	
13	30	20.00%	
14	29	24.14%	
15	28	28.57%	
16	27	33.33%	
17	26	38.46%	
18	25	44.00%	
19	23	56.52%	
20	20	80.00%	
21	19	89.47%	

How about the regular, 37-slot European (Monte Carlo) wheel? Opposite entry 2 we note that, on one number, the casino's advantage *over us* is regularly 2.70%. (On an even chance, like red, even, or high, it's roughly half that, or 1.3878%.)

What if a casino took off all its zeros? Opposite entry 3 we note that on this hypothetical, 36-slot wheel, at the regular payoff of 35 to 1 neither side would have an advantage over the other.

Now we get to the gratifying percentages for a single number on an actual *biased* wheel, which by definition *always favors the player*.

We recall that Allan Wilson ended, just now, by calculating the Jones Boys' advantage over that Las Vegas casino at every spin as between 4 and 8 percent. Glancing down column 2 to entry 8, we see that the value corresponding to Wilson's estimate is 7.46%, signifying that the Jones Boys were enjoying an average relative frequency of 1/33.5.

Elsewhere in his book Wilson estimates that Hibbs and Walford were playing on a number whose frequency was a high 1/30. We observe that opposite entry 13 their advantage over the casino was consequently an enormous 20.00% per spin. When we remember that on the American and European wheels the bank's regular advantages on *unbiased* wheels are the relatively small 5.26% and 2.70% (see again top of column 2), and bear in mind how these percentages conspire easily to ruin most players, we realize how extraordinarily powerful is a relative frequency, when favoring a player, of 1/30.

Thus in Las Vegas with a frequency of 1/30 Hibbs and Walford won $15,000, and with one there of 1/33.5 the Jones Boys won $20,000 (but their bets were higher).

And finally we recall that the frequency we calculated for W. Duppa-Crotch's single number was $(1,000)$ $(1/48)$ $=$ $1/20.8$, and we note that opposite entry 20 is the whopping advantage of 80.00%.

Such is the extraordinary power of playing a biased wheel, and as we proceed, Table 6 (p. 79) will be referred to again, for we'll discover that, as some biased-wheel players have enjoyed even higher frequencies over the bank, they have consequently won not just a thousand, a hundred thousand, or even a million dollars from the casino, but *millions* of dollars in only a single session!

Chapter 7

Modern Biased-Wheel Players: Mar del Plata

Artemeo Delgado, The Helmut-Berlin Syndicate

On the night of January 16, 1946, a mob of Argentine vacationers protested their oppressive military government, which owned and operated the world's largest gambling casino in the Atlantic seacoast resort city of Mar del Plata. In a prearranged demonstration, at 8:30 P.M. hundreds of gamblers stopped betting at the 50 roulette tables and marched grimly down to the front doors. Waiting for them on the beachfront avenue were scores of police in full riot gear, who sprayed the gamblers with tear gas, forcing them back into the casino. More irate and obstinate than ever, the gamblers refused to go back to the roulette tables and decided to wait until the Atlantic breezes blew away the tear gas. Then they gradually left the casino and considered themselves victorious.

In Argentina they take their gambling seriously.

While all this was going on, Artemeo Delgado wasn't the least bit disturbed. Unaware of the gambling drama 85 miles to the northeast, this Argentinian was sitting quietly at a roulette table in the small casino in the Atlantic beach town of Necochea. Tall and corpulent, Delgado

81

operated a little movie theater there and in his off-hours enjoyed playing roulette. Curious as to the identity of the winning and losing numbers, he began in 1946 keeping a profile of the three roulette wheels in the little Necochea casino, making modest bets while recording thousands of spins over a year's time. By wagering only on eight or nine numbers that seemed to occur continually above their rightful average Delgado found that he could supplement his living from the small movie theater. Why did the same eight or nine numbers keep maintaining their slight lead? The tall Argentinian didn't know, but by 1948 he was sufficiently sure of his system to have trained four assistants and moved operations to the huge coastal city of Mar del Plata.

Argentina's largest resort, Mar del Plata, is 250 miles southeast of Buenos Aires, and in the summer months, from October to April, the city is jammed with more than 2,500,000 vacationers. To reach it from the capital takes either 40 minutes by plane or 5 hours by train, bus, or automobile.

Built prior to World War I, the Central Casino at Mar del Plata has tall windows facing the city's five miles of oceanfront. In its two rooms and annex the casino contains an enormous number of gaming tables: 60 double-layout tables for single-zero roulette, 30 tables for punto y banca (baccarat), 9 for the card game of trente-et-quarante, 9 for blackjack, and 7 for craps. Decorated with pillars of white Carrara marble, its walls agleam with old tapestries, its floors hushed by thick red carpets, the roulette room alone is 330 feet by 170. As many as 20,000 gamblers a day jam into the casino, raising its temperature to a sweltering 90 degrees, and the young pages in blue uniforms with brass buttons, on one side of the red-velvet ropes, struggle to contain the crowds pushing eagerly to get in.

Such was the raucous scene greeting Artemeo Delgado and his four assistants in the summer of 1948 when they drifted with the mob into the elegant roulette room. Drawing a statistical profile of various wheels as he had at Necochea, Delgado and his four assistants again found a few wheels with eight or nine numbers continually in the lead, and by betting just at those tables they became consistent winners.

Then the inevitable happened. After a few months of such success the four assistants abandoned their boss and formed gambling syndicates of their own. As revenue from various roulette tables began to drop during 1949, a worried casino management alerted table chiefs to keep records of the growing number of consistent winners. But by the beginning of

1950 the losses to the syndicates were so high the irate Argentine military government fired the casino manager.

Enter at this point a German refugee whose own syndicate was to be responsible for one of the largest roulette wins in casino history. His name was Helmut Bruno Berlin, and he had been a machinist's mate on the Nazi pocket battleship *Graf Spee* when in December 1939, after the Battle of the Río de la Plata against three victorious British cruisers, its captain ordered the ship scuttled in the mouth of the river, a few miles off Montevideo, Uruguay. After seeing that his crew were interned in Argentina, the Nazi captain committed suicide.

In January 1950, when Helmut Berlin walked into the casino at Mar del Plata, like Joseph Jaggers at Monte Carlo he'd never been in a gambling house before, but as an ex-lathe operator he was attracted to the mechanism of the roulette wheel. By this time news of the big losses at the casino, which the management still couldn't comprehend, had leaked out, and Berlin had read about them in the Argentine newspapers. Of normal height, blond and blue-eyed, cold and calculating, the ex-sailor obtained a miniature camera disguised as a cigarette lighter and began secretly photographing various roulette wheels in motion. At times he would stand so long observing a single wheel, however, that a page would become unwittingly suspicious and ask him to move on. In addition, Berlin asked his wife, Clara, and brother-in-law, Paul, to clock various wheels for thousands of spins. At night Berlin would study enlarged photographs of the wheels that kept producing the same winning numbers, noting down distinguishing characteristics—the signatures—such as scratches on the wheel heads, or round or linear indentations in the metal around the numbers.

The casino at Mar del Plata operated from 3 P.M. to 3 A.M., and at peak hours as many as 10,000 gamblers crowded into the cavernous roulette salon alone. In this hubbub Berlin took his turn clocking wheels, arriving at three in the afternoon and leaving exhausted at nine, at which hour he would relinquish his place to one of two others of his team, likewise ex-sailors off the *Graf Spee,* either Hermann Bieger or a man surnamed Otto, who would clock the wheel for another six hours until closing time.

To keep their seat, the team naturally had to make at least minimal bets here and there. With more than a hundred gamblers typically mobbing each roulette table, the harried croupiers took a long time raking in losing bets and paying off winners, and if at Monte Carlo the average number of daily spins is 550, at Mar del Plata the croupiers could produce only half as many, or about 270 spins in as many as ten hours. But the croupiers at least spun both wheel and ball quite slowly, which always favors biased-wheel players, for if the wheel is spun fast, it makes the falling ball ricochet.

At the end of his first stint at one of Berlin's wheels, Hermann Bieger discovered that, out of 270 spins, whose average should be about 135 winners and 135 losers, the wheel produced 148 winners and 122 losers, for a gain of 13. (See discussion of Table 2, p. 45, and Table 28, p. 190.)

"The average is promising," reported Bieger to Berlin the next day. "We won 910 pesos [$65]."

"But the sample is still too small," retorted the ex-machinist's mate, and returning to examining his blown-up photographs, added, "To make sure of a continuing percentage we must clock many more wheels."

Although the Berlin team initially wagered on as many as 16 numbers a spin, they soon found it more profitable to play only the four or five most biased ones (in contrast to the method of Victor Bethell at Ostend, who, in my opinion, always played too many—as many as 18).

While the Helmut-Berlin team was carefully preparing its assault, the four syndicates spawned by the movie-theater proprietor, Artemeo Delgado, who had been rudely pushed aside, were now winning hundreds of thousands of dollars. These syndicates, consisting of fruit hucksters, waiters, and farmers, were soon buying brand-new Cadillacs, Buicks, and beachfront property. Known to the distressed casino only by nicknames like *El Crespo* (Curly), *El Basquito* (Little Basque), or *Juancito* (Johnny), each team member had his own assigned wheel which he had thoroughly studied. These biased-wheel players had naturally never heard of Joseph Jaggers at Monte Carlo, but at Mar del Plata the management's standard countermeasure of shuffling wheels, during down time, from one table to another, failed, because like Jaggers, these gamblers knew their wheels so well they could identify the signatures by the tiniest mar or scratch, the faintest off-shade color in the varnish.

At one point, in desperation, the management transferred two of its losing wheels to the little casino 25 miles southwest in the coastal resort of Miramar; but getting wind of the subterfuge, three of the biased-wheel players traveled down there, identified the signatures, and proceeded to break the bank in Miramar too. In addition, the casino at Mar del Plata tried to harass suspected team members by having the croupiers speed up both wheel and ball, and then pay off winners with agonizing slowness. None of these countermeasures worked.

Once the Helmut-Berlin team had launched itself in the spring of 1950, however, it far outstripped its competitors, owing first to assiduous preparation by wheel clocking and consequent identification of exactly which numbers on which of the 50 wheels were the most lucrative, and then to efficient exploitation by the team's 20 well organized and faithful clockers and players, who included a Spanish hotel proprietor, a taxi driver, a house painter, a retired judge, a trombone player, a retired sanitation official, and a circus contortionist, besides assorted workmen and housewives. (In democratic ways the 20-member Argentine team of 1950 in Mar del Plata mirrored the 18-member Italian team of 1880 in Monte Carlo.) In addition, the Helmut-Berlin syndicate cloaked all its operations in frustrating secrecy. During the team's predatory 13 months of operation, from January 1950 to February 1951, the panicked casino was unable to find out even Helmut Berlin's name, to whom his syndicate referred mysteriously as *El Alemán* (The German), so that the management was forever confounding him with his ex-shipmate, Hermann Bieger, whom they finally managed to identify.

One of the reasons the Berlin team lasted so long was its leader's foresight concerning the flexibility of the five biased numbers to be played. Thus when it finally dawned on the casino that the way to identify syndicate players was to notice if one player, after taking a prior gambler's seat, proceeded to play exactly the same five numbers as his predecessor, Berlin countered by having the second player bet on a second, if not so favorable, set of five biased numbers. That way the casino was prevented from knowing whether the second gambler was actually a team member or just another member of the general roulette public who had whimsically chosen to play a totally different set of numbers.

How much did all the syndicates win at biased-wheel play at Mar del Plata? By the end of January 1951, the 20-member Helmut-Berlin syndicate had won, in only 13 months, 6,000,000 pesos or $420,000— that is, $21,000 apiece. As for all the other syndicates, they had won, in toto, more than $600,000.

At their wits' end, and facing ruin, in the last week of January 1951, the government-owned casino called in the Argentine federal police. We recall that in January 1946, using tear gas, the federal police had tried to force the players back into the building to play roulette, whereas in January 1951, they tried to force them out of the building to stop playing it. In neither case were they very successful. In 1951 the police herded into the manager's office 80 gamblers, whom they accused of being members of either one roulette syndicate or another, classified them as professional gamblers with bad records (even though none of them had broken a single law), and barred them permanently from all Argentine gambling casinos. But naturally the police couldn't confiscate their winnings, which had been won ethically and legally.

Was this the way the mysterious Helmut Berlin was finally apprehended? Not at all. Not surprisingly, the ghostly leader himself slipped through the net thrown over the 80 gamblers. With his well-gotten gains *El Alemán* eventually bought a charming country house in Mar del Plata, where he lived out his life, contentedly tending his garden. He died in 1980, his wife, Clara, soon following him.

Then there were Berlin's teammates, the two ex-sailors off the *Graf Spee*. With his share of the $420,000 Hermann Bieger bought a small textile factory, designed modish children's clothes, and made prudent financial investments. On the outskirts of town, he too bought a country house, where he lived quietly with his wife. On the other hand, Otto didn't fare so well. First he tried more biased-roulette play across the Río de la Plata in the seaside-resort casinos of Punta del Este, Uruguay. But he failed there, for knowing of his success in Mar del Plata, the casinos immediately expelled him. And when Otto tried other casinos in Latin America, he was barred from those also after playing for only a short while.

And what of Artemeo Delgado, the movie-theater owner from the town of Necochea, who on his own in 1946 had discovered biased-wheel play for Latin America? What of the man who had started the ball literally rolling toward the $420,000 + $600,000 = $1,020,000? Abandoned by his assistants, bankrupt and forgotten, Delgado died in misery.

Our story doesn't end there, however. After waiting cautiously as long as 24 years, some of the other gamblers in Helmut Berlin's former syndicate decided in 1975 to have another try at biased-wheel play.

The Argentine Enrique David Borthiry was for 13 years, from 1949 to 1962, an employee in the casino at Mar del Plata, first as the humblest croupier at the end of the roulette table, finally as table chief on a high chair. During the tumultuous 13 months when Helmut Berlin and his associates were winning their $420,000, Borthiry often worked at their tables as croupier and later, in a social way, knew Berlin, his wife, Clara, and his brother-in-law, Paul, both team members.

While earning his living as a croupier, Borthiry was also rising as a newspaper reporter and is today editor-in-chief of the Mar del Plata daily, *La Capital*.

When in 1975 he heard that ex-teammates of Berlin, through the use of proxy players (who hadn't been barred), were reorganizing themselves in several competitive groups for another biased-wheel assault on the Mar del Plata Casino, Borthiry managed, in a friendly capacity, to attach himself to one of these groups in order to assess their plans.

Although at first the Mar del Plata Casino was again petrified, not knowing how to defend itself against a second assault by a horde of anonymous gamblers, this time around its management evolved a countermeasure, justifiable in its own eyes, to prevent a repetition of the earlier Berlin disaster. (They didn't want to call in the federal police again.)

After the gambling assault by *El Alemán* in 1950, wrote Borthiry in his book, *El Alemán Que Venció a la Ruleta* (1979), "in all Latin-American casinos, the staff developed a paranoia toward system players and kept an especially vigilant watch over any gambler who kept wagering on the same numbers over and over again. Since that time, in the Mar del Plata Casino the staff severely inhibits any player who, over several days, carefully writes down the numbers produced by either one roulette wheel or several. Thus in the winter of 1978, as a warning to everybody, the casino expelled many gamblers who were caught continually clocking wheels for several days at a time, an activity now strictly against casino regulations. Before these gamblers were barred, however, the casino made them all sign papers in which they confessed that they had not only been clocking roulette wheels but were entirely aware at the time that this was prohibited by casino regulations. In beneficent contrast, however, the casino never bothers the ordinary casual player who inconsequentially clocks a wheel merely to aid his betting inspiration of the moment....

"Just the same, in February 1979, resorting to all kinds of stratagems to elude the staff's vigilant surveillance, there were several ingenious gamblers in the Mar del Plata Casino who were working not as a syndicate but as independent individuals. One of them indeed worked every day from 3 P.M. to 3 A.M., winning every month substantial sums. With many varieties of approach and surreptitiously losing themselves in the mob of ordinary players, these particular gamblers were unquestionably applying the known methods of biased-wheel play. This system includes first thoroughly clocking a wheel to disclose any steady winners and then exploiting their bias with sufficient capital and lots of patience. Wagering on four or five numbers simultaneously, most of these solitary gamblers, heirs to *El Alemán,* always stick to two fundamentals: knowing how, through its signature, to recognize their cylinder immediately, and knowing how to make the staff think they're ordinary players."

Such, in the Mar del Plata Casino, is the legacy of Artemeo Delgado and Helmut Berlin, whose astute efforts there caused a loss to the bank of over $1,000,000.

Yet despite the casino's regulation against wheel clocking, each year, there and elsewhere in Latin America, some gamblers continue to win through biased-wheel play.

Chapter 8

Modern Biased-Wheel Players: Monte Carlo and San Remo

Dr. Richard W. Jarecki

When we think of outstanding biased-wheel players, we think of a triumph at a particular casino: Joseph Jaggers at Monte Carlo, Albert R. Hibbs and Dr. Roy Walford at the Golden Nugget in Las Vegas, and Helmut Berlin at Mar del Plata.

To win moderate amounts, of course, usually attracts no attention. But what if we want to win large sums, not just at one casino, but to go on exploiting biased-wheel play from one casino to another? Then we may no longer keep our success a secret, either from the intrusively admiring public, who will flock not only to watch us play but joyously bet and win along with us, much to the consternation of the casino, or from the press, who will trumpet our success daily in the media the way they did that of Albert R. Hibbs and Dr. Roy Walford.

Given this almost inevitable scenario, how do we postpone as long as possible our being barred? If we manage to defer it long enough, we may win our huge sum bit by bit by going from one casino to another until that unfortunate day when, alas, our excessive success blows up in our faces and we're barred everywhere. But, of course, why should we complain? We shall have already made our million.

Such was the strategic problem faced in the mid-1960s by a young American physician named Dr. Richard W. Jarecki, who solved it, to some extent, by hiding behind his oft-repeated explanation that the way he won his hundreds of thousands of dollars at roulette was through the ingenious computations of his colleague, a giant computer. This was very clever. We must recall that in the 1960s computers were just coming of age. Outside a relatively sophisticated circle, few persons, including casino managers, the European gaming police, as well as the general public, were vocationally qualified to distinguish myth from reality. Computers were looked upon as creatures from outer space, and the wonders they were to perform, both for good and ill, were thought to be almost infinite. Dr. Jarecki was aware of this, and every time he was interviewed by the press he would modestly attribute his bewildering success at roulette to the giant computer at his disposal at the University of London. After all, hadn't Professor Edward O. Thorp, in his 1962 best-seller, *Beat the Dealer,* explained how he had used a computer to construct his strategy to beat blackjack? Then why couldn't a computer be similarly used to beat roulette?

Dr. Richard W. Jarecki was born in Germany in 1932. Later he became an American citizen and moved to the United States, where from 1964 to 1966 he worked in Newark as a research assistant at the New Jersey State College of Medicine (now the University of Medicine and Dentistry). During these years he evolved his system, first unobtrusively at the roulette tables in Las Vegas, then at various European casinos, where, it was claimed, he and his wife, Carol, and their associates eventually won more than $1,250,000.

The first the public heard about all this was in the summer of 1964, when Dr. Richard and Carol Jarecki put up at Monte Carlo's most prestigious hostelry, the Hotel de Paris. At the casino, just across the way, they both played day and night so successfully at roulette that crowds gathered just to watch them gamble toward that most famous of all roulette goals—breaking the bank at Monte Carlo.

The Jareckis never achieved their goal there, however, because after a few weeks of its suffering substantial losses, the Monte Carlo Casino politely barred them. (It was, after all, at the Monte Carlo Casino that Joseph Jaggers had had his big win in 1873 and the Italian syndicate theirs in 1880. The casino has a long memory.)

Just the same, how had Dr. Jarecki and his roulette team, the press asked, managed thus far to win so many hundreds of thousands of dollars? What was his system?

Well, you see, replied Dr. Jarecki in 1964, his system was based on his own private mathematical calculations. First, his coworkers—he didn't use the revelatory term wheel clockers, but that's what they were— would record every day the numbers at particular roulette tables in the Monte Carlo Casino, and then at night he, Dr. Jarecki, would telephone their results to fellow scientists at the University of London, where the roulette totals were consumed by a huge Atlas computer which responded by producing the winning numbers that he would play the next day at the tables.

Let's examine this explanation. At the end of each day a roulette wheel has produced two kinds of numbers: winners and losers—those above average, those below. (See Table 2, p. 46.) If we program the winning numbers into a computer, what is the machine supposed to tell us? That they've been winning numbers? We already know that. And what may it tell us about the losing numbers? The same, of course. And if we program a computer with a group of roulette numbers which have kept a winning average over a long period of time, all the computer again can tell us is that that's what the group has already done. But, once more, we already know that—it's gratuitous information. Assuming that we program it with the correct data and algorithms, of course, the computer can calculate for us the probability that such an average will continue—but so may a mathematician with only a pencil and piece of paper. It's just that a computer may accelerate the process (excluding programming time). But no machine can predict *tomorrow's* winning roulette numbers.

As early as 1964, when Dr. Jarecki and his wife were barred from the Monte Carlo Casino, insiders were no more fooled about his system than was the casino itself. His wheel clockers, it was claimed, recorded the results, at the tables of their choice, of as many as 20,000 consecutive spins. Given the daily average of 550 spins for a wheel at Monte Carlo, this comes to about $(20,000/550) = 36.36\ldots$ or 36 days' work. Then Dr. Jarecki would make out some kind of frequency-distribution table— similar to my Table 2 (p. 46) for W. Duppa-Crotch—and simply play the lead numbers the next day. There was nothing original in his method— only in the successful way he employed his fanciful computer explanation to delude the managements of European casinos, the gaming police, and the general public. (Of course, his friends at the University of London were consequently operating the Atlas computer for show.)

In 1967 Dr. Jarecki left the New Jersey State College of Medicine in Newark to become a research professor in forensic medicine at

Heidelberg University in Germany, where in 1971 he received a degree in internal medicine and forensic pathology. (It's a curious coincidence that two of America's three most successful biased-wheel players are both physicians, both specializing in pathology. The other, of course, is Dr. Roy Walford of Los Angeles.)

In 1968 Dr. Jarecki purchased for his wife and three daughters an apartment in San Remo on the Italian Riviera, only about an hour's train ride east of Monte Carlo, where they spent their summers.

Barred in 1964 from the Monte Carlo Casino, Dr. Jarecki was determined, nonetheless, to continue supplementing his professorial salary by winning handsomely at roulette. And wasn't San Remo, on the mild shores of the Mediterranean, a beautiful place in which to achieve this? All the 37-year-old, soft-spoken physician had to do was stroll down to the casino for a short time after dinner.

So while taking a rest from the intellectual rigors of forensic medicine, on January 6, 1969, Dr. Jarecki walked down to the casino, played roulette with hardly a break for 48 hours, and left with an incredible $192,000. This amount exceeded by many times that won by any previous biased-wheel player anywhere in the world for such a short period. It was estimated by casino sources that during the prior two years Dr. Jarecki had already won over $1,000,000 from the San Remo Casino alone. As no research professor could possibly finance on his salary such an escapade, and as Dr. Jarecki often placed maximum wagers, even in his earlier period at Monte Carlo it was assumed that he was backed by a consortium of gamblers.

On January 6, after the professor had cashed in his chips for $192,000, to protect themselves from further onslaughts the San Remo Casino asked him politely to stay away for a period of two weeks. In other words, they were instigating a temporary barring. "Dr. Jarecki is a very nice man with a very clear mind and strong nerves," Luigi Bartolini, the manager of the casino, explained to the press, "but he wins too much."

"It's absurd. It's unbelievable. I just don't know how it started," explained Dr. Jarecki without cracking a smile. When the press then asked him to what he owed these enormous roulette wins, Dr. Jarecki carefully explained that at the University of London he had a colleague, an Atlas computer, operated by friends, and that every night after the San Remo Casino closed, he would telephone the day's sequences of numbers to the computer, which...etc., etc.

But if Dr. Jarecki declared his roulette wins absurd and unbelievable,

Luigi Bartolini considered them only painful. "In two days we've lost 170 million lire [$272,000]," sighed the manager. "Of that, Dr. Jarecki must have won at least 120 million lire [$192,000]. So we've asked him politely not to come back for 15 days. It's the first time we've ever had to do that."

Not that the San Remo Casino, in order to protect themselves, hadn't already tried the usual countermeasures. During the December just past, explained one press report, "it got so bad for the casino that they decided to move Jarecki's favorite wheel to a different table each night. Jarecki outfoxed them, however, by spotting the veins in the wood. He was thus able to keep up his computerized law of averages."

Veins of wood: Joseph Jaggers, S. R. Beresford, and Helmut Berlin would have smiled.

"He's very clever," declared Luigi Bartolini with what may be only described as inexplicable naiveté. "We found out later that these roulette wheels have a small, invisible defect. We cannot trace it ourselves, but he has a system. One night he was losing 100 million lire [$160,000], and by closing time he won nearly all of it back again." In addition, complained the manager, the casino was being drained of money by countless spectators who wagered wherever Dr. Jarecki bet.

So what did Dr. Jarecki do as his temporary barring period expired? The professor returned to the San Remo Casino and in a single day won $100,000.

At that point the casino threw up its hands, and on February 6, 1969, the San Remo city council, which overseas the state-authorized casino, voted to extend indefinitely Dr. Jarecki's period of barring.

Complained the exasperated Dr. Jarecki to the press: "If the casino directors don't like to lose, they should sell vegetables."

Asked if his system and other scientific methods might spell the end of gambling, Dr. Jarecki replied, "No, because as soon as you have a scientific method, they throw you out."

After the San Remo Casino relented and rescinded its indefinite period of barring, the whole Jarecki question boiled over again when the professor rewarded the casino's generosity two years later by going back in April, 1971, and winning still another $150,000, bringing his net at that casino alone, it was asserted, to $720,000.

Again the media had a field day. They said that the physician didn't walk mundanely to the casino any more but was driven there in a white Rolls-Royce.

As the public kept asking how Dr. Jarecki could go on breaking the bank, however, the media interviewed various authorities, requesting their own explanations.

One such authority was Inspector Michel Gonzalez of the Brigade des Jeux, the French gaming-police department in Paris, and as he related in his 1980 memoirs:

"In April of 1971 the press, radio, and television were constantly headlining the success of an American named Dr. Richard Jarecki, who, they said, had broken the bank at San Remo. So then, roulette had been conquered at last. The genius of one player, helped by a computer and four collaborators [the wheel clockers], had succeeded in mastering chance. Day after day Dr. Jarecki's coworkers noted down the order of the numbers produced by three roulette wheels, each of which necessitated a special study.

"Then every evening Dr. Jarecki would telephone lists of numbers to a computer in London. After an interval the computer would respond with precision to the question put to it: what are the most frequently occurring numbers, and what is the rhythm of their occurrence? The computer's answers, it was said, permitted him to determine at what tables, and how much, he should bet.

"Strictly speaking, this isn't impossible.

"Given, to quote Vauban [Louis XIV's military engineer], that materials are only materials, regardless of the care with which it is manufactured, one must realize that a roulette wheel may still favor one sector over another.... It's quite possible, for instance, that a cylinder [wheel head] may be made of an unhomogeneous metal containing flaws and weaknesses, a metal whose variations in density consequently cause in practice an imperceptible disequilibrium. Accordingly, this metal may cause an unbalance that favors one sector over another.

"Such elements are naturally to be considered as independent of and complementary to the following facts: that the croupier never spins either the ball, or the wheel itself in the opposite direction, at a constant speed; that [by regulation] the ball must circle the bowl at least seven times [four in the United States] before falling into a pocket; and that the cylinder must be sufficiently well balanced to be able to spin twelve minutes at a normal rate of speed when spun by a croupier's normal impulse.

"As the media were making an enormous fuss about the accomplishments of Dr. Jarecki, radio station *Europe 1* asked my department [the Brigade des Jeux] for an interview.

"During the interview that night, one of my colleagues brought matters into focus by pointing out that Dr. Jarecki's computer analysis of the roulette numbers, even if gathered by his group of coworkers, was entirely feasible and legal, and that anyway [at the San Remo Casino] his win of 750,000 francs [$150,000], with or without the help of a computer, isn't at all unusual in gambling houses, where fluctuations even larger than that sum, either in the plus or minus direction, are often seen and don't need the help of extraneous computers. This being the case, my colleague emphasized that Dr. Jarecki's enormous wins were causing no anxiety among French casino directors, who had never experienced any trouble at all thwarting mathematical systems designed to conquer chance. One of their countermeasures, for example, is simply to shift roulette wheels from one table to another. By this means any bias of a wheel at one table is erased by its position at the new table. In addition, the number of spins produced in a single evening at a particular table is never enough to foster exploitable runs or frequencies."

Inspector Gonzalez's passage typifies the controversial discussions surrounding Dr. Jarecki's play, none of which ever clearly answered the public's one simple question: but how did this professor of medicine manage to win so much money so frequently?

The secret of Dr. Jarecki's success was not and is not, of course, the least bit mysterious. Take, for instance, his extended escapade at the San Remo Casino alone. After his wheel clockers had discovered there a biased wheel, the physician played it for all it was worth. Then when the casino moved it to a different table, like Jaggers and Berlin, Jarecki merely found it, via its signature, at its new location. When the San Remo Casino temporarily barred him, he waited until the expulsion expired and then went back and began all over again.

As I mentioned at the outset, Dr. Jarecki's strategy was to repeat this procedure—which was conceptually but not actually simple—in one European casino after another, disregarding the inevitable blaze of irksome publicity, until he'd succeeded in winning a large fortune. How much? No one really knows, but given the facts set before us, I believe that, for himself, a net of $500,000 is a reasonable figure. Until 1971 this was the largest sum ever won in any casino by a single biased-wheel player.

From 1971 to 1973, while Dr. Jarecki pursued forensic research at the University of Heidelberg, his coworkers continued to seek out biased roulette wheels in casinos other than that at San Remo but were apparently unsuccessful. At any rate, by this time Dr. Jarecki had been banned from most European casinos.

In 1974, with his well-gotten gains, Dr. Jarecki left Heidelberg and returned to the United States—to Red Bank, New Jersey, whence he continues his specialty in forensic medicine.

We close our tale with an edifying news release from Rome on July 7, 1973, just before Dr. Jarecki returned to the United States:

"According to the Italian news agency ANSA, a thorough examination of the San Remo Casino's gaming paraphernalia has given support to the suspicion that Dr. Richard W. Jarecki owed his incredible 'hot streak' to the worn-out condition of their roulette wheels. In other words, each of the instruments there favored certain numbers and neglected others. The casino's responsible management now allege that Dr. Jarecki and his coworkers, through careful, statistical detective work, tracked down and laid bare the weaknesses of their roulette wheels.

"In San Remo, casino sources declared that Dr. Jarecki had won at the time approximately 800,000,000 lire [$1,280,000]. After his second period of exclusion from the San Remo Casino, its management finally readmitted him there last December, but this man, who had fostered his own luck, lingered in the casino for only a short while.

"Owing to Dr. Jarecki's huge win there in the late 1960s, the San Remo city council, as the administrator of the casino, has recently withdrawn 24 roulette wheels from play and banished them for good to its warehouse."

In other words, what the Monte Carlo Casino figured out in 1964 in only a few weeks took the San Remo Casino as long as five years.

So much for how to win $1,280,000.

Chapter 9

Modern Biased-Wheel Players: Bad Wiessee

The Pierre Basieux Syndicate

The Bad Wiessee Casino is a charming, modern, two-story building, looking onto Lake Tegern, nestled in the Bavarian Alps 45 minutes south of Munich.

Pierre Basieux is a Belgian gambler and mathematician (for whose two books on various aspects of roulette see my bibliography). In February 1981, Basieux collected a team of five assistants living in Bad Wiessee and Munich, westward in Constance and Lindau, Germany, and eastward in Salzburg and Vienna, Austria, whence they commuted while gambling at the Bad Wiessee Casino. Rather than gad about, searching from casino to casino for a good biased wheel in the manner of similar players in Las Vegas and along the French Riviera, Basieux decided to pick just one casino and study its wheels very carefully. It was several months before the casino realized that their roulette wheels were being clocked and played by a six-man syndicate.

Relieving one another in three-man shifts, the team spent about seven hours a day for three months clocking every wheel for a conservative minimum of 3,700 spins each. Of the twelve wheels, after clocking five of them for double that number—or 7,400 spins each—the team aban-

doned them as producing only random fluctuations. As all clocking—
sometimes by a single clocker standing between two tables, which he
monitored simultaneously—was done standing up, during the whole
period the team didn't waste a single penny having to be seated and
pretending to be ordinary gamblers.

The remaining seven wheels, however, were all biased, and their
statistical significance Basieux found by applying the following simple
three-sigma formula of $(n/37) + 3.0\sqrt{npq}$, and when $p = 1/37$, as in the
case of a single-zero roulette with 37 slots, then the formula reduces
simply to $(n/37) + .5\sqrt{n}$, where n signifies the number of spins in one's
clocked sample. (For more about the formula see the last chapter. For
additional statistical confirmation Basieux also used the so-called runa-
way test by Nalimov.) Of these seven biased wheels, on four of them the p
values of certain biased numbers ranged quite favorably between 1/32
and 1/28, giving at every spin a large advantage over the Bank of between 12.50% and 28.57% (see Table 6, p. 79).

From the foregoing we may adduce evidence strongly supporting one
side of an oft-debated argument. Of the 12 wheels in the casino, as many
as 7—more than half of them—were found to be biased, and as many as
4—exactly 1 out of 3—sufficiently so as to be profitably playable. Such a
high frequency contradicts those doubting Thomases who say that
biased roulette wheels are infrequent.

At the beginning of the fourth month Basieux and his team began
playing the four most biased of the seven favorable wheels. At every spin
they played on five biased numbers, which were not located together in a
sector but were scattered about the wheel. (It is statistically interesting
that many biased-wheel players bet on five biased numbers per spin
rather than on fewer or more.)

Prudence was the watchword. On the most outstandingly biased
wheel of the four, a wheel they had had to clock for six weeks for a total of
5,000 spins, the team began wagering $3 on each of the five biased
numbers, for a total of $15 per spin. Not surprisingly, they began to win
steadily on this outstanding wheel, which, along with the others, they
could recognize (in case it were moved) by its distinctive imperfections in
appearance. The casino, however, never tried to switch this wheel
covertly.

After Basieux and his team had won steadily for three days, the casino
removed the wheel after closing time and did something to it that is a
perfectly legal countermeasure. Then the management put the wheel
back onto the same table for the next day's play. (We recall that in 1873

Joseph Jaggers at the Monte Carlo Casino had experienced a similar after-hours countermeasure: but there they had shuffled all the wheels around on different tables.) After returning and recognizing the outstanding wheel the next day, Basieux continued to gamble, but instead of winning, for the next two days he lost, and realizing that something had happened, stopped play.

What had the casino done? They hadn't switched the wheel overnight: he recognized its distinctive marks. But it so happened that the wheel was equipped with a special device to counter biased play of the kind Basieux was following. This device is found rarely on American wheels but sometimes on European ones. It is called a movable-*number* ring (as opposed to a movable-*fret* ring, of which more anon in the next chapter on Billy Walters). Ordinarily on a roulette wheel the number pertinent to each slot is individually affixed to the wheel head behind and above the slot, but on a wheel equipped with the countermeasure, all the numbers are fixed instead collaterally to one another on a seamless circle of metal, which the pit boss or roulette mechanic may rotate in its entirety clockwise by as many slots as desired.

Basieux was not aware of this device, but after two days of studying the 5,000-spin sample of his outstanding wheel he figured out what had happened. He noticed that during his last two days, when he was constantly losing on his five numbers, five *other* numbers were constantly winning—and that each of these five new winning numbers was located *exactly* two number away from each of the old ones: which was simply too coincidental from the statistical standpoint.

Thus Basieux and his team returned to the Bad Wiessee Casino and began placing their $3 wagers on the five *new* biased numbers, which were, of course, merely the five old ones under new numerical names behind the old defective slots.

Thus for a gambler to counter the clever device of the movable-number ring (in which all the numbers, when moved, must be rotated as a single unit) he must *keep clocking his wheel* and saving his cumulative sample on a day-to-day basis for purposes of comparison, should he begin to lose. If only one or two of his numbers change their frequencies, that is one thing, but if *all* of them do, and the displacement is the *same* in relation to all new winning numbers, then he may suspect the wheel he's betting on is equipped with a movable-number ring—which the pit boss, in his absence, has ordered rotated some number of slots.

After returning to the fray and again betting on his five biased numbers, Basieux immediately began to win again. Continuing to wager cautiously $3 per spin on each of five numbers for 100 to 150 spins a day during the fourth month, the team began steadily and prudently increasing their bets on all of the four biased wheels they were playing. (See anon Chapter 15 on proportional betting.)

As the outstanding wheel had by definition the most biased number, where $p = 1/28$, they naturally raised their stakes the most on that particular number, and during the last three days of the fifth and final month of their biased-wheel battle, their wager on that particular number reached consistently the high sum of $180 per spin. Like Albert R. Hibbs and Dr. Roy Walford at the Pioneer Club in Las Vegas, Basieux and his team won most of their money in the last few days of their attack (see Chapter 5). At the beginning of their fifth month they were wagering, at three or four tables, $3 a number simultaneously on five numbers and thereby won $2,500. During their last three days, however, as their winnings increased, by proportionately increasing their bets to as much as $180 on each number, they won the enormous amount of $153,000—their total net win for the whole five months, including expenses.

At this point the management of the Bad Wiessee Casino, staggering under the financial blow, removed the outstanding wheel entirely from play, and fearing that the casino would invoke new and unknown countermeasures—including barring—Basieux and his victorious five-man team decided to leave the field with their winnings.

But for five months' work, or 153 days, to win $153,000, or a whopping $1,000 a day, who could complain?

Chapter 10

Modern Biased-Wheel Players: Atlantic City and Las Vegas

The Billy Walters Syndicate

In June 1986, a Las Vegas gambler in his mid-forties named William T. (Billy) Walters, an ex-used car salesman from Kentucky and well known at the best casinos, asked the management of Caesars Atlantic City Casino if they would be interested in the following high-rolling proposition: If Caesars would allow him to exceed their usual betting limits at roulette, Walters would deposit in their cashier's cage the sum of $2 million in cash to match an identical sum deposited by the casino. In other words, the game would be what gamblers call a freeze-out. It would be double or nothing. The roulette game would last until either the casino won Walters's $2 million or Walters won theirs.

Although Walters is a well-known Las Vegas high roller, who has at least twice lost $1 million at blackjack, and the larger casinos all eagerly solicit high-rolling customers, nonetheless, Caesars Atlantic City got cold feet and politely declined.

Billy Walters next took his freeze-out proposition down to the foot of the Atlantic City boardwalk to the management of the Golden Nugget (now Bally's Grand), who thought it over and accepted.

Thus on a Friday night in June 1986 Walters and one of his male gambling partners flew from Las Vegas and deposited in cash the sum of $2 million in the cage of the Golden Nugget Casino.

On the following afternoon Billy Walters and his partner appeared at the roulette pit of the Golden Nugget. At the time there were 12 double-zero roulette wheels on the floor of the casino. (A high roller has the privilege of requesting that a mathematically more favorable, single-zero wheel be put into action, to which a casino usually accedes. Interestingly, however, Walters didn't request such a wheel.) Prior to his appearance Walters had insisted on two stipulations, to which the Golden Nugget agreed: that he be allowed to select freely the roulette wheel on which he would play, and that the dealers of that particular wheel never be changed.

Surrounded by the usual crowd that gapes at a high roller, Walters proceeded to place a single bet of $2,000 on each of five numbers, none of which he ever varied, for a total of $10,000 per spin.

Here are the five numbers on which Walters played:
7-10-20-27-36
... of which, on the double-zero American wheel, numbers 7 and 20 are neighbors, 10 and 27 are also neighbors, and 36 is a single.

While the management of the Golden Nugget looked on with growing consternation, Walters and his partner played from Saturday into Sunday during a period of 38 hours, of which 18 were those of actual play.

At the end of 38 hours the roulette game, by mutual agreement, was terminated, and Walters and his partner flew back to Las Vegas.

Together they had won the largest sum ever won at biased-roulette play: $3,800,000!

If we use the figure of 38 hours, this means that Walters's rate of return was exactly $100,000 an hour, or $1,667 a minute, or $28 a second. If we use the figure 18—representing the actual hours of play at the roulette wheel when the two gamblers were neither eating nor sleeping—the results are even more astonishing: Walters's rate of return was $211,111 an hour, or $3,519 a minute, or $59 a second.

Nothing even approaching Walters's enormous win has ever before been recorded in the roulette world.

Hence the understandable consternation of the Golden Nugget's management—although the gambler was quite popular with the dealers themselves, to whom he left a generous $25,000 tip.

The newspapers always enjoy trumpeting the successes of winners:

"The Golden Nugget reported a $3 million loss at its roulette wheels during June, which Alfred Luciani, an executive vice president, termed 'unusual,'" reported one paper.

"Luciani said the loss was attributable to a pair of gamblers who, through a combination of a system and luck, won $3 million at roulette.

" 'The percentages are always in the house's favor, but that doesn't mean there won't be aberrations,' Luciani said. He declared that play by other patrons was not enough to offset the huge win by the pair, who started betting $1,000 to $1,500 a spin as their winnings mounted."

Indeed in the prior June (of 1985) the Golden Nugget had grossed $966,000 from all 12 of their Atlantic City roulette tables versus their huge $3,800,000 loss in June of 1986.

Although it was much later reported that, prior to his having made his freeze-out proposition to Caesars and the Golden Nugget, Walters had had six wheel clockers working unobtrusively in Atlantic City, fairly soon after his enormous win the press began to associate Walters with biased-wheel play:

"Three Million Follow Up: We reported earlier on the Golden Nugget's $3 million loss to a single gambler in the game of roulette during June....The gambler, who won that amount over a two-day period of time, is the same man who lost a million dollars playing blackjack in Las Vegas shortly before that....The Casino Control Commission and the Division of Gaming Enforcement staffs have checked the roulette wheels at the Golden Nugget and found them all to be in compliance with accepted standards for proper balance....But even a balanced wheel develops a bias for certain numbers, or to be more exact, a certain area of the wheel....It appears that the gambler won legitimately....To solve the problem casinos may have to purchase wheels like the ones used in London [manufactured by John Huxley Ltd.], which tend to stay in more perfect balance, or to get the state agencies to permit more frequent adjustments to the present wheels so that patterns cannot be detected so easily...."

Professor Stewart N. Ethier of the University of Utah, who specializes in mathematical problems pertaining to casino gambling, became interested in Billy Walters's sensational win and used a computer to calculate its probability. Assuming that the wheel at the Golden Nugget had been totally *unbiased*, Professor Ethier calculated that the probability that Walters, betting on a 38-slot wheel $2,000 on each of five numbers for a total of $10,000 per spin, would have won $2,000,000 lies between .0278 and .0309. In other words, the probability that Walters would have succeeded in doubling his original capital through chance alone is only about 3 chances out of 100. As Professor Ethier concluded, "Though not out of the question, this is unlikely." And the probability of Walters's being allowed to continue betting and win an additional $1,800,000 for a total win of $3,800,000 is, of course, even smaller than 3 chances out of a hundred.

Given the press statement just cited that "even a balanced wheel develops a bias for certain numbers," what might be the physical causes of bias today in any Atlantic City (or Nevada) roulette wheels?

To answer that question, let's first remember that in Monte Carlo in 1873 Joseph Jaggers won his $325,000 by playing a roulette wheel in which the bias had been caused by a *single metal ring* of consequently immovable frets or partitions between the pockets. (It's helpful to think of frets as walls.) We recall that the casino finally solved that particular problem of bias by replacing this single metal ring with *individual* metal frets which are *individually movable*, so that if a fret is suspected of causing a bias for, say, number 2, during down time it may be shifted over to, say, number 10, thereby forestalling any biased-wheel player.

In the United States, until the 1940s, roulette wheels always had frets simply stamped out of metal and inserted into slits in the wood between the numbers to form the walls of the pockets.

In the late 1950s the manufacturers of gaming equipment, B. C. Wills of Reno, and later John Huxley Ltd. of London, made frets that were, from below, more securely anchored by two small vertical screws. In this respect we recall the story of Vladimir Granec, who, on certain European wheels, managed to have the manufacturer's two screws illicitly and secretly replaced by slightly smaller, thinner pairs so that the frets at a chosen pocket would be looser and bounce the ball out less, thus causing a bias there that would trap the ball with greater frequency. Today frets of all American and most European wheels are anchored by one vertical screw.

Besides coming loose, frets pose another problem—that of height. Up until the late 1980s all American wheels always had *high* frets (about the width of one's thumb), called *deep-pocket* frets, which tend subtly to trap a ball more than the relatively *low* frets (about the width of a little finger— roughly a third lower) featured on European wheels all the way back to about 1796, when roulette was invented in Paris at a Palais Royal gaming club.

Beginning in the 1960s, John Huxley Ltd. of London, for their so-called French, single-zero wheel, began manufacturing frets not as single pieces of metal but by casting them into one single metal unit, known as a *movable ring*. European manufacturers, like G. Caro and Son of Paris, also began offering the movable-ring feature.

Is the return to a single cast ring of frets not a return to the very condition of the bias that allowed Joseph Jaggers to win a fortune at

Monte Carlo in 1873? Gaming manufacturers say no, pointing out that the *movable* feature of the cast ring redistributes any bias and therefore counters any biased-wheel players.

This is how the movable feature works. After the casino mechanic partially unscrews and thus loosens the central, vertical ornament and then similarly the circular, horizontal metal cone, he turns clockwise the whole solid metal ring of 37 frets (on a 38-pocket wheel), which works on a ratchet and clicks every time he turns the ring the width of an additional pocket. If he wishes, he may ratchet the ring around the width of just one pocket or as many as 37 pockets, whatever the pit boss has ordered. Thus as in the case of interchanging individual frets (which ultimately stymied Jaggers), by rotating the entire cast ring the pocket of today's number 18 becomes, say, the pocket of tomorrow's number 3. Hence by adopting a wheel with the movable ring feature a casino may counter bias owing to loose, individual frets.

But, alas, the countermeasure of the movable ring may itself ironically become the cause of bias for a different reason, thereby nullifying the very purpose for which it was manufactured. Because its pocket walls are so rigidly cast in metal, they themselves have too little vibration and thus resilience, which results in a relatively dead bounce when the ball hits them, so that it tends to become trapped in whichever pocket it initially falls into. In other words, now the ball too seldom bounces out randomly into neighboring pockets. Accordingly, if one section of a wheel becomes warped along the wooden lower ball track (the motionless, slanted area of the bowl down which the ball rolls), the ball will constantly tend to descend along this sector, and, owing to the dead bounce, isn't cata-pulted away from it. This type of bias, for instance, may be exploited by players using a wheel-watcher system that predicts into which numbers the ball will not only fall but stay in. Hence relatively few American casinos have so far ordered wheels with the movable-ring feature.

Up until the sensational $3,800,000 assault by Billy Walters on the Golden Nugget in 1986, almost all Atlantic City casinos had American wheels with the old-fashioned, high, deep-pocket frets that subtly tend to trap a ball. As Walters had won all his money from such a high-fret wheel (and even though, as the press reported, that wheel was subse-quently examined with care by the agents of both the New Jersey Casino Control Commission and the Division of Gaming Enforcement and found to be correct for balance as well as for other technical aspects), numerous anxious Atlantic City casino managers scrambled to protect themselves from biased-wheel play by ordering from John Huxley Ltd. of London their new-style wheels featuring shallow pockets and low frets, which tend more to randomize the ball's destination, inasmuch as low walls, rather than high ones, are obviously easier to hurdle over. Such wheels with low frets are called *low-profile* wheels.

Not to be outdone by their British competitor, the two remaining American roulette-wheel manufacturers, Paul Tramble of Reno and Paulson of Las Vegas, now also offer low-profile wheels, and models from all three companies may be seen at both Atlantic City and Nevada casinos.

To assure a roulette wheel's proper balance, in Atlantic City each casino maintains its own security schedule. Thus, to redistribute any bias, some casinos require daily that a mechanic turn the whole wheel a quarter turn clockwise one day, then a half-turn counterclockwise the next day. But some casinos follow this procedure rather infrequently. In addition, some casinos demand that each wheel on every table be shifted once a month to another table. Accordingly, in a year one wheel may travel around all of the tables.

Sometimes curious lapses occur. Recently one casino discovered that the serial number on the cylinder or wheel head of one roulette wheel didn't match the one on the bowl. Roulette wheels are regularly 32 inches in diameter and quite heavy, and two mechanics are usually required to lift and move them. Thus, to speed up the process, one mechanic had decided merely to interchange wheel heads rather than to have to move the entire apparatus.

Here is an illustration of how the slightest disequilibrium may cause bias. If we take two coins, each only an eighth of an inch thick, and insert them under the edge of the bowl of a standard roulette wheel, this causes sufficient tilt such that now the ball will fall 85% of the time off only 15% of the ball track, a predictable regularity exploitable by a player using the visual wheel-watcher system, especially one involving an electronic signaling device between watcher and player.

In contrast to the informality and lack of bureaucratic controls by Carson City on a casino floor in Nevada, in Atlantic City if a mechanic must in any way adjust a roulette wheel, this may not occur during play hours but only during down time; and what the mechanic does to the wheel must be witnessed by an inspector from the New Jersey Casino Control Commission, along with one uniformed casino security guard, and the whole procedure recorded by an overhead surveillance camera. The State of New Jersey isn't interested in someone with criminal intent sneaking up to a roulette wheel during down time and, with a pair of pliers, bending a fret or two to the subsequent advantage of a confederate player.

In Nevada, so that a roulette wheel may be quickly serviced right on the casino floor, a pit boss may shoo players from one wheel to another at any time of day or night, and in back rooms roulette wheels aren't necessarily kept under lock and key. In Atlantic City, by regulation a wheel may never be serviced on the casino floor, and all wheels, whether new or repaired, must first be certified by a state inspector and then kept in a security vault under lock and key. When one wheel is brought out of security to replace another on the casino floor, their serial numbers must be recorded and the whole procedure filmed by surveillance cameras.

Casino security schedules regularly require a mechanic, using an aluminum spirit level, to adjust a roulette bowl to approach the true horizontal. If the bubble reading doesn't satisfy him, the mechanic rotates the knob on the bottom of either of the two table legs under the wheel to raise or lower it to the horizontal. By the end of a gambling day, four seated players' constantly leaning on the edge of the table (whose legs rest on a rug) may easily cause its disequilibrium and a consequent bias in the roulette wheel.

And finally, after months of intense use, if a roulette wheel needs fundamental overhauling, it's often shipped to a specialist in Las Vegas who, with several assistants, takes 14 work days requiring 32 distinct steps in order to restore the wheel to original, smooth-running precision.

Given all the foregoing security schedules and assiduous maintenance procedures, one would assume that biased-wheel play in Atlantic City would be almost impossible.

Not for the redoubtable Billy Walters syndicate!

After an absence of almost three years to the day, on Tuesday, June 27, 1989, the Billy Walters syndicate made its reappearance in Atlantic City, this time at the Claridge Casino. Whereas in June 1986, at the Golden Nugget, Walters's wheel clockers accomplished their crucial, preliminary task inconspicuously, at the Claridge in 1989 the four men and two women, sporting casual baseball caps and work shirts, proceeded with overt unconcern to clock all eight roulette wheels on the casino floor. For four days, from Monday, June 19, to Thursday, June 22, they stood for hours around the eight wheels and, on clipboards, recorded all the numbers that came up. This unnerved the casino management and the pit personnel, but there is no law against wheel clocking. When curious gamblers playing at the roulette tables asked the Walters's clockers what they were doing, the six coworkers merely replied politely that they were writing down the numbers.

Then having finished their task, the wheel clockers retired, and the syndicate's four players themselves arrived. This team stayed farther down along the Boardwalk at the TropWorld Hotel and Casino, and consisted of the daring Billy Walters himself plus his three partners, Robert Litt and his wife from Tennessee, and a gentleman named Chung.

Recalling the record $3,800,000 that Billy Walters had won in 1986 from the Golden Nugget, its management not surprisingly steeled itself for disaster when he and his three partners meandered into the Claridge Casino on Friday, June 23. How many millions would the Las Vegas gambler win this time?

As at the Golden Nugget, so at the Claridge scores of wide-eyed gamblers congregated around the table where the high-rolling syndicate, after buying in for $50,000, played for a total of eight continuous hours over Friday and Saturday, June 23 and 24. To the usual financial distress of the casino, outsider gamblers wagered along with the syndicate and consequently won too. The four syndicate partners played at one particular wheel in two-partner relays of two hours on, two off.

At each spin a syndicate gambler bet a total of $1,000, placing a wager of $200 on each of five biased numbers, and he never made another wager of any kind. Whenever one of his numbers hit, the syndicate would win ($200) (35) = $7,000 minus four losing bets of $200 each, for a net of $6,200. Of course, on the $38 - 5 = 33$ spins when they didn't win, they'd lose the whole $1,000. On an ordinary, unbiased wheel, owing to the zero and double zero, this would mean the expected average mathematical loss of $2,000 during every cycle of 38 spins.

At the end of this roulette session the final two syndicate players rose from their table, thanked the Claridge pit personnel, tipped them as generously as usual, and returned to their suites at the TropWorld Hotel and Casino.

After only eight hours of play the syndicate had won $200,000.

Galvanizing themselves into what they considered appropriate reaction, the Claridge management immediately ordered their duty mechanic to service thoroughly the losing roulette wheel, which was a deep-pocket, high-fret model made by a Nevada firm. The mechanic proceeded to change and oil its bearings.

Still concerned about their $200,000 loss, however, on Tuesday, June 27, the Claridge enlisted the investigative service of Ron Shelley, an outside, roulette-wheel specialist, who lived nearby.

An Englishman, 6 feet 2 inches tall, Shelley spent two days carefully examining all eight Claridge roulette wheels. When examining the losing

TABLE 7

Biased-Wheel Players: Honor Roll

1	Monte Carlo	1873	Joseph Jaggers	$	325,000
2	Monte Carlo	1880	Italian Syndicate	$	160,000
3	Reno	1947	Albert Hibbs/Roy Walford	$	6,500
4	Las Vegas	1948	Albert Hibbs/Roy Walford	$	15,000
5	Mar del Plata	1951	Helmut Berlin Syndicate	$	420,000
6	Mar del Plata	1951	Other Syndicates	$	600,000
7	Las Vegas	1958	The Jones Boys	$	32,000
8	Monte Carlo/San Remo	1971	Richard Jarecki*		$1,280,000
9	Bad Wiessee	1981	Pierre Basieux Syndicate	$	153,000
10	Atlantic City	1986	Billy Walters Syndicate		$3,800,000
11	Las Vegas	1989	Billy Walters Syndicate	$	400,000
12	Atlantic City	1989	Billy Walters Syndicate	$	610,000
					$6,801,500

*More precisely, Dr. Richard W. Jarecki's forays at the San Remo Casino occurred in 1969 as well as in 1971; in addition, from the Monte Carlo Casino he won a substantial, unknown sum in 1964.

Note: No adjustment in this table has been made for inflation: all figures are in money of the year cited.

wheel, he found that it was in faulty condition. One entire side of the bowl was a significant quarter of an inch higher than the opposite side. And the wheel head wobbled.

A second of the remaining seven wheels was in even worse shape, this time owing to manufacture rather than to maintenance. Using an inside caliper gauge, Shelley found that all the frets on one semicircle of the wheel head were thicker by as much as 1/64 to 1/32 inch, compared to those on the opposite semicircle, thus creating in the latter slightly wider pockets that consequently trapped a higher percentage of balls.

On Wednesday night, June 28, when Shelley made his report to the Claridge management, he warned them to remove the two defective wheels immediately. Inexplicably, the Claridge management chose to ignore his recommendation and left the two biased wheels on the casino floor.

During the four days from Tuesday, June 27, to Friday, June 30, the six informally dressed syndicate clockers returned, and after again clocking all eight Claridge wheels, discovered the second biased wheel.

Then over Friday, June 30, and Saturday, July 1, Billy Walters and his three partners again meandered into the Claridge, sat down at the second biased wheel, and in only one brief period proceeded to win another $300,000 in partner play.

After the Claridge closed early Sunday morning, the chagrined management removed the two biased wheels from the casino floor.

Based on Billy Walters's two forays to Atlantic City, the first in 1986, the second in 1989, the important lesson here for all of us is that the most modern security measures, manufacturing advances, and putatively strict maintenance procedures are still totally futile in forestalling this enormously successful, intelligent, resourceful, and disciplined syndicate of biased-wheel players.

For this one trip to Atlantic City the Billy Walters syndicate had won $200,000 + $300,000 = $500,000. As this was more than $10,000, the syndicate's four players had to record it with the casino, along with their names and addresses—not that their reputable identities hadn't been known for years. But $500,000 still wasn't evidently the syndicate's total roulette winnings for the year 1989. It's reported that in January of that year Robert Litt, one of its premier partners, came up from Tennessee to head the syndicate's team that won, at the former Atlantis Casino in Atlantic City, the sum of $110,000. And it's also reported that in May of the same year Billy Walters himself headed the syndicate's team who won, at the Dunes Casino on the Las Vegas Strip, as much as $400,000.

Accordingly, for the year 1989 alone the total known win of the Billy Walters syndicate for biased-roulette play was $500,000 + $110,000 + $400,000 = $1,010,000.

And if we add to this the syndicate's record 1986 win of $3,800,000, we get a grand total of $3,800,000 + $1,010,000 = $4,810,000, a sum that's unquestionably the largest ever won anywhere in the world by a syndicate from biased-wheel play.

We may conclude from the Billy Walters' syndicate's astounding achievement that the time-honored system of biased-roulette play has not only reached a new peak but will continue to prosper.

Chapter 11

Arithmetic of an Unbiased Wheel

Playing on One Even Chance: The Theory of Runs

The Even Chances and the Bank's Advantage

Mathematicians have long known that our gain or loss at ordinary, *unbiased* roulette, whether on the even chances or the numbers, increases at a rate that is proportional to the square root of the number of spins on which we bet. Thus our first formula is simply $\sqrt{n}$, where n signifies the number of trials or spins.

Let's assume three things: that we exclude momentarily the bank's advantage from zero or double zero, that we bet on an even chance like red (or high or even), and that at each spin we bet only one unit of money, say $1.

Here are two examples.

First example:

How much will we gain or lose if we bet on red for 100 spins (about an hour in Las Vegas or Atlantic City, two hours in Monte Carlo)?

Using the formula, we take the square root of 100 (one standard deviation), which is 10. This signifies that 68% of the time, i.e., in two

111

games out of three, our *gain* or *loss* will be $10 or less, i.e., either $0 (breaking even), $1, $2...or $10.

And if we multiply this answer by 2 (obtaining 2 standard deviations), we get $(2)(\$10) = \$20$. This signifies that 95% of the time, i.e., in 9.5 games out of 10, our gain or loss will be $20 or less, i.e., either $0, $1, $2...or $20.

Nothing is more important than knowing how much *capital* to bring into the casino, so we may last through a losing streak. Thus if we wager on red for 100 spins, 68% of the time a capital of $10 will be enough, and 95% of the time one of $20 will suffice.

Second example:

How much will we gain or lose if we bet on red for 1,000 spins (about 10 hours at 5 hours a day for 2 days in Las Vegas or Atlantic City, or about 20 hours at 5 hours a day for 4 days in Monte Carlo)?

Again we take the square root of 1,000 spins, which is 31.62 or about 32. Thus 68% of the time—in 2 games out of 3—our gain or loss will be $32 or less.

And if we multiply this answer by 2, we get $(2)(\$32) = \$64$. Accordingly 95% of the time—9.5 games out of 10—our gain or loss will be $64 or less.

Once more these answers let us know how much capital to bring into the casino to ride out a losing streak. Thus for a game of 1,000 spins 68% of the time a capital of $32 will be enough, and 95% of the time one of $64 will suffice.

But, alas, for any even chance, like the red, we must also factor in the matter of the bank's advantage in the form of zero or double zero.

At roulette in Nevada on any even chance the bank's percentage or PC is 1/19 or .0526315..., hence 5.26% of each wager. (And in Nevada it's 5.26% on the numbers too.) In Atlantic City on any even chance the PC is half that, or .0263157..., hence 2.63%, for when zero or double zero occurs, the dealer takes half your bet on an even chance—your whole bet on the numbers. (In Nevada and Atlantic City on single-zero wheels the dealer always takes your whole bet, so the PC on both an even chance and the numbers is always 1/37 or .027027027..., or 2.70%.) And finally in Monte Carlo and Europe in general on any even chance the bank's PC is .013878743..., hence 1.39%, for when zero occurs, the croupier takes half your bet (or you may let it go "into prison"; in either case the PC is almost identical). (And in Monte Carlo and Europe the PC is 2.70% on the numbers.

How do these PC's at roulette affect our gain or loss? The simple rule is that we first multiply the number of spins by the PC in order to get our average *rate* of loss. Then we subtract this amount from our average gain and add it to our average loss.

Let's use the answer from our first example and pretend we're at Monte Carlo, where the even-chance PC is 1.39%. In 100 spins 68% of the time (2 games out of 3) our gain or loss will be $10 or less. And 100 spins × .0139 = $1.39. Accordingly, if we're lucky and ahead at the 100th spin, our ultimate gain is not $10 but only $10 − $1.39 = $8.61. And if we're unlucky and behind at the 100th spin, our ultimate loss is not just $10 but $10 + $1.39 = $11.39.

Obviously, if in half of our sessions, each 100 spins long, we win on average only $8.61, and in the other half lose on average $11.39, alas, we're gradually betting ourselves into the poorhouse.

Let's use the answer from our second example and pretend we're in Las Vegas (or Reno), where the even-chance PC is the much larger 5.26%. In 1,000 spins, 68% of the time our gain or loss will be $32 or less. And 1,000 × .0526 = $52.60. Accordingly, at the 1,000th spin our ultimate gain *becomes a loss*, because $32 − $52.60 is *minus* $20.60, and our ultimate loss becomes $32 + $52.60 = $84.60.

These two answers show what an erosive effect a PC as large as 5.26% per spin has on any even chance, for it means that in half our sessions 1,000 spins long we *lose* $20.60, and in the other half we *lose* $84.60, both on average.

How much less deleterious is the Monte Carlo PC on an even chance of only 1.39%, where in 1,000 spins our average rate of loss is only 1,000 spins × .0139 = $13.90, which yields us an average ultimate gain of $32 − $13.90 = $18.10, or an average loss of $32 + $13.90 = $45.90.

For gamblers who want to bet very long on the even chances the lesson is obvious. Always look for a single-zero wheel, and this is not especially difficult.

For instance, on a recent July afternoon I was in Atlantic City talking to the roulette pit boss in the Trump Plaza Casino. There are 12 roulette wheels in this casino. One of these is a single-zero wheel located near the baccarat table in the baccarat pit. Anyone is welcome to play this wheel; it's not reserved for high rollers. On this afternoon the 11 double-zero tables were absolutely mobbed with players both seated and standing. At the single-zero table there were only two seated players and none standing. The dealer was bored.

I asked the pit boss what fostered this situation. "I don't think most players know we offer a single-zero wheel, and when they come in through the front door, they don't look around."

And several years before, on a March evening, I asked the same question on the third floor of the erstwhile Atlantis Casino, where there were three double-zero wheels and one single-zero wheel comprising the roulette pit. The double-zero tables were full, and nobody was playing the single-zero wheel, which on the numbers alone is $5.26\% - 2.70\% = 2.66\%$ more advantageous to the players. "I've never understood why," replied the pit boss resignedly. "It makes no sense."

At any rate, at the present time a player may find a single-zero roulette wheel at as many as five casinos in Atlantic City—the Taj Mahal, Resorts International, Trump Plaza, Showboat and TropWorld. In Las Vegas there is one downtown at the Hotel Nevada & Casino and another out on the Strip at the Mirage.

Runs on the Even Chances

On the other hand, who at roulette is going to plod along betting $1 for 100 spins, let alone for 1,000? What we're probably looking for is a *run* on an even chance, i.e., an *uninterrupted sequence* of, say, reds, on which we may double up our gains or at least increase them, using some sort of progression.

How often does a run of some particular length occur? That depends on how long we play. Suppose we take a game lasting 1,024 spins (rather than 1,000, because 1,024 is a power of $2 - 2^{10}$ – and avoids bothersome fractions). This is $(1,024/110) = 9.3$, or about nine hours in Las Vegas or Atlantic City, or $(1,024/55) = 18.62...$ or 19 hours, spread out over a couple of days, in Monte Carlo.

Table 8 (p. 115) gives us the picture of the average number of runs of any length in our session of 1,024 spins. Let's examine columns 1 and 2. As players we'll encounter 128 runs of exactly 1 red (identified by being preceded and followed by a black), 64 runs of exactly 2 reds, 32 runs of exactly 3 reds, and so on: obviously each longer run is only 1/2 as frequent as its predecessor. At the foot of column 1 the last number $(1+)$ signifies that there will be on average one run longer than 8 reds. It may be comprised of 9, 15, 21, or an infinite number of reds, but as we note from the foot of column 2, its average length is 10 reds.

From column 3 we note that the 128 runs of 1 red and 64 runs of 2 reds each absorb 128 red spins, and that together they sum to 256 reds or exactly half of all the 512 red spins in the total sample of 1,024 red *and*

TABLE 8

Average number of winning runs of red at the end the end of 1,024 spins
(excluding zero)

1 Number of runs		2 Length of run: r		3 Number of red spins absorbed	
128	×	1	=	128	} 256 reds
64	×	2	=	128	
32	×	3	=	96	
16	×	4	=	64	
8	×	5	=	40	
4	×	6	=	24	} 256 reds
2	×	7	=	14	
1	×	8	=	8	
1+	×	10	=	10	
256 runs				512 reds	

black spins. This is always true for any even-chance bet, regardless of the sample size—the combined runs of *1 and 2* reds always absorb on average one half of the red spins, while the runs of *3 reds or longer* absorb the remaining half.

Suppose we've adopted a staking system that requires four winning bets in a row. A typical system of this kind is the paroli of 3, where we allow our winnings to double three times for a win of $1 + 2 + 4 + 8 = 15$ units or dollars.

In our session of 1,024 spins, how often on average will a run of 4 reds occur? If we look at columns 1 and 2 of Table 8 it says there are on average 16 runs of exactly 4 reds. But, as gamblers, we'll win also on every run *longer* than 4 reds—for we'll win too on runs that are 5, 6, 7, 8, *or more* reds long. So in 1,024 spins, how many runs are there of four or more reds? From column 1 we merely add up the runs of exactly 4 , exactly 5, exactly 6, etc., and all these exactlies come to a total of $16 + 8 + 4 + 2 + 1 + 1 = 32$ runs of 4 or more reds. If we use 32 runs as the numerator and 1,024 spins as the denominator of a fraction, then the probability p that at any spin the run of four or more reds *will occur* or begin is $(32/1024) = 1/32$. And the probability q that it *will not occur* is $1 - (1/32) = 31/32$. Accordingly, on average, a run of four or more reds will occur once every 32 spins.

Although Table 8 (p. 115) gives us adequate information about the frequency of winning runs, it's nice to know that there's a simple formula that answers directly the question of their probability. For a winning run on an even chance, a dozen or column, or on a particular number, etc., the formula is qp^r, and for specifically an even-chance wager this reduces to $(1/2)^{r+1}$, where r signifies the number of reds comprising the winning run. The formula answers this question. At any spin, what is the probability that a run of *r or more* reds (blacks, highs, evens) will occur or begin?

From Table 8 we just learned that for a run of four or more reds the answer is $p = 1/32$, and $q = 31/32$. Using the formula for winning runs, I've constructed Table 9 below, showing how we'll fare by adopting the paroli or double-up progression on red (or on any even chance), i.e., if we let our wins ride or double on runs from r equals 2 to 7 reds long. (The fractions of column 3 always apply, regardless of the length of our session, whether it's a game that is 1, 50, 100, 1,024, or 10,000 spins long.)

So if we double up *once*, we need a run of 2 or more reds ($r = 2$), and on average we'll lose per spin about $1/2$ unit of money (.43) for 7 spins (q) and then on the 8th spin (p) win 3 units (thereby breaking even).

If we double up *twice* in a row, we need a run of 3 or more reds ($r = 3$), and on average we'll again lose per spin about $1/2$ unit (.47) for the first 15 spins (q) and then on the 16th spin (p) win 7 units (again breaking even).

TABLE 9

Paroli on red: doubling up after a win

1	2	3		4	5
Length of run: r	Bets	p	q	Win	Lose
2	1 + 2	$1/8$	$7/8$	3	.43
3	1 + 2 + 4	$1/16$	$15/16$	7	.47
4	1 + 2 + 4 + 8	$1/32$	$31/32$	15	.48
5	1 + 2 + 4 + 8 + 16	$1/64$	$63/64$	31	.49
6	1 + 2 + 4 + 8 + 16 + 32	$1/128$	$127/128$	63	.50
7	1 + 2 + 4 + 8 + 16 + 32 + 64	$1/256$	$255/256$	127	.50

Note: p signifies the probability of winning at any spin.
q signifies the probability of losing at any spin.

And so on up to a run of 7 reds (r = 7), which occurs once every 256 spins (p), when we win 127 units (breaking even).

Tables 8 (p. 115) and 9 opposite tell us in theory what happens to winning runs. What happens to them in actuality?

In Chapter 5 the reader will recall that for Table 3 (p. 55) (concerning the longest *losing* run on a single number, zero) I drew on the Hans Hartman sample of 46,080 spins recorded at a Monte Carlo wheel in 1933 for three consecutive months.

In Table 10 (p. 118) I've again divided these 46,080 actual spins into 47 games, each 1,024 spins long, and counted the number of runs of length 1, 2, 3…15. (We note that in 46,080 spins the longest run was one of 15 during the 22nd game. There were also 5 runs of length 14, and so on.)

In Table 9 we note that when r = 2, when we double up once, this winning run occurs once every 8 spins (p). To calculate the expected number of this run in 1,024 spins we have np = (1024) (1/8) = 128, and from column 2 of Table 10 (p. 118) we see that in theory there should be indeed 128 runs of length 2.

Did I count through 46,080 spins just to prove theory? Of course not. My goal was to discover by how much the number of *actual* winning runs, in each game of 1,024 spins, *fluctuated* from the *theoretical* number of 128. As gamblers, that's what we definitely need and want to know.

In the first 7 columns the 2 games in each column representing the *most* and *fewest* number of winning runs of the given length are in bold type. Given that the expected number of runs of length 2 should be 128 in each game of 1,024 spins, we note accordingly that we meet the fewest number of such runs—111—during the 20th game and the largest number—155—during the 35th game. So in 46,080 spins the lower and upper limits for length 2 were 111 and 155 winning runs.

But given that 111 and 155 winning runs were respectively two extremes, if we had gambled through the whole 46,080 spins, what would have been the *actual average fluctuation* from the theoretical expected number of 128 runs of length 2?

There are two ways of solving this, the hard way and the easy way (and it's advisable to understand both).

In the hard way we note from column 2 that there were exactly two games (the 8th and 12th) when the number of runs was exactly the expected number of 128, and on these two games we broke even.

As for *winning* streaks, there were 22 games when the number of winning runs was *above* 128 (anywhere from 129 to 155) for a total of 3,010

TABLE 10

Actual runs of **red** and **black** in 47 consecutive games each 1,024 spins long.

Runs:	1	2	3	4	5	6	7	8	9	10	11	12	13	14	15
Theory:	256	128	64	32	16	8	4	2	1	1/2	1/4	1/8	1/16	1/32	1/64

Game															
1	251	132	**51**	35	26	5	1	1	0	3	1	0	0	0	0
2	253	147	72	26	13	6	5	0	1	0	0	1	0	0	0
3	236	148	68	28	12	6	3	1	2	1	1	1	0	0	0
4	219	124	64	27	25	6	**9**	0	1	1	0	0	0	1	0
5	235	123	64	35	21	7	4	2	0	2	0	0	0	0	0
6	226	121	75	32	11	**14**	6	1	0	0	0	0	0	1	0
7	248	112	64	35	17	11	6	1	1	1	0	0	0	0	0
8	243	128	60	28	21	13	3	1	0	0	0	0	0	0	0
9	251	139	73	37	12	**1**	4	2	2	0	0	0	0	0	0
10	255	122	70	34	15	6	5	3	1	0	0	0	0	0	0
11	271	115	61	35	10	10	7	4	1	0	0	0	0	0	0
12	270	128	63	34	10	11	4	1	0	1	1	0	0	0	0
13	271	136	67	25	16	10	2	1	2	0	0	0	0	0	0
14	290	114	62	28	12	9	8	1	0	3	0	0	0	0	0
15	266	133	61	30	16	8	5	2	0	1	0	0	0	0	0
16	249	130	63	35	22	6	1	3	1	0	0	0	0	0	0
17	**216**	130	63	31	20	7	8	2	0	1	1	0	0	0	0
18	265	135	69	33	**6**	6	4	7	0	0	0	0	0	0	0
19	276	121	63	33	14	9	1	3	1	1	1	0	0	0	0
20	262	**111**	62	28	19	11	5	4	0	0	0	0	0	1	0
21	269	112	67	42	10	10	2	2	1	0	0	0	1	0	0
22	239	135	61	28	24	5	1	0	1	2	1	0	0	0	**1**
23	245	142	59	34	18	6	3	2	1	1	0	0	0	0	0
24	237	117	72	35	18	8	4	0	0	2	1	0	0	0	0
25	255	134	66	30	14	9	2	2	2	0	1	0	0	0	0
26	254	123	53	34	16	7	7	3	0	1	1	0	1	0	0
27	**292**	117	55	36	13	8	6	3	0	1	0	0	0	0	0
28	264	122	66	27	17	12	4	2	1	0	0	0	0	0	0
29	255	134	61	33	16	5	6	2	2	0	0	0	0	0	0
30	255	133	59	24	13	12	6	1	1	1	0	2	0	0	0
31	254	124	60	29	22	8	4	1	2	0	0	0	0	1	0
32	269	147	54	39	16	8	1	1	0	0	0	0	0	0	0
33	271	124	65	40	10	9	4	0	2	0	0	0	0	0	0
34	234	121	54	34	17	10	**9**	3	2	0	0	0	0	0	0
35	222	**155**	72	**23**	15	4	3	3	2	0	2	0	0	0	0
36	245	130	52	34	18	7	3	4	2	1	0	0	0	1	0

TABLE 10 (continued)

Runs:	1	2	3	4	5	6	7	8	9	10	11	12	13	14	15
Theory:	256	128	64	32	16	8	4	2	1	1/2	1/4	1/8	1/16	1/32	1/64
37	236	129	61	35	17	9	5	3	1	0	0	0	0	0	0
38	265	141	70	30	9	11	2	0	0	1	0	1	0	0	0
39	264	135	62	30	18	7	6	0	0	1	0	0	0	0	0
40	271	114	61	35	21	11	3	0	0	1	0	0	0	0	0
41	245	124	74	28	9	10	4	4	1	0	1	1	0	0	0
42	257	118	70	37	16	4	7	0	1	0	1	0	0	0	0
43	236	116	59	**45**	17	11	4	0	1	0	1	0	0	0	0
44	255	131	61	34	13	9	3	0	3	1	1	0	0	0	0
45	263	115	67	27	**27**	7	4	1	1	0	0	0	0	0	0
46	244	134	**79**	**23**	16	8	3	2	2	0	0	0	0	0	0
47	269	127	74	32	15	5	**0**	2	1	1	1	0	0	0	0

1	2	3	4	5	6
Runs		Theory	Actuality		
1	(47)(256) =	12032	11918	− 114	253.58
2	(47)128 =	6016	6003	− 13	127.72
3	(47)(64) =	3008	3009	+ 1	64.02
4	(47)(32) =	1504	1507	+ 3	32.06
5	(47)(16) =	752	753	+ 1	16.02
6	(47)(8) =	376	382	+ 6	8.13
7	(47)(4) =	188	197	+ 9	4.19
8	(47)(2) =	94	82	− 12	1.75
9	(47)(1) =	47	43	− 4	0.915
10	(47)(1/2) =	23.5	30	+ 6.5	0.638
11	(47)(1/4) =	11.75	17	+ 5.25	0.362
12	(47)(1/8) =	5.88	6	+ 0.125	0.128
13	(47)(1/16) =	2.94	2	− 0.938	0.043
14	(47)(1/32) =	1.47	5	+ 3.530	0.106
15	(47)(1/64) =	0.73	1	+ 0.266	0.021

such runs, and $(3010/22) = 136.82$ or 137. So if we play *any* kind of system based on a run of length 2, in a game of 1,024 spins the *average* number of winning runs in the *plus* direction will be 137.

As for *losing* streaks, there were 23 games when the number of winning runs fell *below* 128 (anywhere from 127 to 111) for a total of 2,737 such runs, and $(2737/23) = 119$. So in a game of 1,024 spins the *average* number of winning runs of length 2 in the *minus* direction will be 119.

(The total of 256 + 3,010 + 2,737 = 6,003 runs of length 2 we will find in the second half of Table 10 (p. 118) in column 4 under *Actuality.*)

So these two are our *actual* averages: 137 runs in the plus direction, and 119 in the minus direction.

And what is the easy way to calculate these two average fluctuations? It's to use the following formula, which gives us the answers *in theory:* $x = .8\sqrt{npq}$, where x signifies the fluctuation or deviation in winning runs from the expected number pn.

This is all we do. In a roulette game 1,024 spins long we know (Table 9, column 3, p. 116) that at any given spin the probability of a run of length 2 or more occurring is $p = 1/8$, and of its not occurring is $q = 7/8$. So first we have…$x = .8\sqrt{(1024)(1/8)(7/8)} = 8.47 = 9$.

Whence we get: 128 + 9 = 137 runs above average

and: 128 − 9 = 119 runs below average

So that's how we know that actuality and theory are identical.

If we glance down column 2, we may observe how *volatile* would be the fluctuations, in both the plus and minus directions, from actual game to game. We must always bear in mind that, excluding zero, the chance that we'll end up ahead or behind at the end of any game of 1,024 spins is invariably fifty-fifty.

Given that 128 runs are the expected number, we observe that in games 1, 2, and 3 we would have won respectively 132, 147, and 148 runs: wonderful! Alas, now comes the downturn after (3)(1,024) = 3,072 spins. In games 4, 5, 6, and 7 we would have won only 124, 123, 121, and 112 winning runs during (4)(1,024) = 4,096 spins.

And so on down column 2 for all 47 games: sometimes it's up, sometimes it's down, and because *unbiased* roulette is a game of *random* events, there is absolutely *no predictable trend* whatsoever to be drawn from any chain of its events, for it is not really a chain: *events in random roulette are a chain of disconnected links.*

Perhaps the most important lesson to be drawn from Tables 8, 9, and 10 is that, if we adopt a system based on a winning run of 2, 3, 4…*r or more* reds, whether we have just won or lost our last game has absolutely *no bearing whatsoever* on whether we will win or lose our next game.

But why should we be surprised by this? Isn't that what gambling is all about? If we could predict even slightly the next random event, there wouldn't be any gamble.

Chapter 12

Arithmetic of an Unbiased Wheel

Playing on a Single Number

Betting on an Even Chance versus a Single Number

If we exclude the problem of the bank's advantage from zero, which should we choose—to bet on an even chance, like red, or on a single number?

Every gambler even superficially acquainted with roulette knows that on a single number the swings of fortune, whether in the plus or minus direction, are much more volatile, much more extreme than on an even chance. It's like comparing the swings of a clock pendulum only 2 inches long ($p = 1/2$) with one 37 inches long ($p = 1/37$). When the shorter pendulum swings to the left into the winning side, it stays there no longer on average than when it swings to the right into the losing side. This short roulette pendulum swings *symmetrically*.

In contrast, when the longer pendulum swings left into the winning side—during which our single number hits typically several times—this abundance of riches must unfortunately be compensated for after the pendulum swings to the right into the losing side, *where it must stay for a much longer period of time* (during which, of course, our number, by

121

definition, doesn't hit at all), in order, as I said, to compensate for the aforesaid abundance of riches during the briefer winning period. Thus this longer roulette pendulum, unlike a true clock pendulum, swings *asymmetrically*.

In my own opinion, it's not the gnawing effect of the bank's percentage, represented by zero, but the fact of this *asymmetrical swing* that is the primary cause of most gamblers' losses, zero being their secondary cause. It's during these periods of drought, when our number disappears into a void, that we may lose substantial amounts of money. This is why the problem must be examined.

In Table 11 (below) I contrast (excluding zero) how *much longer* we would have to bet on red in order to win or lose the *same* (unspecified) amount of *money* from a bet on a single number. As we note from column 1, we would have to bet on red for 100 spins to win or lose the same fixed amount that we would win or lose betting on a single number in only 3 spins (because a single number comes up on average so seldom in only the first 3 spins). We would have to wager on red 500 spins to match an equivalent gain or loss on a single number in only 14 spins. And we would have to bet on red for as many as 20,000 spins to match our gain or loss on a single number in only 556 spins. I'm not making any recommendation, of course, for the long-odds bet on a single number versus the short-odds one on red. I'm just contrasting here the difference in the swings of their two pendulums. In Table 11 the (unspecified) amount of money is fixed and the number of spins is variable.

In Table 12 opposite matters are reversed—the number of spins

TABLE 11

Comparison by *spins* of a bet on an even chance (red) versus one on a single number (excluding zero)

1 By betting on red (p = q = 1/2) our n spins are:	2 By betting on a single number (p = 1/37) our n spins are:
100	3
500	14
1,000	28
5,000	139
10,000	278
20,000	556

remains fixed and the amount of money is variable (zero again excluded). The two columns contrast, in the *same* number of *spins*, our average win or loss on red versus that on a single number. As we observe from comparing the three columns, at the end of 100 spins, on average we would win or lose on red 8 units to 48 on a single number. At the end of 10,000 spins, on average we would win or lose only 80 units on red to as many as 480 on a single number.

If we compare horizontally the results of columns 2 and 3, we may draw the following rule: a wager on a single number will always win or lose on average 6 times the amount bet on an even chance (like red).

Again, what a difference in the swings of the two pendulums!

At the beginning of the last chapter on the Even Chances, I stated that, whether on the even chances or the numbers, our gain or loss increases at a rate that is (only) proportional to the square root of the number of spins on which we bet, i.e., as $\sqrt{n}$. A vertical comparison of the columns in Table 12 (below) illustrates this. Accordingly, although the proportion of 10,000 spins to 100 spins is as much as $(10,000/100) = 100$ to 1, the ratio of either 80 units to 8 on red or 480 units to 48 on a number is only 10 to 1. In other words, compared to the number of spins we play, the rate of our gains or losses (large though they become absolutely) is relatively slow.

The Probability of Ruin

In the beginning of the last chapter I explained that, to calculate for an even-chance wager the amount of capital necessary to ride out a

TABLE 12

Comparison by *units* of a bet on an even chance (red) versus one on a single number (excluding zero); at the end of n spins our average gain or loss is z units:

1	2	3
n spins	z units on red	z units on one number
100	8	48
500	17	107
1,000	25	151
5,000	56	339
10,000	80	480
20,000	113	678

losing streak, we merely take the square root of the number of spins, i.e., $\sqrt{n}$. Thus 68% of the time we will ride out a losing streak on red by bringing to the roulette table $\sqrt{n}$ units. In 100 spins this would be $\sqrt{100} = 10$ units.

This is a very simple estimation and involves what mathematicians call the *probability of ruin*, which may become quite complicated.

The French mathematician Louis Bachelier pointed out in 1912, however, that for the amount of money *during* (not just at the end of) an even-chance game, we should multiply $\sqrt{n}$ by the factor 1.625. Thus, in 100 spins we must have not just 10 but $(10)(1.625) = 16.25$ units to ride out a losing streak *during* the game.

Concerning a bet on a single number, if our number doesn't come up *at least once*, i.e., if it *doesn't occur at all*, and we thereby lose our entire capital, then by definition we say we are bankrupt or *ruined* and out of the game.

What is the frequency of this misfortune occurring *during n* spins?

Losing Runs: At Least Once versus Not at All

As I mentioned, I consider losing runs—that asymmetrical swing—to be the primary cause, as opposed to zero, of loss for most roulette players. So what is the frequency of those runs?

The whole question is aptly answered by Table 3 (p. 55), which lists the length of the *longest* losing run in each of 45 consecutive games in the Hartman sample of 46,080 spins. Each game was 1,024 spins long.

During the first game the longest losing run for the chosen number (zero) was exactly 159 spins, and had we been betting on it, we would have obviously lost exactly that many units. During the second game the longest losing run was 153 spins. The longest run of all—268 spins— occurred sometime during the 17th game. The average of all 45 of these longest losing runs is 148 spins—let's call it 150. Accordingly, when we play roulette game after roulette game, each about 1,000 spins long, we must expect somewhere during the course of each game to lose on average 150 units when our chosen number *doesn't occur at all* (i.e., doesn't occur at least once).

In Table 13 opposite I've divided the 45 losing runs into segments of 50 losing spins at a time. Thus the longest losing run in each game was never once so short as from 0 to 49 spins. There were 5 longest-losing runs lying in length somewhere between 50 and 99 spins, 23 lying in length somewhere between 100 and 149 spins, and so on. Notice that this

TABLE 13

In 46,080 spins the *longest losing run* somewhere during each of the 45 games, each game 1,024 spins long, was *exactly r* spins in length as follows:

1 Exactly r spins long		2 Quantity	3 Percentage	
1.	0-49	0		
2.	50-99	5	11	
3.	100-149	23	51	} 75
4.	150-199	11	24	
5.	200-249	3	7	
6.	250-299	3	7	
7.	300-349	0		
		45	100%	

Note: Average length of all the 45 losing runs was 148 spins (about 150).

last group of 23 accounts for .51 or about 50% of all the longest losing runs in all 45 games. And if we add to that the 11 runs lying in length between 150 and 199 spins (accounting for 24%), we may say that every time we go to the roulette table and play for about 1,000 spins, 75% of the time, i.e., in 3 such games out of 4, the longest losing run will be between as many as 100 and 200 spins in length. All gamblers expect losing runs, but it's the 75% *regularity* of this longest losing run that might surprise many players. Yet there it is—and the actuality of the Hartman sample can't be argued against.

To most of us, of course, it's the *position* of the disastrous losing run that we next want to know about. Will this longest losing run come at the beginning, middle, or end of the 1,024 spins? From the mathematical standpoint it may unfortunately occur permutationally at any time or spin. But let's see what actually happened during the 46,080 spins of the Hartman sample.

Suppose we define a *long* (not necessarily *longest*) losing run as one over 100 spins in length. In going through the 45 games of the Hartman sample I found that the 13th, 20th, 21st, 24th, 27th, 28th, 31st, 35th, 40th, 41st, and 42nd games all *immediately started* with *long* losing runs which were respectively 192, 160, (120), (123), 223, (112), 259, 140, 104, 136, and (102) spins long. (Those runs in parentheses are not in Table 3, p. 55, because they weren't the *longest* in their game.) The average of these 11 games *starting* with a *long* run was 152 spins—let's call it 150. And (11/45) = .2444...or about 25%.

Hence to sum up, in 75% of the games, about 1,000 spins long, we'll have somewhere to face a losing run—when our number *doesn't occur at all*—averaging 150 spins in length. And in 25% of these games—1 out of 4—this 150-spin losing run actually starts the game.

Once more, so much for what happens during the course of a large sample of 46,080 spins.

And complementarily, what is the *theoretical* frequency of such losing runs—when our chosen number *doesn't occur at all* for 10, 25, 50...even 350 spins?

In Table 14 opposite I have listed the answers to this question. Accordingly, a losing run of 10 *or more* spins occurs once every 49 spins (q = 1/49, p = 48/49). A losing run of 100 *or more* spins occurs once every 573 spins. And a losing run of 300 *or more* spins occurs once every 137,457 spins. (In connection with Table 3 [p. 55] we recall our discussion of the losing run of 300 or more spins, on a 38-slot wheel, that so disastrously beset Albert R. Hibbs and Dr. Roy Walford at Harolds Club in November 1947.)

Like Tables 3 (p. 55) and 13 (p. 125), Table 14 opposite should serve as a warning to us of how statistically normal and frequent are relatively long losing runs on a single number.

We recall that at Monte Carlo 550 spins—say 573—are the typical total number of daily spins produced by any given wheel. In Table 14 we observe that, for a gambler playing any chosen number, a losing run of 100 or more spins will occur consequently as often as *once a day*. A three-day stay in Las Vegas or Atlantic City is typical, where a wheel produces 110 spins an hour (twice the European rate). Let's say a gambler plays a wheel seven hours a day for three days, for a total of 2,310 spins—let's say only 2,255. From Table 14 we note that a losing run of 150 or more spins will occur on average, therefore, *once during his three-day visit*.

For both our examples these losing runs—100 and 150 spins—are entirely normal, yet I suspect that the two gamblers might complain that their luck had been unusually bad.

The *constants c* in Table 15 (p. 128) allow us to move from the averages in Table 14 to the calculation of specific probabilities themselves. Averages give us the larger picture. Probabilities allow us to focus on the likelihood of the specific event, favorable or unfavorable, at each spin.

The opposite of an event's occurring *not at all* is when it occurs *at least once*. First let's calculate the probability of our number's occurring at least once—then we'll see how the same calculation applies to a losing run.

TABLE 14

On a single number, a *losing* run *r or more* spins long occurs on average once every *n* spins (*q* equals 1 over the following denominators) as follows:

r	n
10	49
25	73
50	146
75	289
100	573
150	2,255
200	8,873
250	41,112
300	137,457
350	541,126

Note: When *n* is less than 65, a slight error occurs.

We sit down at a roulette table and begin betting on a chosen number—say zero.

First example. How long do we bet on our number before it reaches a probability *Pat* of .50 (the fifty-fifty point) of occurring at least once during the *very next r* spins, i.e., during the *r* spins on which we're betting?

The answer involves two simple steps. First, in Table 15 (p. 128) we look under *Pat* for .50. Opposite this probability is the constant .693 or .7. We subtract 1 from the denominator of the probability of occurrence in a single spin of a roulette number (which is p = 1/37), which gives 36. Second, we multiply 36 by .7, which gives 25 spins, the answer.

Accordingly, if we bet on our single number for 25 spins, it will have a probability of .50 of occurring *at least once* any time *during* those 25 spins—or, rephrased, a probability of fifty-fifty of occurring *before* the 25th spin from now.

And conversely and most importantly, our number has a probability of 1 - .50 = .50 of *not occurring at all during* those 25 spins.

Second example. How long do we have to bet on our number before it reaches a probability of *Pat* of .90 of occurring at least once during (the very next) *r* spins? Again using Table 15, we follow the same two steps. Opposite Pat = .90 is the constant 2.303. This value, multiplied by 36, gives 83 spins, the answer. Thus if we bet on our single number for as long as 83 spins, it will have a probability of .90 of occurring *at least once* any time during those 83 spins.

TABLE 15

List of constants c with which to calculate the probability *Pat* of an event's occurring *at least once* during a certain number of spins.

Pat	Constant c
.05	.051
.10	.105
.25	.288
.33	.398
.50	$.693\ldots = .7$
.63	1.028
.67	1.146
.75	1.386
.90	2.303
.95	$2.996\ldots = 3.00$
.99	4.605
.999	6.908
.9999	9.210

Note: The constants should not be used when p is larger than 1/12.

And conversely, it will have a probability of $1 - .90 = .10$ of *not occurring at all during* those 83 spins.

In Table 16 opposite I have listed 9 typical answers for *Pat* concerning a single number at roulette. Accordingly, if we want a probability of .67—two games out of three—of seeing our number occur at least once, we have to bet for 40 spins. If we want the larger probability of .95—9.5 games out of 10—of seeing it occur at least once, we must wager much longer—for the very next 108 spins.

When we read Table 16, however, we must always bear in mind the warnings explicit in the actual roulette results of the Hartman sample of 46,080 spins.

Thus, let's take the last example. To most of us, examining Table 16, to have as many as 95 chances out of 100 of having our number occur sometime during the very next 108 spins—suppose we say 100 spins— seems an overwhelming assurance that we'll win. What are the trifling $100 - 95 = 5$ chances against us? Yet we recall from the Hartman sample that sometime during each 1,024-spin game we would have had to face a losing run (our number's not occurring at all) of as long as 150

TABLE 16

The probability *Pat* that a chosen number (p = 1/37) will occur *at least once* sometime during the very next r spins.

Pat	r spins
.50	25
.63	37
.67	41
.75	50
.90	83
.95	108
.99	166
.999	249
.9999	332

Note: When r is less than 65, a slight error occurs.

spins (and that this unfortunate event started 25% of the games). And 150 is much longer than 108.

Suppose we take a last example. To most of us to have 99 chances out of 100—a so-called quasi-certitude—of having our number occur at least once during the very next 166 spins (see Table 16) practically guarantees our success. What's a tiny 1 chance out of 100 against us? Yet we remember from the Hartman sample (see Table 13, p. 125) that in 75% of its games—3 out of 4—we would have had to face a losing run as long as between 100 and 200 spins in length—and it's within that segment that a losing run of 166 spins falls.

The mathematically astute will rightfully complain that I shouldn't compare an event in any 1,024-spin sample with one in a sample of specifically *the very next* 108—or 166—spins, and they're justified. I merely wish to warn any reader against using Table 16 with thoughtless optimism, and the results of the Hartman sample always return us to sober actuality.

We're now in a position to apply the constants of Table 15 opposite to the probabilities of those especially long and disastrous losing runs listed in the lower half of Table 14 (p. 127).

The reader will recall my conviction that it's this type of losing run, rather than the bank's percentage advantage from zero, that ruins most players. We can't deny that zero doesn't have its adverse, cumulative effect, but in my opinion these *losing runs* wipe out most players long *before* this cumulative effect of zero is realized.

Concerning Table 14 (p. 127), the reader will recall my first example of a gambler who spends one day in Monte Carlo playing all 573 spins produced by one wheel, and that Table 14 indicates that he will encounter a losing run of 100 or more spins *on average* once.

But what if we don't want to play all day long? Instead of 7 hours, suppose we decide to play only 3, a typical session at a roulette table. That would be $(55)(3) = 165$ spins. During only 165 spins what is the probability (as opposed to the average) that we will encounter this losing run—when our number doesn't occur at all—of 100 spins?

First we go to Table 14 (p. 127), then Table 15 (p. 128), and follow the same two simple steps as before.

In Table 14 it says that the probability q of a losing run 100 or more spins long is $q = 1/573$. In Table 15 we may pick out any probability, but suppose we pick Pat $= .25$, for which $c = .288$ (merely because it makes the answer come out conveniently to 165; in addition, although the second step is to subtract 1 from the denominator, when the latter is larger than 50 or so, it's insignificant, and as the denominator here is 573, let's omit this step).

Then we multiply 573 by .288, getting 165 spins. Opposite $c = .288$ is Pat $= .25$—the probability that our event will happen at least once. But that isn't what we asked. We asked for the converse probability—that of our event's not occurring at all. For this answer we just subtract .25 from 1, viz., $1 - .25 = .75$, the answer.

Accordingly, if we want a 75% probability of a losing run of 100 or more spins *not occurring*, we will have to play for 165 spins. But again, let's not forget the probability of ruin—there is a 25% chance here that such a disastrous losing run *will occur* during these 165 spins.

As we see, the application of the constants in Table 15 (p. 128) is extremely easy, and they give us the tool we need in order to assess the risk of gambling *for a certain length of time*, for who goes to a roulette wheel to bet on just one spin?

For my own practical use I long ago memorized two handy constants giving the probability *Pat* that an event, *favorable* or *unfavorable*, will happen at least once (or conversely, not at all). These are $c = .7$ for Pat $= .50$ (the fifty-fifty point) and $c = 3.00$ for Pat $= .95$ (a reasonable certainty).

Here's a last example. In discussing Table 14 (p. 127) I used as my second example a gambler who, on a typical visit, spends three days in

Las Vegas or Atlantic City playing seven hours a day for a total of 2,255 spins.

But what if we don't want to gamble that much? Instead of a total of 21 hours, suppose we want to play only $2^1/_2$ hours a day. In three days that gives $(3)(2.5) = 7.5$, or about eight hours, for a total of $(110)(8) = 880$ spins—let's say 898. During 898 spins, what is the probability that we will encounter a disastrous losing run as long as 150 spins?

In Table 14 it says that the probability q of a losing run of 150 or more spins is $q = 1/2,255$. And 2,255 times $c = .398$ gives 898 spins. Opposite $c = .398$ is Pat $= .33$, and this is the probability that the disastrous event *will occur* at least once.

Conversely, $1 -$ Pat $= 1 - .33 = .67$, i.e., that in two games out of three this losing run of 150 or more spins *will not occur* at all during these 898 spins.

Once more, let's not forget the probability of ruin that we just calculated here. There's a 33% chance that during these 898 spins the losing run of 150 or more spins *will occur at least once*. Many gamblers would prudently conclude that that's simply too large and unsafe a chance to take.

Here are three quick examples. How long do we have to play before acquiring a fifty-fifty chance of seeing occur at least once in the next r spins a losing run as long as 100, 200, or 300 spins? For the probability of fifty-fifty, Table 15 (p. 128) gives $c = .7$, so using Table 14 (p. 127), we get $(.7)(573) = 401$ spins, $(.7)(8,873) = 6,211$ spins, and $(.7)(137,457) = 96,220$ spins, the answers.

I know—who's going to play 96,220 spins?

But how about 6,211? In Las Vegas or Atlantic City, at 110 spins an hour, that's $(6,211/110) = 56.464...$or 57 hours, and at 8 hours a day, that's $(57/8) = 7.1$ or only 7 days needed to have a fifty-fifty chance of encountering a losing run of 200 or more spins. Thousands of gamblers *regularly* spend a week or ten days in Las Vegas, yet I suspect most of them would consider a disastrous run of as many as 200 or more spins as almost bordering on the impossible.

And before we began this study, many of us probably thought that an adverse run of 100 or more spins is quite rare. In Las Vegas or Atlantic City it takes only *three and a half hours* to have a fifty-fifty chance of seeing one occur on the number that we're playing.

Such are the attributes of the roulette pendulum when it swings to the losing side. As I mentioned, the pendulum's swing is asymmetrical, because it must stay on the losing side for a much longer period in order

to compensate for the abundance of riches during the briefer winning
period.

Winning Runs: At Least Once versus Not at All

Well, what about the briefer winning period? Now that we've
investigated losing runs, the calculations for winning runs are a simple
matter. Besides, because a winning run on a single number is indeed so
rare, most gamblers don't try systematically to wager on its occurrence—and I think this strategy is wise. What we should obviously
gamble on is an *excess* of our number over its theoretical average, not on a
rare event like a winning run of our number occurring two or three times
in a row.

What of the Hartman sample of 46,080 spins and its number of
winning runs of exactly one zero (i.e., preceded and followed by a number
other than zero), exactly two zeros in a row, and exactly three zeros in a
row? (There were no runs of four consecutive zeros: to have a chance of
seeing one would require a sample of roughly 1,800,000 spins.) Table 17
below shows how closely the actual results accord with theory and needs
no comment.

In Table 18 opposite I've listed the *theoretical* probability p of winning
runs for one number. (The observant will note that this table is the
complement of Table 14 [p. 127] listing the probability q of losing runs.)

Reading the figures for n from the bottom up, we see that a winning
run of 3 (or more) zeros occurs only once on average every 52,062 spins.
This event is obviously so rare that it's never worth betting on. In other
words, if your number has already come up twice in a row, take down
your winnings and take a walk.

On the other hand, a run of two (or more) zeros occurs on average
once very 1,407 spins, and as a long shot this is certainly worth

TABLE 17

Actual number of *winning* runs exactly r zeros long at the end of the 46,080
spins of the Hartman sample.

Exactly r	Actual	Theory	Difference
1	1190	1179	+ 11
2	34	32	+ 2
3	1	1	0
	1,225	1,212	+ 13

TABLE 18

On a single number, a *winning* run *r or more* spins long...	...occurs on average once every n spins (p equals 1 over the following denominators) as follows:
r	n
1	38
2	1,407
3	52,062

considering. Many players customarily remove all of their winnings after one win on their number, except for a single-unit wager for a possible repeat.

Given this custom, in Table 19 (p. 134) I've listed ten answers for the probability *Pat* that our chosen number will occur twice in a row at least once during the very next n spins, i.e., that there will be a winning run of two (or more). (This table is comparable to Table 16 [p. 129], except that the latter focuses on a winning run of one isolated zero, where p = 1/37.)

In other words, to have a 10% chance of seeing our number repeat twice in a row (at least once) we'll have to bet for 149 spins; to have a 50% chance we'll have to bet for 985 spins; and to have a 95% chance we'll have to bet for as many as 4,221 spins.

Conversely, to learn the various probabilities of our number's not occurring at all, one need merely subtract from 1 the decimal fraction in the *Pat* column. I leave this trifle to the reader.

Such are some of the important aspects of the roulette pendulum as it oscillates asymmetrically and lengthily among the losing runs and more briefly among the winning runs; and lest the reader decry my analytical emphasis of the former, let me close on a delightful and optimistic note from my old Monte Carlo friend, Alois Szabo.

As a preliminary, the reader should know that the chance of any given number's repeating itself in the very next two spins of the wheel is 1 in $(37)(37) = 1,369$. So the odds against its happening, if one simply walks up to the table, are 1,368 to 1.

Here is Alois Szabo's amusing anecdote:

"A cool-headed, shrewd gambler knows that *one cannot win all the time* and will play accordingly. A good gambler figures like this: 'If I have luck today, I'll win. If I'm unlucky, I'll lose just so much *and no more!* Tomorrow, or the day after, I'll try again.' He knows that it is only a

TABLE 19

The probability *Pat* that our chosen number will occur *twice* in a row (p = 1/1407) at least once during the very next *n* spins, i.e., that there will occur a *winning* run of r = 2 (or more).

Pat	*n* spins
.10	149
.25	405
.33	560
.50	985
.67	1,563
.75	1,954
.90	3,244
.95	4,221
.99	6,566
.999	9,880

question of time before his luck will return and that then he will be rewarded for having been patient and having limited his risks.

"All the foregoing is based on years of experience, and while I could cite thousands of examples, I shall limit myself to a personal experience. My niece, whom I consider to be one of the best gamblers I know, was unable to win for several months. Day after day she tried in vain—but nothing doing. So she built her game down in proportion, and it was amusing to watch her struggling with measly 50-cent chips instead of the 10- and 20-dollar ones which she was accustomed to throw on the numbers *en plein* [straight up].

"One fine day, however, the Wheel of Fortune turned, and unwittingly she demonstrated how a hazard game ought to be played. I remember it as though it happened today. She arrived in the [Monte Carlo] Casino with only one dollar in her purse—which, as you know, is not unusual with women! Out of this 'capital' she lost 50 cents on the spot. The remaining 50 she threw on the zero as cold-bloodedly as if she had another thousand in her pocket. The zero failed to turn up, but as luck would have it, her chip was not raked in. (Errors like this are common occurrences during the rush hours in crowded casinos.) In the next *coup* zero did show up, and she was paid! Without turning a hair she added a 10-dollar chip from her winnings to the stake. And the zero came again!

"From then on she played only with tens and twenties, and in a few minutes her winnings mounted to well over $2,000!

"All she had lost during the long months was but a fraction of what she won in half an hour.

"The conclusions to be drawn from this experience are:

1. When once winning, *ride your luck*, and take every advantage of the game of hazard!

2. When chance is against you, be strong enough to call it a day, and *limit your losses*! Without this the best, the most daring and shrewdest gambler will bleed away."

And I myself certainly agree with Alois Szabo: in a losing streak always reduce your stake to a bare minimum until your luck turns. If you're going to bet big, always bet big, as his niece did, with your winnings—*never with your own capital.*

Chapter 13

Arithmetic of an Unbiased Wheel

Three Months at Monte Carlo

Three Months at Monte Carlo

May I ask the reader to join me on a trip to Monte Carlo to play roulette for three months? In respect of which, would we win or lose? From our vicarious venture it won't be difficult to find out.

Again I draw on the Hartman sample of 46,080 spins, which accounts for all the spins at Roulette Table Number 2 at the Monte Carlo Casino from January 1, 1933, through March 25, 1933—a total of 84 days.

Now we mustn't suppose that Dr. Hartman, a Riviera resident, sat in the casino's Salle Schmit every day from 10:00 A.M. till midnight, carefully writing down, in the manner of a wheel clocker, every number as it occurred (although he might have done that). That chore was actually accomplished by the professional recorder for the gaming journal, *La Revue de Monte Carlo* (edited just across the frontier in Beausoleil, France), which existed as an aid to Monte Carlo gamblers between the two world wars. For a pittance roulette players could buy the weekly issue, listing all the numbers (a sample gamblers call a *permanence*) in the exact order of their occurrence, on which they could then practice their staking or other systems for the forthcoming week. What Dr. Hartman did was merely to take three months of the *Revue* and republish them in hardcover. (For readers seeking similar samples of roulette numbers two addresses are listed in Miscellanea at the end of this book.)

As the reader has become aware, what I myself have done is to divide its 46,080 spins into 45 games, each 1,024 spins long, analyzing the results to illuminate important winning and losing events which every roulette player is sure to encounter, even in a short game of 25 to 50 spins.

In Table 3 (p. 55) I listed the *longest* losing run in each of these 45 games. We now learn where I obtained this information, because Table 20 (pp. 138-142) lists not just the longest losing run but *all* the losing runs, of whatever length, for each game *in the exact order* in which they occurred. In Table 3, for instance, we saw that the longest losing run for the first game was 159 spins; and in Table 20 we note that this was the sixth losing run of all. The reader will recall I stated that 11 out of the 45 games (25%) immediately started with a losing run of 100 or more spins, and the prudent reader may now profitably check through Table 20 to see exactly where these disasters occurred. It's a most instructive experiment. (He will find the first such run—192 spins long—at the start of the 12th game.)

In the Monte Carlo Casino how long will it take us to play a game of 1,024 spins? At an average of 55 spins an hour that would be $(55)(10) = 550$ spins a day, or about two whole days, playing relentlessly morning, noon, and night. But we prefer to enjoy ourselves and gamble just a reasonable three hours a day. That would yield $(3)(55) = 165$ spins a day for $(1024/165) = 6.2$ days, or about a week.

So there we are. *Each* of the 45 games of Table 20 represents a *whole week* at Monte Carlo, whereas on paper each of these games will take us from only 30 seconds to 2 minutes to play!

As we learned from the theory outlined simply in the last chapter, there are only two kinds of runs, *winning* and *losing*, and during any roulette game, however short, we inevitably encounter both.

First of all, the *losing* runs: how many of these misfortunes do we encounter during the first game of 1,024 spins? If we count in Table 20 in the first game, all its listed numbers—1-39-21-4...51-93-51-32—we'll find that there are 26 losing runs, and their lengths are signified by each of these consecutive numbers. Thus the first losing run is just 1 spin long (it's actually, of course, the first spin of the whole 46,080-spin sample).

TABLE 20

Actual number of *losing* runs exactly *r* spins long at the end of 46,080 spins in the actual order of the runs' occurrences. The Hartman sample divided into 45 sessions each 1,024 spins long.

THE RESULT OF THREE MONTHS: 46,080 SPINS

1	17	9	38	5	17	7	43
39	23	46	46	54	9	38	2
21	3	42	9	1	1	13	45
4	113	20	20	66	3	8	0
49	20	36	11	11	87	6	22
159	3	38	63	26	39	14	1
8	77	84	38	5	33	8 <u>108</u>	52
44	21	46	30	20	0	80	71
3	58	3 <u>16</u>	2	19	61	12	44
66	13	25	59	28	18	61	12
14	30	9	12	82	23	9	9
62	5	33	2	32	184	37	17
25	26	22	30	22	7 <u>16</u>	45	8
57	36	131	1	35	58	57	8
5	38	0	17	45	35	0	25
2	44	49	84	0	1	33	38
91	0	32	82	65	30	52	12
32	32	37	10	0	0	1	48
7	2 <u>42</u>	20	43	73	64	44	8
46	19	20	63	56	134	24	36
46	15	12	22	6 <u>21</u>	26	38	14
5	17	55	59	25	19	36	29
51	59	24	100	6	20	69	4
93	35	31	11	4	6	68	28
51	39	40	33	15	97	24	5
1 <u>32</u>	11	70	3	10	14	134	35
17	92	6	5 <u>17</u>	14	35	94	17
69	5	119	43	11	31	33	23
16	6	15	59	44	12	28	31
8	11	71	17	14	26	10	33
5	100	27	18	4	14	9 <u>65</u>	44
39	7	77	53	27	6	34	0
63	38	56	6	1	61	0	17
153	7	4 <u>48</u>	13	232	82	4	61
45	17	40	85	17	3	2	27
1	12	33	30	36	16	29	44
16	185	0	60	62	36	20	10 <u>26</u>

8	0	13	35	22	121	9	43
6	11	9	123	45	136	19 31	40
61	20	13 43	15	6	32	160	9
60	40	72	0	11	7	28	10
1	7	41	137	15	52	5	24
31	9	89	38	32	5	57	36
88	23	6	35	28	4	16	22
49	55	68	7	16 5	40	22	168
20	14	19	35	78	13	4	79
7	21	14	15 3	43	45	9	74
20	82	1	40	9	8	3	21 20
9	47	66	28	16	23	21	24
149	128	55	77	205	10	7	55
23	4	1	2	46	76	47	18
3	6	25	32	87	4	7	15
52	12 30	31	4	19	0	24	25
10	192	23	17	11	4	30	16
5	22	17	7	9	18 63	15	3
49	27	19	37	7	79	27	202
19	28	85	18	10	19	7	5
30	0	39	6	3	6	37	20
49	16	83	10	21	66	132	19
61	11	120	24	33	18	12	10
85	74	9	10	74	135	43	1
99	8	11	48	62	1	25	31
11 4	5	10	13	268	19	13	22
22	84	6	72	1	13	22	82
16	100	6	23	17 49	9	33	35
18	10	66	35	38	121	9	64
36	57	15	24	9	2	73	35
39	27	14 35	14	23	5	19	92
59	13	25	21	6	16	30	68
58	21	15	94	8	16	20 114	26
2	58	44	34	31	57	120	71
12	4	52	15	13	89	19	22 98
11	2	22	5	13	31	15	7
14	45	6	11	27	90	16	33
1	30	37	0	18	55	80	20
26	25	6	3	3	0	84	6
75	78	37	23	8	21	20	65
7	79	9	4	66	8	112	54
24	17	260	42	38	35	13	49
24	0	26	13	15	21	3	28
3	10	28	46	21	63	28	85

46	21	103	71	94	34	50	46
49	93	74	116	82	28	16	23
30	33	8	63	108	58	16	2
22	11	38	112	53	30 62	98	7
12	13	2	27 76	29	259	89	33 21
34	12	14	112	32	55	55	91
42	16	14	0	26	67	25	31
56	1	25 58	31	87	15	26	98
32	38	44	82	7	60	11	4
5	12	14	0	8	79	33	21
16	38	49	25	33	14	7	37
42	14	35	80	6	44	66	22
16	15	3	6	108	22	52	18
0	7	7	10	1	1	13	0
11	39	93	25	23	64	0	3
8	27	6	99	19	75	32 10	2
49	6	194	43	59	3	23	72
17	24 4	35	22	31	31	8	85
10	19	5	7	2	30	32	34
52	12	49	61	149	47	26	19
13	39	22	0	5	21	90	43
3	83	8	8	8	18	6	11
58	14	20	117	7	60	125	8
2	12	82	5	1	11	79	2
2	14	16	29	2	50	105	2
28	2	2	31	29 48	6	2	5
23 11	19	63	16	21	110	5	2
123	27	3	2	3	1	19	2
13	16	50	1	33	5	50	5
172	50	6	28	18	90	4	17
17	16	66	39	14	12	93	21
57	7	13	2	98	31 0	17	23
31	4	24	20	65	91	11	68
7	75	128	12	35	12	54	0
11	47	14	9	79	37	11	19
91	1	0	51	42	43	41	0
10	7	26 9	8	12	80	9	3
2	20	223	11	37	101	9	7
15	4	4	0	30	47	51	30
21	116	68	19	95	3	10	4
26	30	78	17	11	21	32	1
16	50	105	28 89	106	15	36	14

90	18	46	5	54	39	44	16
5	32	10	1	7	171	76	3
42	68	13	16	32	7	182	58
11	54	34	23	18	14	30	21
13	33	2	4	<u>40</u> 80	67	29	<u>45</u> 58
<u>34</u> 18	99	106	0	136	148	147	31
140	44	25	115	1	53	19	5
101	26	53	33	67	47	89	4
23	<u>36</u> 25	27	16	12	70	86	22
1	62	98	<u>39</u> 5	37	13	10	31
19	25	18	104	49	15	19	24
4	63	41	32	12	11	19	17
40	22	30	44	76	81	0	19
57	42	8	59	18	15	5	8
2	6	89	12	5	<u>42</u> 58	30	6
74	145	7	17	8	34	3	8
103	39	46	10	44	4	47	56
4	4	6	41	23	13	103	186
38	115	<u>38</u> 4	0	2	170	46	49
35	55	95	0	89	9	3	9
78	96	25	45	0	35	<u>44</u> 7	42
150	1	8	6	7	8	8	30
53	2	98	67	40	12	78	50
52	40	67	2	50	27	1	59
4	36	27	19	4	52	29	74
42	58	18	8	27	10	115	41
<u>35</u> 24	66	0	51	4	84	122	36
18	23	7	3	69	92	48	63
10	101	44	8	4	5	38	15
30	33	17	36	10	57	31	48
5	19	27	10	23	99	18	5
19	<u>37</u> 23	18	56	1	33	71	4
8	63	40	10	37	51	46	71
120	14	11	50	40	33	47	0
11	30	45	9	58	10	4	<u>46</u> 3
100	11	19	19	52	8	5	125
46	1	15	12	<u>41</u> 55	21	62	47
130	99	19	0	102	79	38	32
4	21	14	13	76	14	23	31
36	34	61	6	7	<u>43</u> 71	23	4
18	47	25	53	4	31	40	66
22	36	52	17	45	4	6	11

10	179		42	73	40	<u>16</u>
43	166		27	40	16	
20	18	47	26	11	231	
167	8		35	7	26	

The second losing run is 39 spins long. And the last losing run is 32 spins long. As I pointed out, the longest losing run in this game is the sixth—159 spins long.

But how about the *winning* runs—where are they? Well, we don't have to list them overtly, for in Table 20 every losing run *must end* with a winning run—i.e., with the occurrence of our chosen number, zero—because by definition that's how we tell, obviously enough, when a losing run terminates. If a losing run never ended with a zero, then our game would consist, rather discouragingly, of only a single losing run to infinity. Accordingly, between the first and second losing runs of length 1 and 39 the first zero occurred. Between the second and third losing runs of length 39 and 21 the second zero occurred…and so on.

Hence the following simple rule: for every *losing* run there is always a (terminating) *winning* run of 1 zero. (Of course, upon rare occasion—34 in the Hartman sample—2 zeros in a row occur, and even more rarely, 3. In Table 20 a single 0 signifies a (winning) run of 2 zeros, and two 0's signify the only (winning) run of 3 zeros—in the middle of the 40th game.)

How many losing runs are there in any given game? If we count the losing runs in the first game, there are, as I mentioned, 26. If we count those in the second game, there are 30. Here I list the number of losing runs for the first five games: 26-30-27-30, whose average is 28.

To calculate the average number of losing (or winning) runs, however, there is a much easier way. We simply multiply out the simple expression npq, where n signifies the number of trials or spins in the game, and p and q the usual probabilities for winning and losing our bet at each spin. Accordingly, in a game 1,024 spins long we have $(1024)(1/37)(36/37) = 26.927…$or a theoretical average of 27 losing (or winning) runs—close to the actual average of the first five games.

We're now in the enviable position of being able easily to calculate our gains or losses from any of the 45 games during our three-months stay in Monte Carlo.

Suppose we take the first game as an example. We counted that it consists of 26 winning (or losing) runs, and as we win 35 units from each of these zeros, our *gross gain* is simply $(35)(26) = 910$ units. And as we lose a single-unit bet every time a spin occurs except for these 26 winning zeros, our *gross loss* is $1024 - 26 = 998$ units. Our *net gain* or *loss* is obviously the difference. Here it's a *net loss* of $998 - 910 = 88$ units.

Thus as it takes only about 30 seconds to count the number of losing runs listed in any of the 45 games, and at most a minute and a half to perform the foregoing simple arithmetic, that's why, a moment ago, I promised that we could easily play a whole week at Monte Carlo—or 1,024 spins—in only a couple of minutes!

In the prior chapter, on the simple theory of winning and losing runs, one of the reasons that I didn't discuss the gnawing effect on our pocketbook of the bank's percentage—which is 2.70% at every spin—is that the subject is so much more illuminated in the context of Table 20 (pp. 138-142). As we know, given a wheel of 37 numbers, when we win, the bank should pay us not 35 units to 1 but 36 units to 1. So if we substitute in our first example the mathematically fair odds of 36 to 1, our gross gain would become a larger $(36)(26) = 936$ units (rather than only 910), which would reduce our net loss to only $998 - 936 = 62$ units (rather than 88).

At any rate, why did we lose actually 88 units? Because the first game of 1,024 spins had only 26 zeros—1 fewer than the theoretical average calculated at 27 zeros.

Suppose we take the second game as our last example. As the 1,024 spins contained 30 winning (or losing) runs, our gross gain is $(35)(30) = 1050$ units, our gross loss is $1024 - 30 = 994$ units, yielding a *net gain* of $1050 - 994 = 56$ units. (And this calculation, representing a whole week at Monte Carlo, three hours a day, didn't take us even two minutes!)

Given the mathematically unfair payoff odds of 35 to 1, why did we win even 56 units by the end of the second week? Because the second game of 1,024 actual spins contained 30 zeros—3 more than the theoretical average of 27.

And so we could proceed, calculating our net gain or loss from each of the 45 games that we'd play at Monte Carlo, but quick though this may be, there's an even faster way to discover if we'd be ahead after each 1,024-spin game.

We know that the theoretical expected number of zeros per game is npq = (1,024)(1/37)(36/37) = 26.927...or about 27 zeros. So for all 45 games we have only to count the number of actual winning (losing) runs. When these total 29 or more, we *win something* (actually at least 20 units). When these total 28 or fewer, we *lose something*. (The number of actual wins must be 29 or more—rather than just 28 or more—in order to allow us to beat the bank's PC of paying us only 35 to 1 rather than 36 to 1.) The reader will recall that for the first five games the actual number of zeros was 26-30-27-25-30, so as 30 and 30 were above 29, and 26, 27, and 25 were below, we would have here won two games and lost three.

Following the foregoing simple method, it takes only about 30 seconds to find out if we would win or lose a whole one-week game at Monte Carlo! For instance, in the tenth game we found 43 winning (losing) runs—way above 29. Whereas in the 15th game we count 23—way below.

Would we have to perform even this second, lightning procedure, which is on a month-to-month basis, to find out our net gain or loss at the end of the whole three months of 46,080 spins? Of course not. Applying the first method, we may use the far fewer figures of Table 17 (p. 132), representing the actual winning runs of zero during the whole three months.

Here's the quick calculation to discover how much we'd win or lose actually betting on zero for as long as 46,080 spins.

Accordingly, 1,190 winning runs of 1 zero times 35 gives 41,650 units; 34 winning runs of 2 zeros times 35 gives 2,380 units; and 1 winning run of 3 zeros times 35 gives 105 units: for a total of 44,135 units, our *gross gain*.

And 1,190 winning runs of 1 zero account for 1,190 spins; 34 winning runs of 2 zeros account for 68 spins, and 1 winning run of 3 zeros accounts for 3 spins: for a total of 1,261 winning spins. So 46,080 spins minus the 1,261 winning spins gives 44,819 losing spins *or* units, our *gross loss*.

So 44,819 gross units lost minus 44,135 gross units won yields 684 units, our final *net loss* for the whole three months.

Glancing again at the right-hand column of Table 17 (p. 132), we see that there even occurred a *surplus* of 13 zeros during the three months, so we can't complain about the pendulum's not swinging positively in our favor—indeed, it gave us an extra (13)(35) = 455 units.

So where was the villain? This time I'm afraid we'll have to point to the bank's advantage of 2.70% at each spin. For 46,080 spins that's an expected loss of pn = (46080)(.027027) = 1,245 units.

From this we may draw a crucial lesson: in the *short* run (say a game of 1,024 spins) the bank's advantage at roulette may be a relatively minor detraction, but in the *long* run—and three months at Monte Carlo is a long run—the probability of the pendulum's having a positive swing sufficiently capable to overcome the PC's constantly gnawing effect is unfortunately very small.

How typical is a loss of 684 units?

Here theory again provides the quickest route to the answer. (The reader will recall our using the following formula to calculate the theoretical average plus or minus fluctuation of runs of red listed in Table 10, p. 118.) At the end of 46,080 spins what will be our average gain or loss in units if we bet on one number? We have...x = $.8\sqrt{(46,080)(1/37)(36/37)}$ = 27.89, and in a mathematically fair game this plus or minus fluctuation or swing, in units is (x/p) = (27.89)(37) = 1031.93..., or 1032 units, the answer.

As roulette is a mathematically unfair game, however, we must *add* to our average loss the expected loss of 1,245 units and *subtract* from our average gain the same amount, i.e., $-1,245 - 1,032 = -2,277$ units, and $-1245 + 1032 = -213$ units.

An unpleasant dilemma, isn't it? At the end of 46,080 spins we have a fifty-fifty chance of either *losing* 213 units or *losing* 2,277 units.

So again—how typical would have been a loss of 684 units? Obviously it would lie somewhere in between—and as the theoretical expected loss here is pn = 1,245 units, to have lost only 684—roughly only half the expected loss—is doing very well. Indeed, that's only (684/84) = 8.14 units a day. (We remember that the three months were actually 84 days.)

Accordingly, to lose 8.14 units would have been the price we would have had to pay to gamble every day at Monte Carlo, and for some gamblers this is a trifling amount to pay for the thrills experienced at the gaming tables of this famous casino.

Given all these lucubrations, the best thing we can say for betting on one or more random numbers on an unbiased roulette wheel is the advisability of keeping our game down to only 1,024 spins, representing about a week at Monte Carlo or three days at Las Vegas or Atlantic City. That way we have a reasonable chance to win.

But to play longer...

Chapter 14

Arithmetic of an Unbiased Wheel

The Probability of Long Runs

A few years ago I was sitting in the Salle Schmit of the Monte Carlo Casino, chatting with a retired British army major. Our mundane topic was the agreeability of the Riviera climate. "A remarkable thing happened here last winter," he said. "I woke up one February morning, peered out my hotel window, and saw snow on the casino gardens." "Heavens," I replied, "snow in Monte Carlo—I've never seen anything like that!" "Oh, but *that's* not what was remarkable," he murmured, squinting off as though recollecting an other-worldly vision. "I came over here, and a run of 12 reds occurred right here at this very roulette table!"

Speaking of a run of 12 reds, I recall an amusing anecdote about the Bad Homburg Casino in the 1860s. Attached to the casino was a charming theater, which was packed one afternoon with an audience entranced by the famous coloratura soprano, Adelina Patti. Suddenly the rear door of the theater burst open, and a breathless gambler hurried halfway down the center aisle, where he paused dramatically, thereby halting the concert: "There's a run of 12 on red!" he shouted.

Amid gasps of astonishment the audience rose as one and rushed down the hall to gamble at roulette, leaving Patti in tears.

Is a run of 12 on red very uncommon? Not really, but my British friend

146

remembered it glowingly, of course, because it had happened to *him*. But isn't that the way with all of us? If we look at column 4 of Table 10 (p. 118), we see that during the three months of the Hartman sample 6 runs of 12 reds *and* blacks actually occurred (close to the theoretical average of 5.88 runs listed in column 3), so half of these—or 3 runs—would have been on red, i.e., about one a month, and as my British friend spent most every day in the casino, it would have been more surprising if he had *not* seen the run of 12 reds.

We observe also from column 4 of Table 10 (p. 118) that the longest run during the 46,080 spins was one of 15 (blacks, as it so happened), which occurred (as we note from the second half of the table) sometime during the 22nd game. (From my extraneous records I find that this run happened to occur near the end of the sample, at the 42,941st spin.) But 15 isn't a *very long* run, only a *long* run.

The Hartman sample aside, is there any way we may appraise the probability of any run at all (including a run of exactly 1)?

Here is the simple rule: if the probability of an event is a fraction whose numerator is 1, the probability of the event's *not occurring at all* during spins equal to the denominator in number is always .37 (or close to); and conversely, the probability of the event's occurring at least once is $1 - .37 = .63$. (When the denominator is less than 65, a slight error occurs.)

Suppose we take an easy example of a run of exactly one number. We know that the probability at each spin of our chosen number's occurring is $p = 1/37$. Accordingly, without having to perform any calculation at all we know that during the first 37 spins (37 is the denominator) the probability of our number's not occurring at all is .37. And conversely, the probability of its occurring at least once is .63. Or for rough gambling purposes, every time we sit down and play a certain number for 37 spins there is always about 1 chance out of 3 that it won't come up at all and 2 chances out of 3 that it will come up.

Here's a second example. The probability of a winning run of 15 (or more) reds is $qp^r = (1/2)(1/2)^{15} = 1/65,536$, so its chance of not occurring during 65,536 spins is .37, and of occurring at least once is .63.

Here's a last example. The probability of a winning run of four (or more) reds is $qp^r = (1/2)(1/2)^4 = 1/32$, so the chance of its not occurring during our first 32 spins of play is .37, and of its occurring at least once is .63.

The simplicity of this rule provoked an amusing incident some years ago. In Nice I walked into Henri Daniel's editorial office, where the *genius loci* himself was seated struggling with his latest betting progression on the dozens, which he planned to publish in his gaming magazine. "The probability of one dozen's repeating five times in a row is $(1/3)^5$ or $1/243$," he explained. "If I use the normal approximation to the binomial distribution and the *theta* function, I could calculate the fluctuations around the mean, but it takes too long, and I want to go to lunch." Frowning as though performing lightning calculations, I declared, "Your progression has exactly a 63% chance of succeeding at least once during the 243 spins." "Really?" he gasped, quite impressed. "Why, that's remarkable. How did you figure that out?" To get him to go to lunch I had to tell him.

Some gamblers don't believe that *very long* runs ever actually occur in casino games. Their argument is simple: runs of 12 or 15 have perhaps been seen thousands of times, but who has ever actually witnessed a run as long as, say, 28 (or more)?

Let's approach the answer via actuality and theory.

First of all, the longest recorded run on one number was on July 9, 1959, at the El San Juan Hotel in Puerto Rico, when number 10 occurred 6 times in a row. If we step up to the table, the probability of this occurring is $1/(38)^6 = 1/3,010,936,384$.

In 1988 at the Bad Durkheim Casino in Germany, on Table No. 2, number 23 occurred five times in a row, the probability being $(1/37)^5 = 1/69,343,957$. In this sequence number 23 occurred seven times in 18 spins.

In addition, in June 1950, a gambler threw 28 consecutive passes at a craps table at the Desert Inn in Las Vegas. (Like the probability of each red at roulette, that of a pass at craps, excluding the bank's advantage of 1.41%, is $1/2$.)

The longest recorded run at any table game at all was perhaps one of 34 consecutive passes in August 1979. One Jack Davison made exactly 34 consecutive passes at craps at Binion's Horseshoe Casino in downtown Las Vegas.

In theory the basics of runs are easy to grasp. In Table 21 (opposite) I've listed the frequency of runs on an even chance.

So then, what *is* the probability of a run of, say, 28 or more? It's $qp^r = (1/2)(1/2)^{28} = (1/2)^{29} = 1/536,870,912$, the answer. So the event, obviously enough, is very infrequent.

It's helpful and profitable to realize that during these 536,870,912 spins there is a 63% chance that this run will occur at least once, and

TABLE 21

Frequency of Runs on an Even Chance

A run of r reds (blacks, passes, etc.)	occurs on average once *during* these many spins (powers of 2):
R	
1	2
2	4
3	8
4	16
5	32
....	....
10	1,024
15	32,768
20	1,048,576
25	33,554,432
....	....
26	67,108,864
27	134,217,728
28	268,435,456
29	536,870,912
30	1,073,741,824

conversely a 37% chance that it won't occur at all (and a 37% chance is large).

In the Monte Carlo Casino, at 550 spins a day, this run will occur on average once every $(536,870,912/550) = 976,129$ days, or $(976,129/365) = 2,674$ years.

As there are six even chances (red, black, high, low, odd, and even) on every roulette wheel, a run of 28 or more on *any one* of these six chances will occur on average once every $(2,674/6) = 446$ years.

From here matters are more difficult to estimate. In the Monte Carlo Casino there are two main gambling rooms. In the first, the Salle Schmit, which opens at 10:00 A.M., there have averaged historically about four roulette tables, and in the second, the Salle Privée, which opens at 3:00 P.M., there have averaged about three roulette tables. Thus a run of 28 or more will occur on average once every $(446/7) = 64$ years.

As of 1939 the Monte Carlo Casino had existed since 1863, but with the above average of seven roulette tables in operation, from, say, 1870. And 1939 − 1870 = 69 years.

In 1939 the American mathematician Horace C. Levinson reported that sometime during these 69 years, at one roulette table, a run of 28 had actually occurred on even.

And as the actuality of 69 years accords with the theory of 64 years, there we are.

Given that the overwhelming source of reports of very long runs at the Monte Carlo Casino came from the *permanence* magazine, *La Revue de Monte Carlo* (and I suspect it was the source of Levinson's information), which ceased publication at World War II, and that since then magazines listing the numbers of a single Monte Carlo roulette table, like *La Revue Scientifique* in the 1960s, have enjoyed only a fitful publication, I believe that for these reasons we no longer receive verified reports of very long runs from that casino. And to me the probability seems small that either player or croupier there, each with his preoccupations, would perforce remark the occurrence of a very long run and insist further that it be recorded for posterity in some book or journal.

It should be mentioned that from the 1840s to 1872 about a dozen German casinos offered the banking card game of trente-et-quarante, with its four even chances of red, black, color, and inverse. Although in 1882, in his magisterial work on gambling, *La Roulette et le Trente-et-Quarante*, Martin Gall reported nothing about very long runs specifically at roulette, he did state that he had once met a young gambler who claimed to have witnessed a run of 28 on color at trente-et-quarante. "Although I myself have never seen or heard reported a run longer than 22," commented the scholarly and cautious Gall, "one does meet travelers who have seen their share of marvels; they believe what they have seen, and our only duty is to seem to believe them."

Chapter 15

When the Gambler Has the Advantage

Capital Requirements for Winning, and Proportional Betting

Capital Requirements for Winning

Given a certain duration of play—100 spins, 1,024 spins, etc.—how much money should we bring to the casino to get through the worst losing streak? We don't want the inconvenience of continually returning to our hotel safe or the casino cage, yet on the other hand, for security reasons, we don't want to bring to the tables more capital than needed.

With considerable inconvenience to themselves many gamblers either under- or overestimate the required sum. As we'll discover, a very simple calculation yields the answer, which depends on two things: whether we have or the bank has the percent advantage, and the betting strategy that we adopt for play.

When the Casino Has the Advantage

Suppose we're going to play on a single number of an *unbiased* wheel, where the casino's conventional PC of 2.70% at Monte Carlo or 5.26%

in the United States is by definition *against* us. We decide to play a game of 1,024 spins. Regardless of whether we do or do not quit winners at the end of the game, how much money need we have to survive the worst losing streak during the game? Put differently, what will be the *strain*, as gamblers term it, i.e., our worst cumulative net loss *during* the game?

Again let's draw on the 45 games of Table 20 (pp. 138-142), the step-by-step results of whose first game of 26 winning (losing) runs I've listed in Table 22 opposite.

Column 1: as each of the 26 losing runs ends in a *winning* run of 1 zero, our gross gain is always 35 units per run.

Column 2: these lengths of the 26 *losing* runs are naturally identical to those comprising the first game of the 45 games of Table 20 (pp. 138-42); a winning run should occur once every 37 spins, and as the total of column 2 is 1,013 losing spins (units), we have $(1013/26) = 38.96...$ or 39, quite close.

Column 3: as there is close to a fifty-fifty chance of our winning or losing net at the end of each run segment, in this column there are as many pluses as minuses—13 of each (though ordinarily there would be some fluctuation around this exact mean of $(26/2) = 13$).

Column 4: as we note at its bottom, our game of 1,024 spins results in a final *cumulative net loss* of 103 units.

Column 4 obviously yields the most interesting results. We see that during the course of the 1,024 spins our *largest cumulative net gain* is 75 units at the end of the fourth run, and that our *largest cumulative net loss* is 106 units at the end of the 25th (next-to-the-last) run.

But are 106 units so *typical* a net loss during a game of 1,024 spins that that sum is all we'd ever have to bring to a casino to get through every game, or at least most games, of that length? And what about a game of just 100 or 500 spins, etc.?

As we can't mathematically depend on the results, for being indicative, of just one game, here's a simple formula answering the question of our capital requirements on a single number of a game of *any* length. (For simplicity I'm excluding the matter of the bank's PC.) The formula is: $(n/37) + 5.838 \sqrt{n}$, which gives the amount of capital we should bring to the casino to get through 84% (one standard deviation) of all losing streaks on a single number in a game of *any* length, and $(n/37) + 9.5 \sqrt{n}$, which gives the amount of capital we should bring to the casino to get through 95% (two standard deviations) of all such losing streaks.

Here's an example. What is the sum we need to get through the worst losing streak of 84% of games that are 1,024 spins long? Using the

TABLE 22

The Hartman sample: results of 1st game of 1,024 spins (here Column 2 is identical to 1st game of Table 20, pp. 138–142).

Winning/ Losing Run	1 Gross Gain	2 Gross Loss	3 Net This Game	4 Cumulative Net
1	+ 35	− 1	+ 34	+ 34
2	+ 35	− 39	− 4	+ 30
3	+ 35	− 21	+ 14	+ 44
4	+ 35	− 4	+ 31	+ **75**
5	+ 35	− 49	− 14	+ 61
6	+ 35	− **159**	− 124	− 63
7	+ 35	− 8	+ 27	− 36
8	+ 35	− 44	− 9	− 45
9	+ 35	− 3	+ 32	− 13
10	+ 35	− 66	− 31	− 44
11	+ 35	− 14	+ 21	− 23
12	+ 35	− 62	− 27	− 50
13	+ 35	− 25	+ 10	− 40
14	+ 35	− 57	− 22	− 62
15	+ 35	− 5	+ 30	− 32
16	+ 35	− 2	+ 33	+ 1
17	+ 35	− 91	− 56	− 55
18	+ 35	− 32	+ 3	− 52
19	+ 35	− 7	+ 28	− 24
20	+ 35	− 46	− 11	− 35
21	+ 35	− 46	− 11	− 46
22	+ 35	− 5	+ 30	− 16
23	+ 35	− 51	− 16	− 32
24	+ 35	− 93	− 58	− 90
25	+ 35	− 51	− 16	− **106**
26	+ 35	− 32	+ 3	− 103
		(− 1,013)	(+ 296-399)	(− 103)

formula, we find the needed sum is 215 units (appropriately more than our cumulative net loss of 103 units of the first Hartman game).

So if we bet on a single number for 1,024 spins, with a capital of 215 units, we'll have to leave the table for more money during 100% − 84%

= 16% of the games we play. If we want less inconvenience, we'll have to bring to the table 332 units, which will satisfy our capital requirements 95% of the time. Frankly, I myself prefer bringing to a casino only 215 units and inconveniencing myself 16% of the time rather than suffering the insecurity of carrying around on my person 332 units (speaking figuratively), but that's just my own choice.

Independent of capital requirements, however, Table 22 (p. 153) serves as an excellent illustration of what we *typically* go through if we bet on a single number for 1,024 spins. Thus, glancing down column 2, we realize that the villain of our game is not all the small and medium losing runs, which are balanced by the corresponding winning runs of 1 zero (each paying us 35 units), but the *single very long* losing run of 159 spins, which isn't cancelled out by anything at all. From column 4 we note that at the end of this sixth run our cumulative net gain becomes for the rest of the game a net loss (excluding a trifling net gain of 1 unit at the end of the 16th run).

The important point for us to grasp is the *typicality* of this circumstance. If we glance in Table 20 (pp. 138-142) at only the first ten games, we see from the three-digit numbers (that obtrude and are thus easily located) that *only* two of the games (the sixth and the tenth) are without *at least one* killer losing run, and as we previously found, their average is about 150 spins. If we could avoid only this *one* disastrous run, how many of these games, even with the vaunted bank's percentage against us, would result in net wins! Unfortunately, however, the killer run is impossible to avoid, because there's absolutely no way to predict when it's going to begin. Thus in this 1st game of the Hartman sample there are 26 winning (losing) runs. From the permutational standpoint, the very long run of 159 spins had as much chance of beginning at the 6th position as at *any other* position from the 1st to the 26th. In other words, the 6th losing run was as likely to have turned out to be only 1 spin long as 159 spins long.

When the Gambler Has the Advantage

After we've clocked a wheel and discovered that through a *bias* we have the mathematical advantage over the casino, everything changes almost from black to white.

From the standpoint of capital requirements we have two choices: do we minimize our risk or maximize our gain?

To *minimize risk*, at each spin we must bet *no more than* the casino's posted *minimal* wager on a single number. Suppose we call this 1 unit. As

Professor Edward O. Thorp has remarked, "Timid play [minimal betting] is the one and only strategy...which minimizes the probability of ruin."

Yet even though the biased wheel gives us a definite *average* advantage, we may still very easily go broke *before* winning. Recall the valiant struggles over *thousands* of spins in Las Vegas by Albert Hibbs and Dr. Roy Walford to win $15,000 (see Chapter 5), and in Reno by Allan N. Wilson and Robert Bowers to win $300 (see Chapter 6). In this regard, bearing in mind that Allan N. Wilson is both a mathematician and a successful biased-wheel player, we could profitably follow his suggestion if we have an advantage over the casino of 5.88% on a single number. (This is when $p = 1/34$.) If we back ourselves with a capital of 700 units, we have as high as a 90% chance here of *not* going broke in the process of doubling our capital. But Wilson reminds us that when Robert Bowers and he were making substantial (not minimal) wagers in Reno, for safety's sake they increased their bank-to-bet ratio to a more conservative 2,500 units-to-1.

In addition, we should bear in mind the bank-to-bet ratio of Billy Walters in Atlantic City. When in 1986 Walters and his partner won their record $3,800,000 in only 18 hours of actual play, the bank they had deposited in the casino cage was $2,000,000, and their total beginning wager on five biased numbers was $10,000 a spin ($2,000 on each number). Accordingly, their bank-to-bet ratio was $(2,000,000/10,000) = 200$ to 1, i.e., their initial wager, though large in absolute value, was only $1/200 = .005$, or *half a percent* of their capital.

Why didn't Billy Walters and his partner, like Wilson and Bowers, adopt an even safer ratio of 700 units-to-1 or even 2,500 units-to-1? Most likely because the five biased numbers that they were playing were *far more biased* than the single number of Wilson and Bowers, which was $p = 1/34$. How much more biased? I have calculated it as perhaps $p = 1/30$ or even stronger.

Walters and his partner, however, had *five* biased numbers going for them as opposed to only *one* for Wilson and Bowers, and as we'll learn in a moment from Edward O. Thorp, our optimal mathematical strategy is always to bet *simultaneously on as many biased numbers as possible*.

Proportional Betting

As we recall, Table 6 (p. 79) lists the gambler's percent advantage over the casino when he's playing a single biased number.

As the other extreme from minimizing risk by wagering timidly or minimally 1 unit per spin (even after we begin winning) is the strategy of *maximizing gain* by wagering our entire bankroll on only a single spin. At a game even mathematically advantageous to us that's *in practice* absurd and suicidal. What we seek is a compromise between the extremes of minimal (long-term) risk and maximal (short-term) gain. What we seek is a wager optimally combining the greatest safety with the greatest growth rate of our capital or bankroll. Given this, what should be our bank-to-bet ratio?

One of the scholars of the optimal ratio, or proportional betting, is an American mathematician, John L. Kelly, Jr., who proposed it in 1956. In simplified form the Kelly system states that, when the game is *favorable to us* (whether on red or on one or more numbers), at every spin we should wager an amount equal to *our current bankroll multiplied by a fixed multiplier.*

On an even chance the fixed multiplier is simply our PC advantage. In accord with Table 6 (p. 79), suppose our PC advantage at every spin on an *even chance* is 20% and our capital is 100 units. Then our first bet is $(100)(.20) = 20$ units. If we win that wager, we now have a bank of $100 + 20 = 120$ units. Accordingly our second wager is $(120)(.20) = 24$ units. If we win that wager, we now have a bank of $120 + 24 = 144$ units. Accordingly our third bet is $(144)(.20) = 28.8$ or 29 units. And if we *lose* that wager, we now have a bank of $144 - 29 = 115$ units. Accordingly our fourth bet is $(115)(.20) = 23$ units. If we lose that wager, we now have a bank of $115 - 23 = 92$ units. And so on and on, always betting after every winning wager 20% of our new bank, and after every losing wager 20% of our remaining bank (or whatever our present advantage from bias may be).

Mathematicians consider the Kelly proportional betting system the best mathematical strategy, constituting, as it does, the perfect compromise between betting, in relation to our capital, too little (overly time-consuming) versus too much (overly risky). The drawback to the Kelly system is not mathematical but practical or psychological. At the gaming table many gamblers simply don't want the inconvenience of doing even its simple multiplication after each spin. That's too bad, because to deviate form the Kelly is always to our financial disadvantage.

In explaining the Kelly proportional betting system, for simplicity I used an even chance (say red), but it's just as valid at roulette for wagering on one or more numbers. Suppose we've clocked a wheel and have discovered five equally biased numbers. The question is, which is advisable—at each spin to put a 5-unit bet arbitrarily on one of the biased numbers, or a 1-unit bet on each of the five numbers? Do we put all our eggs in one basket or spread out? In other words, do we diversify?

The answer is we should *always diversify* on as many significantly biased numbers as available. (I'm excluding the trivially biased ones.) The mathematician who solved the problem for roulette is Edward O. Thorp, who contrasted betting on just one biased number versus five biased numbers.

For illustration purposes, in both cases Thorp assumed a large 44% advantage. (From Table 6, p. 79, we see that in the case of the *single* number this means we have p $= 1/25$.) Because the payoff is not even money but 35 to 1, to find out our wager after each spin, we can't simply multiply our bank each time by our fixed advantage of 44%. There has to be a slight adjustment. Let's say that our formula is (PC/A) and equals our bet multiplier. The *PC* signifies our percent advantage (expressed as a decimal fraction—here .44), and *A* signifies the bank's payoff odds-to-1 (here 35 to 1).

Accordingly, in the case of a *single* number our multiplier is $(.44/35) =$ .01257, or 1.26%. Using a hand electronic calculator supplied with an exponential function, Professor Thorp calculated that after 1,000 wagers we'll have won 11.47 times our starting bankroll!

"Notice the small value of [the fixed multiplier of 1.26%]," wrote Thorp. "That's because the very high risk of loss on each bet makes it too dangerous to bet a large fraction of [our] bankroll. To show the advantages of diversification, suppose instead that we divide our bet equally among the 5 most favored numbers, as [Claude] Shannon and I actually did in the casinos [see Chapter 2]. If one of these numbers comes up, we win an amount equal to [payoff odds of] $(35 - 4)/5$ [or 6.2 to 1] of our amount bet, and if none comes up, we lose our bet. Thus A $= (31/5) = 6.2...$ This corresponds to p $= 1/5$. Then [for (PC/A)]$...(.44/6.2) = .07097$, so you bet about 7 percent of your bankroll. [Thus] this growth rate is about 5.75 times that for the single number. After 1,000 bets, you would have approximately 1.25 million times your starting bankroll. Such is the power of diversification."

Thorp's calculations undoubtedly throw light on why, in Atlantic City in June 1986, Billy Walters and his partner won their record $3,800,000 in only 18 hours of actual play by betting on five biased numbers for about $(18)(110) = 1,980$ or, say, 2,000 spins. As I mentioned, their initial wager of $10,000 was *only* .5% of their $2 million bankroll. Were they using the Kelly system? Because we don't know the percent advantages from their five biased numbers, we can't say for sure, but it's at least recorded that they were using a proportional betting system.

"What is the price of deviating from betting the optimal Kelly fraction...?" continued Thorp. "It turns out that for bet payoffs like blackjack, which can be approximated by coin tossing, the 'performance loss' is not serious over several days play. But for the roulette example, the performance loss from moderate deviations form the Kelly system is considerable."

Based on selected PC values from Table 6 (p. 79) and Thorp's formula, which I've expressed as PC/A equals our initial betting fraction, I've listed in Table 23 opposite what our *initial* Kelly wager should be (columns 2 and 3) for a given PC bias advantage (column 1). In practice at the table, of course, one rounds off all the amounts of columns 2 and 3. Accordingly (see column 2), on one biased number we'd bet, in ascending order of advantage, 1-1-2-3-4-6-10-13-23 units. (And we similarly round off for the sum for five biased numbers in column 3.) Notice how small our initial wagers are for the first four percentages from 1.41% to 9.09%—from only 1 to 3 units. This shows how conservative the Kelly system is.

The figures in Table 23 opposite tell us how much our *first* bet should be on a biased number using the Kelly proportional system. But how much should be bet *after* our first wager, that is, after each gain or loss as we go betting along from spin to spin?

The formula for this *constant multiplier* is simply $p - (1/36)$, where p signifies at each spin the probability of a single biased number.

Thus when we have a number with a *very strong* bias, say with $p = 1/20$, this works out to $.05 - .0278 = .0222...$ Hence, as we go betting along from spin to spin, our constant multiplier is about 2.22%.

By the same token, when we have a number with a *strong* bias, say with $p = 1/27$, this works out to $.037 - .0278 = .0092....$ Thus as we go betting along from spin to spin, our constant multiplier here is about .92%.

We can see that, given at one end a high fraction of $(1/20) = .05$, and at the other end a low one (let's say) of $(1/32) = .03125$, in practice our constant multiplier will always be between roughly 5% on the high side and 3% on the low. No gambler could ask for anything simpler (and in a pinch we may adopt an average multiplier of 4%).

Mathematicians consider the Kelly proportional betting system the best strategy there is, and it's certainly better than constantly resizing

TABLE 23

With a starting bankroll of 1,000 units our initial Kelly (proportional) bet should be:

	1	2	3
p	Our PC Bias	Betting on 1 Biased Number	Betting on 5 Biased Numbers
1/35.5	1.41	.403 unit	2.27 units
35	2.86	.817 unit	4.61
34	5.88	1.68 units	9.48
33	9.09	2.60	14.66
32	12.50	3.57	20.16
30	20.00	5.71	32.26
27	33.33	9.52	53.76
25	44.00	12.57	70.97
20	80.00	22.86	129.03

our bets through intuition, which usually amounts to disastrous overbetting, leading to ruin. Thus, as all biased-wheel players should follow *some* proportional betting system, why shouldn't we adopt the best one there is?

Concerning random roulette, in Las Vegas and Atlantic City a roulette gambler customarily buys a stack of 20 one-dollar chips, and even if he bets only a dollar on one number per spin, he often finds he soon exhausts his capital. But why this ruin? Is the disappearance of his stack in only 20 spins due to unusual bad luck? Not at all.

As we recall, the constants in Table 15 (p. 128)—and their examples in Table 16 (p. 129)—yield the clear and simple explanation. The probability in one spin of a random number on a 38-slot wheel is 1/38, and the odds-to-1 against this are 37 to 1. If we wager a dollar per spin on the same number (or even switch the number after each spin!), how many spins do we have to wait out until we have a fifty-fifty chance of seeing that number occur? From Table 15 (p. 128) we see that when Pat (the probability of an event's occurring at least once) equals .50, the constant c is .7, and .7 × 37 = 25.9, or 26. (In Table 16, p. 129, the first answer is 25 spins rather than 26, because the table pertains to a 37- rather than a 38-slot wheel.) Thus to have a fifty-fifty chance of seeing our number occur at least once we have to wager for 26 spins. On *each* spin the probability of our number's occurring is only 1/38, but taken as a group, the probability (Pat) of it's occurring at least once *any time during the whole series* of 26 spins is fifty-fifty. Hence if we buy the standard stack of 20 chips and bet them one at a time, we have obviously even more than a fifty-fifty chance of exhausting our capital as early as only the 20th spin, when our last chip gives out. And as many gamblers who buy a stack of 20 chips bet on average five of them per spin—a chip on five different numbers—if they don't hit, they've lost their whole capital in only (20/5) = 4 spins.

If we're playing on a biased number, our ruin situation, of course, is improved, for the losing streaks are considerably shorter. Suppose the probability of our biased number is 1/30 rather than the random 1/38. Then applying Table 15 (p. 128), we have .7 × 29 = 20.3, or to have an even chance of seeing our biased number occur we have to play only 20 spins rather than 26.

Regardless of what proportional betting system we adopt for the preservation of our capital, however, in my opinion we should always disguise our biased-number wagering with appropriate expectation-lowering, random-number betting if such camouflage can prevent our being harassed or barred. One advantage to the wheel-watching system so clearly and adequately explained by Laurance Scott (see bibliography) is that at every spin the numbers we bet on *change*, which doesn't attract the attention of the staff. Unfortunately, the Achilles heel of the incomparably easier biased-number system is that the number(s) *doesn't change*. Hence our need in biased roulette for a camouflage act comparable to those of blackjack players who disguise their proportional-betting, card-counting systems. To promote the delusion that they're winning through luck rather than their counting system, some blackjack players pretend that they're extroverted drunks, others that they're sheepish introverts bewildered by their good fortune.

Here in part is the amusing act which a Nevada acquaintance of mine has cultivated to gull the dealer and pit boss into believing he's playing only random numbers. Having already clocked a wheel on a prior visit and determined, for example, that its number 29 is biased, this gentleman ambles into the casino and sits down at the end of the table near the three column spaces. After buying his stack of 20 chips he asks one of the other players—always in a voice just loud enough for the dealer to overhear—what is the date? The 17th? Superstitiously he places one of his chips on number 17—and as he settles back into his chair, abstractedly drops another chip on number 29 as though it were a mere superstitious afterthought. Lastly he places a wager on the middle column (containing numbers 17 and 29).

Throughout his game he earnestly focuses his attention on his column bet, strategically shifting it from one column space to another in an embarrassingly fruitless pursuit of winners. Sometimes he even places a thoughtful wager on the red or black or on some other even chance. In particular, to bemuse the dealer or pit boss even further, he alternates his two superstitious wagers, on one spin betting only on 17, on the next only on 29, then alternating them on each subsequent spin, as though following the dictates of some abstruse astrological plan. As he proceeds, he unfolds and openly consults an astrological chart adorned with planets, moons, and stars, and seems pained if people smirk at him. If not actually addled, he appears slightly deaf, for if you ask him the time, he smiles and says the weather outside is fine, and if you ask him how it is outside, he says he's sorry but he forgot his watch.

Of course, only 29 means anything to him, but to wager only on that one number for spin after spin, especially with a proportional up-and-down betting system, would quickly reveal his true goal. Throughout all this he sacrifices the joys of convivial discourse with both dealer and fellow players in order to ponder the metaphysical significance of the list of roulette numbers that he keeps studiously writing down as they come up. If he ever thinks the pit boss is in any way suspicious of him—after all, he *is* winning steadily on 29—he quietly folds up his chart of planets and wanders out of the casino to return prudently on a later shift. He has never been barred, and if the staff recall him at all, remember him only as another lucky fool.

The success of this gambler would have never been his if he had followed only the dictates of mathematics.

Chapter 16

Wheel Clocking

Clocking a Random Wheel in Search of Biased Numbers

In Search of Biased Numbers

If we look at Table 2 (p. 46), the results of 1,000 spins at Monte Carlo clocked by W. Duppa-Crotch in 1891, we observe that about half the numbers are winners (here 15 numbers) and about half are losers (here 19 numbers), with three numbers occurring 27 times, the theoretical average in his 1,000 spins. This division is always true regardless of the size of any roulette sample: about half will always be above average and half always below.

Accordingly Table 24 (pp. 164–165) lists the results of all 37 numbers of a permanence or sample of 4,456 roulette numbers for 15 consecutive days at the Wiesbaden Casino in 1970. As we note from the right-hand summary column, at the end of 15 days zero occurred 94 times, number 1 occurred 111 times…and number 36 occurred 116 times, etc.

On the first day there were 338 spins, so the expected, theoretical occurrence of each number was pn = $(1/37)(338)$ = 9.14, or 9 times. In actuality, 17 numbers occurred more than 9 times, and 13 occurred fewer than 9 times (and 7 numbers occurred exactly 9 times).

162

Following this method, we find that on the second day (295 spins) 15 numbers were above average, 17 below; on the third day (354 spins) 17 were above average, 17 below; on the fourth day (258 spins) 15 above, 16 below; on the fifth day (288 spins) 14 above, 18 below; on the sixth day (251 spins) 14 above, 19 below; on the seventh day (309 spins) 21 above, 13 below; and so on similarly for days 8 through 15, every day about half the numbers being above average, half being below.

Why am I pointing out such an obvious statistical fact? Because we're looking for *trends*, and there is a very simple mathematical theory about randomness which will explain why, day after day, a certain *few* numbers will be either continuously above average or continuously below, but why *most* numbers will bob up and down, being above average one day and below the next.

The simple theory is merely that for a winning run in the very next n spins. As we've just learned, at the end of any given day about half the numbers will be winners, half losers. Thus the probability that any *given* number will be among the winners is $1/2$. The same is true for the next day, but the probability that that given number will be a winner on *both* the first *and* the second day is only $(1/2)^2 = (1/2)(1/2) = 1/4$. The probability that it will be a winner three days in a row drops to $(1/2)^3 = (1/2)(1/2)(1/2) = 1/8$; that it will be a winner four days in a row drops to $(1/2)^4 = 1/16$; and that it will be above average all seven days of the week is as small as $(1/2)^7 = 1/128$. The important point for us to realize is that, although a random number can indeed go on and on being a winner, every day its chance of remaining so decreases by 50% from the previous day.

So were we to take the trouble of analyzing in this light all of Table 24 (pp. 164–165), we wouldn't be surprised to find that *most* numbers are neither pure winners nor losers but on a day-to-day basis bob up and down, above and below average.

The foregoing is true of ordinary, *random* numbers, but what we're looking for, or course, are extraordinary *biased* numbers whose characteristic is that they *remain winners* more or less continually (i.e., above average). The statistical clocking problem—for which there is often no *immediate* solution—is how to distinguish between a random winner and a biased winner.

For definition's sake let's say a *weak* number is one with p = $1/35.5$ to $1/31$, a *strong* number is one with p = $1/30$ to $1/25$, and a *very strong* number is one with p = $1/24$ and larger.

TABLE 24

WIESBADEN CASINO

Daily totals of numbers from January 1 to 15, 1970

Numbers	Day: 1.	2.	3.	4.	5.	6.	7.	8.	9.	10.	11.	12.	13.	14.	15.	Total
0	9	10	7	3	2	4	3	4	8	7	5	6	8	8	10	94
1	12	10	11	5	10	4	5	12	8	8	5	5	3	7	6	111
2	9	13	11	8	8	9	5	4	8	2	6	12	8	18	7	128
3	6	7	13	7	5	5	11	12	14	15	9	9	3	7	7	130
4	9	1	17	7	8	11	8	9	11	7	11	10	6	6	9	130
5	12	6	12	3	5	10	10	5	5	14	12	4	6	10	4	118
6	12	8	14	11	9	5	7	7	3	6	6	8	4	12	6	118
7	7	5	10	8	7	7	10	7	5	6	5	12	13	5	8	115
8	6	6	10	10	7	4	9	8	6	12	5	10	10	9	4	116
9	14	8	4	6	8	8	9	7	8	9	7	10	13	10	6	127
10	13	8	7	5	7	2	10	6	9	8	10	9	9	10	7	120
11	9	7	8	8	11	8	8	11	8	9	9	7	4	6	8	117
12	15	10	8	10	9	5	14	9	13	11	5	6	8	9	8	142
13	10	7	7	6	9	5	4	8	10	10	9	11	8	10	7	121
14	9	9	7	2	6	7	6	6	3	8	5	7	9	9	9	105
15	7	9	10	7	13	8	12	8	8	8	7	11	7	8	10	126
16	13	11	5	7	13	7	5	9	10	5	6	14	11	10	2	128

																Total
17	11	6	8	6	11	5	12	11	9	7	10	11	8	10	9	134
18	6	11	8	8	9	7	4	9	11	11	8	7	8	10	13	130
19	12	5	9	11	6	5	11	10	9	5	9	8	10	7	8	125
20	7	9	10	5	10	11	11	6	4	4	5	9	4	3	15	113
21	11	7	13	6	8	9	11	6	12	12	7	11	4	11	10	138
22	10	9	10	9	11	9	9	2	10	15	6	10	7	5	7	129
23	9	11	8	9	19	4	12	7	8	10	14	9	8	10	14	152
24	6	4	11	8	7	5	9	2	2	9	4	5	9	5	4	90
25	9	7	15	14	11	6	12	11	7	6	8	12	6	5	8	137
26	8	8	10	6	8	6	6	10	10	10	6	8	6	5	6	113
27	10	7	6	7	9	8	9	4	10	15	4	7	8	14	15	133
28	6	10	8	5	3	6	10	4	14	6	10	7	4	6	3	102
29	4	11	7	8	6	9	3	7	12	4	7	7	3	10	6	104
30	12	5	9	6	4	5	7	6	7	8	9	6	8	5	11	108
31	10	6	7	4	6	5	10	11	6	7	9	6	6	10	4	107
32	10	12	3	5	2	5	8	8	10	6	10	10	5	5	7	106
33	7	10	9	8	6	4	5	11	13	4	10	5	12	9	7	120
34	11	8	21	7	7	11	9	8	13	8	8	9	9	8	1	138
35	6	7	15	10	5	10	6	5	12	11	10	2	6	6	4	115
36	1	7	6	3	9	12	9	11	7	11	10	8	7	7	8	116
Total Daily Spins:	338	295	354	258	288	251	309	281	323	314	286	308	268	305	278	4456

Strong Numbers: p = 1/30 to 1/25

Suppose we take a single example from Table 24 (pp. 165–166), the Wiesbaden sample of 15 days—say number 12, the third rank winner by the end of the first seven days, occurring 73 times in 2,093 spins. Thus number 12 had a *strong* relative frequency of p = (73/2093) = 1/28.7 or 1/29. Let *w* (for winner) signify above the daily average, *l* (for loser) signify below:

Wiesbaden–day:	1	2	3	4	5	6	7
Number 12–rank:	w	w	l	w	w	l	w

Well, now, at p = 1/29, by the end of the first seven days or 2,093 spins, was number 12 a *strong biased* number or only a *lucky* random number? The important point is that *we can't be sure*. But by the end of these 2,093 spins number 12 was rank 3 among the five top winners. By the end of 15 days or 4,456 spins number 12, occurring 142 times, was rank 2 (see Table 24, right-hand column), and after 31 days (from Table 24 extended) or 8,943 spins it was rank 5, with 269 occurrences. Whether it was random or biased, for a number to be consistently among the five top winners for 8,943 spins naturally makes it very appealing to us.

Very Strong Numbers: p = 1/24 or larger

Having no sample with a naturally occurring *very strong* number, I've taken a week's permanence or sample of 3,178 spins from the El Cortez Casino in Las Vegas for from September 1 to 7, 1979, and artificially created such a number. As we know, on an ordinary American wheel with 38 numbers the frequency of any one number is 1/38, so the frequency of two would be 2/38 or 1/19. I combined the actual occurrences of zero and double zero to obtain the artificial number 0/00 (thereby, in addition, reducing the 38 numbers to 37).

Certainly most mathematicians would declare as not only very strong (my term) but very biased any number which keeps coming up on average once every 19 spins! For a gambler to discover so favorable a number would probably be a thrilling, once-in-a-lifetime experience. Accordingly we're not the least bit surprised by our number 0/00 bobbing relentlessly between the very top 2 ranks of the 37 numbers for the first seven days in question (except for the second day):

El Cortez—day:	1	2	3	4	5	6	7
Number 0/00–rank:	2	18	1	1	1	1	2

When p $=$ 1/19, how on earth could such a very strong number drop on the second day to so low a rank as 18th from the top? The answer is that on that day the normal expected frequency for any number was 15 occurrences, and zero occurred only 11 times and double zero a very infrequent three times, for a total of 11 $+$ 3 $=$ 14 times, giving our artificial number 0/00 the abysmally low rank of 18 out of 37 (meaning there were 17 numbers occurring more frequently than it).

But as the very unusual does occur only infrequently, here are the entirely expected results for the second week:

El Cortez—day:	8	9	10	11	12	13	14
Number 0/00–rank:	1	2	1	2	1	1	1

So in clocking a wheel we're obviously never going to have any trouble recognizing a *very strong* number, for in the cumulative total of any sample its *consistently* high rank among the top five winners is simply too obvious to go unobserved—and besides, we're looking for it anyway.

Based on the illustrative stories of the earlier chapters of this book, my opinion is that the majority of playable biased numbers are of the middle or *strong* range, where p $=$ 1/30 to 1/25. But this is just conjecture. Who really knows? Perhaps there are many wheels with *weak* biased numbers, where p $=$ 1/35.5 to 1/31, but I suspect these may be disdained by high-rolling, professional biased-wheel players as simply not worth their financial time or trouble. (Unfortunately for our study, their high-rolling ventures are the only ones that get reported in the newspapers.) If so, I find their disdain somewhat ironic, because the very best blackjack players treasure a count advantage as high as a mere 1.50% per hand, yet a *weak* (to use my term) biased number, where p $=$ 1/35.5 to 1/31, according to Table 6 (p. 79), yields an advantage of between 1.41% and a relatively high 16.13%. How joyously a blackjack player—or indeed a gambler at any casino game—would treasure an advantage over the house in the range of (1.41% $+$ 16.13%)/2 $=$ 8.77%!

The crux of this discussion is that, *without increasing the number of spins* (i.e., the value of *n*), it's statistically very difficult, if not impossible, to distinguish between a *consistently winning*, worthless, fickle, *random* number, which at any moment may drop below average to show itself for what it really is—a terrible loser—and a *consistently winning* worthwhile, faithful, strong *biased* number, which has great difficulty dropping below average, because it's physically and favorably defective.

Suppose we play a particular roulette wheel for only one spin. Obviously some number must come up. Suppose it's 17. Does that mean 17 is a biased number? Of course not—bias needs a sufficient number of spins to prove itself. But how many spins are *sufficient?* That's the obdurate statistical clocking problem.

Suppose we play 338 spins—the total of the first day of the Wiesbaden sample (first column Table 24, pp. 164–165). For that *day* number 12 was the rank-1 winning number, occurring 15 times. Does that mean it was a biased number? We can't tell, because the number of spins or sample size is too small, so we must go to the second day to see how it does.

On the second day we find that the rank-1 winner was number 2, occurring 13 times. Now what do we do? Do we stick with number 12, which occurred 10 times and sank here to rank 9, or switch to the new winner, number 2 at rank 1? Do we switch horses in midstream? We recall that this was the clocking problem that plagued Hibbs and Walford in Las Vegas, and Wilson and Bowers in Reno, both teams solving it—with greater or lesser success—by increasing their sample to many thousands of spins (see Table 4, p. 64, and Table 5, p. 75). When we looked ahead, we found that number 12 for the first 7 days or 2,093 spins was the rank-3 winner, and for the first 15 days or 4,456 spins it was the rank-2 winner (see Table 24, right-hand column). But we know this gratifying piece of information only through *hindsight*. What do we do *before* that? What do we do *now?*

The answer is that we should always base our bets only on *the cumulative total of* all *the spins that we have up to the last minute.*

In the case at hand we have 338 spins for the first day and 295 for the second, making a cumulative total of $338 + 295 = 633$ spins. As we learned, if we make out a cumulative total *only* for the first day, we find that number 12 is rank 1, and if we make out one *only* for the second day, we find that number 2 is rank 1 and number 12 rank 9. But if we make out a cumulative total combining *both* days—i.e., for *all* 633 spins that we have at hand—we find that number 12 is *still* the rank-1 winner and that number 2 is only rank 4. So *that's* why we know we should continue betting on number 12—between the two it's the relative winner.

Similarly if we make out a cumulative total for the first three days, we get $338 + 295 + 354 = 987$ spins, and numbers 12 and 2 have by now both occurred cumulatively 33 times and are consequently both at rank 3. Accordingly we might as well continue betting on number 12.

The first four days give us a cumulative total of 1,245 spins, and number 12 is now at rank 4 and number 2 at rank 5. Hence again we continue wagering on number 12.

The first five days give us a cumulative total of 1,533 spins, and number 12 continues at rank 4, while number 2 has sunk to rank 6. Hence we stick with a wager on 12.

And so on for the rest of the week of 2,093 spins, number 12 attaining rank 3, number 2 sinking to rank 8. And by the end of the first 15 days or 4,456 spins at Wiesbaden, number 12 is rank 2 (at 142 occurrences), and number 2 has fallen to rank 11 (at 128 occurrences).

For simplicity I've explained how we should clock the wheel and then bet by the indicated rank by relating our strategy only to the journeys of the two arbitrary numbers 12 and 2 relative to each other; but that doesn't mean that in practice we should have bet at all on number 12, because whenever it sank from its cumulative rank-1 position, we should have *switched immediately* to the *new* rank-1 winner. For number 12 this began at the end of the third day, when number 34 rose to the cumulative top—where it stayed for the fourth day too. On the fifth cumulative day number 34 gave up the palm to number 25. And so on, not only for the first 7 days, but for the first 15—for our purpose, all 37 numbers fighting to be cumulatively the rank-1 winner. As we see from the right-hand, total column of Table 24, the cumulative rank-1 winner for all 15 days at Wiesbaden was actually number 23, which occurred 152 times. (Number 12 was rank 2 with 142 spins, we recall.) Accordingly at whatever point during the 4,456 spins that number 23 became the rank-1 winner, *then* we should have immediately switched to wagering on it. (To stick, out of faith, to a *former* rank-1 winner, say number 12, means that we egotistically arrogate to ourselves *foresight*— and that's pure gambling, exactly by wheel clocking what we're trying to avoid.) So this is the betting rule we must always follow:

We must always bet rank 1 rather than rank 2, rank 2 rather than rank 3, and rank 1 rather than ranks 2, 3, 4...or 37. And following the rule, our *last* cumulative total of spins *alone* indicates rank 1 (as well as the lesser ranks).

In Table 25 (p. 170) I've listed the first five ranks of winning numbers for the Wiesbaden Casino for 1970—first for the first week, then for days 1-15, 1-31, and for curiosity's sake even days 1-365 (for those who would play all 87,222 spins—see Table 5, p. 75).

It would be gratifying to believe that clocking a wheel and making out a cumulative total today endows us with *foresight*, enabling us to win tomorrow. Unfortunately all this procedure does is give us *hindsight*,

TABLE 25

Wiesbaden 1970: Cumulative top 5 winning numbers; the journey of No. 12
(which may or may not have been biased).

Days:	1	1–2	1–3	1–4	1–5	1–6	1–7
	12	**12**	34	34	23	34	25
	9	16	6	6	25	25	34
	10	1	1	25	6	23	**12**
	16	2	2	**12**	**12**	6	23
	1	9	**12**	2	34	**12**	22

Days:	1–15	1–31	1–365
	23	27	2
	12	23	21
	21	10	30
	34	3	13
	25	**12**	28

enabling us to see which numbers *have been* winners up to the last spin. If
we bet on this past winning trend of a number which is *random*, it will
either slowly or quickly fail us, and we'll lose, but if the winning trend of
a number owes itself to the latter's being veritably *biased*, it will continue
on average to prosper, and we'll win unfailingly.

How do we know the exact spin on which to switch from one winning
number to another which we *hope* is showing a bias? The answer is that
we must follow my stated rule of allowing *only* the cumulative total of *all*
the spins up to the last moment to be our guide, to determine our choice.

Accordingly I have invented for roulette the following procedure for
mathematically optimal wagering. Suppose we want to clock a wheel
and (for simplicity here) bet on only one number. (What follows is
equally valid for wagering on more than one biased number—say five
numbers—in the manner favored by experts like Edward O. Thorp,
Pierre Basieux, and Billy Walters.) We go and sit down at the roulette
wheel.

The first spin results in number 17, so on the second spin we wager on
number 17. As we go along, we keep a cumulative score of all 37
numbers on an ordinary pad, or preferably on the scorecard provided by
the casino. The next number is 10, so on the third spin we bet on 10.
Rule: when the cumulative score between two or more numbers is
identical, just to break the dilemma, always bet on the number last to

occur. The next number is 17 again, so as it has now become the cumulative, rank-1 winner, on the fourth spin we wager on 17. And we will *continue* wagering on number 17 until the cumulative total for another number is either equal to or 1 more than that for number 17.

In sum, that's all there is to this simple procedure. The betting system requires that we bet invariably on the cumulative lead winner, immediately changing to any other lead winner whenever it comes along.

The pitfall, however, is to become *irrationally* enamored of a previous rank-1 winner and not switch when indicated by the cumulative total. Not to switch means we assume foresight and believe the previous rank-1 winner will become rank-1 again. Such an assumption has no statistical justification. The cumulative total of *all* the numbers is invariably the only reliable criterion.

What is the purpose of this mathematically optimal or best betting practice? (By definition something other than optimal is inferior.) It guarantees that on average we'll begin betting *as soon as possible* on the *biased* number rather than on just lucky random numbers. And that's the whole purpose of wheel clocking: *to find biased numbers and exploit them as soon as possible*. If there were no biased numbers on defective wheels, wheel clocking (consequently of only random numbers) would be pointless.

Chapter 17

More About Wheel Clocking

Two Unusual Ways of Wheel Clocking, and Statistics

Two Unusual Ways of Wheel Clocking

The matter of simple arithmetic aside, how does one go about clocking a wheel in an actual casino? On first thought this would seem to offer no problem. One simply goes to any wheel in a casino, sits down, and begins making a cumulative list of numbers as they occur. One preferably asks one of the staff for the blank roulette scorecard which the better casinos conveniently provide players for this very purpose. Naturally to maintain one's seat one must gamble, if only modestly. Some players like making minimal bets on one or two numbers, others on the even chances. I myself prefer wagering simultaneously on two dozens or columns, because although this doesn't in any way improve one's mathematical expectation, one's probability of success at every spin is almost 2/3, and I feel comfortable with the concomitant frequencies of the winning and losing runs, and their standard deviations.

Then where is the problem? For most of us there isn't any problem at all. Casinos welcome evident system players—that's why they provide blank scorecards for roulette and baccarat—and anyone making modest bets and studiously taking down roulette numbers is simply viewed as another harmless, conventional system player. Besides, what other ways of clocking a wheel are there? Offhand, most of us couldn't even imagine any other way. One sits down, one clocks. What variations could there be?

What follows, however, are two other methods I myself have come across during my own casino experience. Both were invented by professional biased-wheel gamblers and demonstrate to what extraordinary and ingenious lengths high-powered team players will go to get cumulative totals either quickly or over a period without the casino's knowledge.

The Short Way: the Camera

The first method of wheel clocking may be described in a few words. I found out about it not too long ago when I was discussing biased-wheel play with a friend who is a pit boss at a large casino on the Las Vegas Strip, where he's in charge of the second-floor cameras and television monitors that observe play at individual tables of craps, blackjack, baccarat, and roulette. I'd asked him how long it takes in practice to clock a wheel. "Eight hours," he replied. "How do you know?" "Because recently a man representing a Venezuelan team of biased-wheel players approached me and told me that that's how long they need to clock a wheel to tell whether or not it's biased. What he wanted me to do was to record on one of my cameras all the numbers coming up for that length of time on each of my roulette wheels. There's nothing illegal or unethical about that, but I told him to get lost."

Now I ask the reader, who but a team of professional biased-wheel players would have thought of something that ingenious?

The Long Way: the Mysterious Stranger

The second way of wheel clocking is, in its way, even more subtle and original, and certainly more comical.

I was sitting at a roulette table in the Salle Privée of the Monte Carlo Casino, plodding away at my modest double-dozens wager, one of whose practical advantages is that, by sitting at the end of the table near the observant croupier, one avoids the troublesome arguments that inevitably occur in the center of the layout from predatory chip claimers. As it takes only a few moments to record the last spin and place one's next wager, however, one has plenty of time to gaze idly about the huge, three-story room.

I first noticed the middle-aged Englishman among the gamblers who meander from table to table. Pausing nonchalantly at one of the four roulette or two trente-et-quarante tables, he would make a subdued, jocular remark to some acquaintance, usually female, about her game. I knew he was English, because he stopped and murmured something amusing to a lady two seats from me. What he actually said I didn't hear, simply because it didn't concern me. There are always in the Monte Carlo Casino a few gamblers who socialize from table to table while pursuing fortune.

This gentleman always carried around a few chips which he would rattle negligently in his hands while peering over some gambler's shoulder in the conventional way of trying to read, from the seated person's scorecard, the numbers that had most recently occurred at that roulette wheel. Only in retrospect did I realize that, except for a couple of times, I'd never seen him actually place a wager, but why initially would anybody notice anything that trifling? One of the exceptions was while I was playing at the first trente-et-quarante table, to which he walked up and put a wager on red. After red failed to show in the next hand, he commented obtrusively to everybody, including the indifferent croupier, that that just wasn't one of his lucky tables. Before he wandered away, however, he quietly winked and smiled at one of his female acquaint-ances, whereby I gathered he was just another of the casino Lotharios.

The next day, however, I changed my mind. Before gambling, I was seated off the Salle Schmit in the Salon Rose, having tea and a sandwich. It was a February afternoon and not crowded, yet when the mysterious stranger materialized in the wide doorway, he meandered over and graciously asked if he might share my table. I acquiesced with equal graciousness. As he studied carefully the short menu which every gambler there knows by heart anyway, he remarked, "Rather busy here at Monte Carlo for this time of the year, isn't it?" I stirred my tea while he discoursed on the weather. I had the vague feeling that I was being cultivated—but for what purpose? Finally after a conventional amount of chitchat, to which I made meager contributions, he said, "I do enjoy a flutter here. I wander from table to table, trying to catch a lucky streak at each one. But most people don't like that system. They prefer to make a study of the wheel at some particular table. I notice you enjoy sitting at one table in the Privée—your lucky table, eh? I have numerous acquaintances here who swear by their luck at one particular table—

simply won't gamble at another." He smiled, but I could see he was disappointed by my indifferent response to his gaming topic. I still had the feeling I was being cultivated, but I couldn't comprehend why. Seeing the waiter approach, he managed to catch sight of an imaginary friend out among the roulette wheels of the Salle Schmit. "Oh, there's Mrs. So-and-So," he declared. "I've got to see her before she leaves the casino." So saying, he smoothly extracted himself from the table and was gone.

I came across this gentleman not only in the gaming rooms. In the evenings he would be ensconced in an armchair in the lounge or bar of the Hotel de Paris, usually chatting with some female acquaintance or some English couple or other. Obviously he was an amusing conversationalist. Perhaps he was an amorous lounger casting his net for a wealthy widow. Perhaps he was just lonely or bored. I didn't think about it.

One afternoon I looked up from what he'd called my lucky roulette table in the Privée. It was a rather crowded session, but I happened to catch sight of the Englishman hovering at another roulette table just as one of his seated lady friends handed up to him her scorecard, for which he thanked her and moved off. That evening I ate dinner alone across the way in the Café de Paris. The mysterious stranger came in by himself and at a couple of tables away sat immured behind the *Daily Telegraph*, but I could see him occasionally glance furtively at me from behind its pages. Now what? I thought.

In a moment I found out. Just as I was finishing my dessert, he paused on his way out. "Hello," he said, in his irritatingly jolly way, "how are things at your lucky table in the Privée?" Unbidden, he sat down at the adjacent table, his feet in the aisle. "I'm afraid my own system of going from table to table isn't working out so well this week," he added gratuitously. He chuckled at the irony of it all. I stirred my tea. Finally, to bring things to a head and possibly to get rid of him, I said, "I noticed this afternoon that one of your lady friends handed you her scorecard. Perhaps the winning numbers that come up will help you win. Lots of people write them down. I do so myself." "I'm glad you brought that up," he said, smiling benevolently, and pulled his chair closer. "I've found that studying the prior day's list of numbers before I play *does* help me, and I've asked one or two of my friends if they wouldn't mind letting me borrow their cards when they've finished playing so I may copy them. I say, I certainly would be grateful if you'd let my copy the ones from your wheel at the end of the day. I say, may I buy you a drink?"

I didn't mind his copying my scorecards whenever it was mutually convenient, so we remained on casual, friendly terms over the next two weeks, but it took me (rather unimaginative on my part, I must admit) that long before I perceived his goal, which was unobtrusively to clock every single roulette wheel in the whole Monte Carlo Casino—the five wheels in the Salle Schmit and the four in the Salle Privée.

My initial glimmer of his goal arose because, although he sedulously collected one or more scorecards from each table at different sessions, he himself would hardly ever gamble, and this being the case, why, I asked myself, would he need a scorecard from one table, let alone from as many as nine? Thus I gradually realized that he was gathering his information for a team of absent biased-wheel players. Following the practice of such teams, they would arrive after he left. No one would see *them* clock the wheel they would play.

Here is what this gambler was actually doing. He'd been attracted to me, I later realized, because he'd noticed that I sat habitually at the same roulette table. Had I kept changing from table to table, he wouldn't have bothered to cultivate me at all. Whenever possible he preferred cultivating women—middle-aged or elderly—evidently because, compared to men, he found them less suspicious of his blandishments. Thus his candidates for cooperation were always gamblers who habitually sat at the same table. If he had to, he would invite them to tea, a sandwich, a drink, even for dinner if necessary. And as he was always good company and never made any designing moves, either flirtatious or monetary, on the people whom he cultivated, why would they ever possibly suspect that their crucial service to him was to let him borrow their silly daily roulette cards?

How did I myself confirm my suspicions? So intrigued did I become that, when he was absent from the casino, I finally got up the courage to ask his acquaintances at all nine roulette tables: "By the way, after you've finished for the day, would you mind if I borrow your scorecard and copy it? I want to know what the lucky numbers are." "I'd love to, but an English gentleman has already asked me to save it for *him*," they would invariably reply. The ironic aspect of the whole thing was that, as he himself hardly ever gambled, his method of wheel clocking wasn't costing him a single penny! It was costing all the rest of us *our* pennies, and often a lot of them too. He was out only some trifle for tea or cocktails.

After a few weeks, just before taking the train back to Paris, I saw him on a cold March evening seated in the Café de Paris, immured as usual behind the pages of the *Daily Telegraph*. I went up to him after dinner and said, "Here's your scorecard for today. I'm afraid it's my last one. I have to leave for Paris tomorrow." I glanced around at all the empty tables and, unbidden, pulled up a chair to his table. "Rather busy here at Monte Carlo for this time of the year, isn't it?" I remarked. Somewhat bemused, he casually put aside the *Telegraph* and took me in suavely. "I'm sorry to hear you're leaving," he said in his airy tone of a man of the world. "The numbers you've already given me have helped me win many times." In three weeks I'd seen him bet twice: once at trente-et-quarante. Irritated by his absurd imposture, his cloyingly cheerful remarks, his ridiculous prevarications on every subject including the weather, I threw care to the winds and asked, "But how can the numbers from *my* roulette table have helped you when you never play at *my* roulette table?" The unimpeachable logic of this question caused him to blink several times. He glanced thoughtfully through the windows onto the Place du Casino. "Oh, but they have helped. You see, I play them when you're not there," he answered, and looked me straight in the eye.

That did it. I'd had enough. "At the same time when you play the eight other wheels you're clocking via the little old ladies?" I muttered. He blanched for a moment and remained silent. The bolt had struck home. His savoir faire suddenly vanished. He eyed me grimly, and for the first time I thought some of the inner man might be coming through. "I see you know some of the lingo," he murmured sardonically. "An occasional word," I replied, and threw my last bolt into the breach: "How soon are the others going to arrive?" He gazed at me a long time in thoughtful appraisal, and I never did know what thoughts passed through his mind. He had to be very careful and discreet, but I suspect he realized that, as I was clearly an American visitor, it was unlikely that I was a detective from the casino. Besides, for the role that he was about to offer me, perhaps an American, a foreigner in those parts, would benefit the team's camouflage. At any rate, I concluded later that what he was about to suggest was probably partly to test me, partly to bribe me, and partly to keep me quiet by inveigling me into his team of players. Finally he made up his mind to risk it: "Would you like to join them? We can always use someone who fits in, you know." Had someone walked in just then, he would have probably thought the Englishman was inviting me to be a fourth at bridge. I rose to go: "As I said, I'm leaving tomorrow on the train." He remained seated and, avoiding eye contact, stared through the window at the Place du Casino. "Perhaps it's just as well for everybody." "Perhaps it is," I said in farewell.

I never saw the man again.

Edifying Statistics

Here are some edifying facts cited in *Las Vegas Behind the Tables* (1988) by Barney Vinson, a Las Vegas pit boss:

In 1984 as many as 12.8 million individuals gambled in Las Vegas casinos. The average player risked $1,068, stayed 4.3 days, gambled a total of 17.8 hours, and averaged $7.54 a wager. After a show each player gambled for 148 minutes, or about 2.5 hours.

Given the foregoing, we may say that a gambler who favored roulette played for $(17.8/4.3) = 4.14$ hours a day. At 110 spins an hour he played a total of $(4.14)(110) = 455.4$ spins a day, or $(4.3)(455.4) = 1,958.22$ spins during his roughly four-day stay.

Thus a typical roulette player in Las Vegas gambled about 450 spins a day for a total of 2,000 spins, a total coincidentally helpful for our discussion, because it's identical to the 2,093 spins of one week at the Wiesbaden Casino (Table 24, pp. 164-165). (As the reader is aware, in Europe casinos aren't open 24 hours a day, and a croupier there averages only 55 spins an hour to the 110 spins in the United States.)

An important book on roulette is *Roulette Wheel Study* (1987), by an Englishman, Ron Shelley. The book is authoritative, because the author is an international expert on the game owing to his position as an insider in the American casino industry. Shelley was the independent consultant hired by the management of the Claridge Casino in Atlantic City to examine, test, and report on their eight roulette wheels after the loss of their first $200,000 to the Billy Walters syndicate in July 1989 (see Chapter 10). In the book he provides many factual details—including the five numbers Walters and his partner actually bet on—concerning their sensational win of $3,800,000 in 18 hours in June 1986, at the Golden Nugget Casino in Atlantic City. He states that 90% of all the wheels in Atlantic City and Nevada are no more than five years old. In Atlantic City they're only three to four years old, and in Las Vegas few are over 20.

A casino typically nets from a roulette gambler 27% of his purchased chips. Accordingly if a gambler buys $100 worth of chips, after an indefinite period at roulette, when he cashes out, he will receive $73. But that's a mean, of course, which admits of large individual fluctuations.

In his book Shelley provides information about supervisor and dealer procedures, mechanical and electronic cheating devices, the size and composition of today's plastic roulette balls and their consequent coefficient of restitution (degree of bounce), the pros and cons of different materials used in roulette wheel construction, large photographs with explanatory captions of the three manufacturers presently supplying American and Caribbean casinos, and innumerable other technical matters of manufacture, service, and maintenance directly affecting a gambler's play on the wheels.

We recall, for instance, that frets have always been a particular bugbear of roulette-wheel manufacturers, and Shelley describes mechanical and electronic gauges used to detect any measurable discrepancy in the height, width, and depth of frets. From a confidential 1982 engineering report by physicists of the University of London, commissioned by John Huxley Ltd., the London roulette wheel and casino equipment manufacturer, Shelley cites the following:

"A player wishing to win by observation [wheel watching] is primarily concerned with the characteristics of a wheel which enhance, or detract from, the wheel's randomness. The height and nature of the separators [frets] are an important factor in this context. A separator which is larger will tend to trap a ball better; hence the player desiring to win by observation will select a wheel with the largest [highest] separators."

In March 1989, I conducted my own survey of roulette wheels in Las Vegas. The ten typical large casinos that I visited on the Strip had a total of 35 wheels and the ten downtown casinos along Fremont Street had 20. So as a rule of thumb, the better Las Vegas casino has between two and three operating roulette wheels (versus about 12 roulette wheels in an Atlantic City casino). And the type of frets? Both on the Strip and downtown half the wheels had the old-style, higher, deep-pocket frets, and half had the new-style, smaller, low-profile frets, so the biased-wheel player looking for higher frets would not be frustrated. In Atlantic City, however, only about four casinos now have wheels with the higher frets that tend, if only subtly, to trap the ball.

To be sure, high frets are usually not used on European wheels, but it should be significantly borne in mind that Dr. Richard W. Jarecki won his $1,280,000 on San Remo wheels having *low* frets. (Accordingly the cause of bias on those San Remo wheels was either the looseness of the frets or lay obviously in defects elsewhere in the wheels. I mention this, because as I explained in an earlier chapter, one may never divine a

biased wheel through casual observation. Looks deceive. Although a
wheel in obviously decrepit condition may be a good candidate for
clocking, just the same, one may detect and confirm bias *only* through
adequate clocking.)

From time to time one hears the baseless conjecture that biased wheels
are far more likely to be found in the smaller, poorer, out-of-the-way
casinos, where budgets are restricted and maintenance procedures lax.
By way of contravention may I remind us all that, if the amount won be
the criterion, the most ill-maintained and notoriously defective wheels in
the world have been found to be in the largest first-class casinos, such as
the Monte Carlo Casino, Monaco; Harolds Club, Reno; the Golden
Nugget in both Las Vegas and Atlantic City; the Mar del Plata Casino,
Argentina; and the San Remo Casino, Italy. It would be equally
ridiculous to hold that biased wheels are more likely to be found in the
large, well-established casinos, because the complacency and overween-
ing confidence of their managements foster laxity. It may not be too often
repeated: regardless of the size or quality of a casino, one may detect bias
in one of its wheels only through sufficient clocking.

I asked Stirling Hawkins, the pit boss and roulette-wheel mechanic at
the Golden Nugget in Las Vegas, about the frequency of maintenance
procedures, and he replied that, although he himself cleans, oils, and
blows out the bearings of his wheels with compressed air quite frequently, most Las Vegas casinos service their wheels only once every six
months.

Be all this as it may, one comforting conclusion about this subject is
that to be practical and successful at clocking and biased-wheel play a
gambler never has to *know* what caused a particular wheel to be biased.
Indeed, even after playing a wheel, much of the time he will simply never
know and never be able to find out, but the jingle of innumerable coins in
his pocket is more than a compensation.

Chapter 18

Playing a Biased Wheel

Combining Clocking with Playing

An Alternative Way of Clocking?

Were one to use an electronic memory device, hidden or otherwise, with which to clock a wheel, one opens oneself to permanent barring or legal or illegal harassment.

Accordingly I asked Harry Lorayne, the American memory expert, whether it would be feasible to clock a roulette wheel through unaided human memory alone. Lorayne concludes that even for him the mnemonic process would be so onerous as probably to be impracticable, because one isn't working with only 37 or 38 changeless numbers but with their ever-changing cumulative totals, for which in one's mind, therefore, one must alter the mnemonic code word after every spin, when one must re-encode the new cumulative total of the last number which has just occurred.

Accordingly it seems that most of us must restrict ourselves to the conventional but at least easy way of clocking a wheel while seated at the table with pencil and scorecard or pad.

The Impossibility of Perfect Wheels

One of the myths of biased-wheel play is that such biased wheels are rare, because roulette-wheel manufacturers, who putatively know their business, go to great lengths to produce wheels without the slightest defect. I have no quarrel with that claim. Manufacturers *do* go to such lengths. There is, however, one insoluble problem: it's technically impossible to manufacture a wheel *without* defects.

Let's glance back over a hundred years. After the Jaggers raid in Monte Carlo in 1873, the casino's Paris manufacturer retooled all its wheels, replacing their single, immovable fret rings with individual, movable frets. A lot of good that change did the casino: look at the large sum the Italian syndicate won from them in 1880.

Now let's move up to the 1960s and early 1970s. The wheels beaten by Dr. Richard W. Jarecki at the Monte Carlo and San Remo casinos were still of this post-Jaggers kind—relatively low, movable frets fastened to the cylinder from below by a small, vertical screw (of the kind tampered with by Vladimir Granec). Such frets are inevitably liable to become loose and therefore biased.

So what should a manufacturer do to solve this dilemma? Regardless of which style he adopts, his wheel is inevitably susceptible to bias—and he knows it.

The reader will recall my quoting Inspector Michel Gonzalez of the French Brigade des Jeux (Gaming Police), who in 1971 was interviewed on Paris television, along with other experts, about the phenomenal successes, over a period of years, of Dr. Richard W. Jarecki. In addition to the words I quoted, Inspector Gonzalez boasted that *henceforth* casinos won't have to lose money through biased wheels, because manufacturers have recently developed a novel option: instead of individual, movable frets, they now offer a single metal ring of immovable frets.

For heaven's sake, what kind of *novel* option is that? What protection is there for a casino to regress to the very type of frets exploited so successfully by Joseph Jaggers over a hundred years ago? As it turns out, these single-unit fret rings (along with movable-number rings) have been quite unpopular with the few casinos in Las Vegas and Atlantic City that have tried them. For one thing, there is little resilience to the ball—only a dead, unrandomizing bounce—and for another, some manufacturers inhibit sales by charging a substantial premium just for this dubious safety feature—as much as 15% of the cost of the whole wheel, and the cost of a new roulette wheel today is approaching $10,000.

I've invoked the problem of defective frets to illustrate the impossibility of technical perfection from the standpoint of *manufacture*.

In addition, once a wheel is delivered to a casino, there is the equally inevitable imperfection caused by *ordinary wear and tear*, for which normal maintenance procedures are often ineffectual. Only a complete overhaul is a solution, and this occurs only at infrequent intervals.

Here are some examples of unavoidable wear.

Every time a roulette dealer picks up the ball from its last pocket, places it on the (upper) ball track, and spins the ball on its way, his fingertip inevitably presses down at a habitual spot on the wooden or plastic track. As each dealer repeats this action over thousands of spins, that spot on the track becomes inevitably worn into an invisible but definite cavity, and as the wheel is rotated a quarter turn from time to time dictated by maintenance procedure, several of these cavities become formed round the track, slightly deflecting the ball in an unrandom way from these areas. In other words, the ball track is no longer that level strip of material that arrived from the manufacturer.

Roulette dealers inevitably cause another defect through normal operation of their wheels. Every time a dealer retrieves the ball from the last pocket into which it fell, the back of one of his fingernails tends to strike the metal fret whence he's retrieving the ball, and over thousands of spins this action gradually wears the chrome off the brass frets unevenly at different numbers. Although the difference is undetectable to the naked eye, some pockets consequently become slightly wider than others, thereby tending to trap the ball.

The successful biased-wheel player naturally tries to find wheels in disrepair. In this respect I mentioned in the last chapter that on the Strip in Las Vegas I surveyed ten casinos, half of which had wheels with high frets. Of the three roulette wheels in the Flamingo Hilton, for example, one was in such disrepair that the ball rattled loudly and ceaselessly round the ball track, in each revolution jumping over not one but two obstructive warps. To quote Ron Shelley on this condition:

"Worn ball tracks will definitely cause a bias. Even at the finest casinos I've seen ball tracks with large crevices in them. Ball tracks made of plastic or vinyl will have a raised edge at the joint…this will cause a bias if too high or if the track becomes loose. The roulette ball itself will eventually cause wear to the ball track—some more than others.

"The molded balls used in roulette, such as acetal or nylon, are very close to being perfectly round. These balls will chatter slightly at one point in their spin, and then as the counteracting forces reach an equilibrium, the ball will settle down into a smooth spin. If this type ball chatters all the time…[then the casino must] change the ball…if the problem continues, then the problem lies in the ball track."

The ball spinning round the Flamingo Hilton's high-fret wheel jumped and chattered like a magpie. Of the ten casinos I visited on the Strip this was the one wheel that begged for maintenance and repair. On the other hand, just south along the street the seven roulette wheels of Bally's Grand all had low-profile frets and ball tracks as smooth as silk.

Need I point out to the reader in which casino, all else being putatively equal, we should begin clocking a wheel?

Here are some further examples of defects, cited by Gino Munari, a Las Vegas consultant to casino managements:

"Upon examining most wheel heads, the numbers around the head have been adhered in a continuous circular piece. In that piece there is a seam that protrudes slightly. A ball falling out of the track across the seam will be affected by the abnormality. Simply by betting those numbers that are favored by the imperfection will allow the player a tremendous advantage..." Regrettably, this is not necessarily so.

Munari adds information concerning the bottoms of roulette pockets, where the ball finally rests. These are usually made from an insert of plastic or vinyl material:

"The inserts where the ball drops are positioned in a continuous red and black pattern around the wheel except for the numbers 0 and 00, which are green. [On a European wheel 0 is violet—a cross of red and black.] What is important here is that the inserts are individually seated with glue, and not a solid piece of material [like the ring of numbers].

"The individual inserts are subject to hot and cold temperatures and affixed in a manner that is subjective to the person doing the construction. Several inserts, for instance, may have the last dab of glue from an old bottle that may not be as bonding as that from a new bottle. There may also be some air pockets in between the inserts and the base of the wheel. Any slight imperfection like this will cause the ball to have less resiliency than normal and therefore stay in certain number pockets more often than normal....

"Roulette teams have scouted for biased wheels and have sent teams out to play them earning 'classical' amounts of money, to use the vernacular of the road hustler. In Lake Tahoe a prominent casino was beaten out of more than $400,000 over the course of the team's play in just a couple of days. The players bet the exact set of numbers each spin of the wheel. The four to six numbers were bet straight up, with no other bets placed.

"To ward off suspicion, the team traveled to Las Vegas and legitimately gambled with the winnings. This ploy is a clever [camouflage] method used by most hustlers to cover their tracks. They figure that after the dirty work is done, why not take a shot with the house's money?

"Another team that we were able to gather more information about played two different sets of numbers straight up in a different Las Vegas casino and won $40,000 in an evening's work in February 1987. The numbers bet were 17, 32, 11, and 0." [17 and 32 are neighbors.]

It goes without saying (see Chapter 10) that Billy Walters is constantly on the lookout for biased wheels, and as described by the writer Ian Thomsen in *The National Sports Daily* on June 8, 1990:

"Billy Walters was winning consistently and holding onto the money. He invested in real estate, fast food franchises and other ventures. His confidence was such that he could play golf matches for thousands of dollars. He even captured the 1986 Super Bowl of Poker in Lake Tahoe. There has been recent talk that he won more than $3 million in one day [two days] of roulette in Atlantic City [in 1986]. Apparently Walters hired agents [clockers] to take notes at the roulette tables in an attempt to locate 'biases' or patterns in the wheels. Sources at Caesars Palace [in Las Vegas] say that after Walters beat them for more than $1 million in one sitting the wheel was sent to NASA for an examination and dissection that revealed specific biases—but not for the numbers Walters had been playing [?]. Nobody knows his secret, and he isn't saying, though he admits he has been barred from playing in the major casinos."

It should be mentioned that in March 1989, when I surveyed Las Vegas roulette wheels, at Caesars Palace I found that its six wheels were manufactured by B. C. Wills of Reno, Nevada, and all were of the high-fret variety.

If we add the $1 million win at Caesars Palace to the $3.8 million listed in the Honor Roll of Table 7 (p. 109), that brings Billy Walters' total win thus far to $4.8 million at roulette alone, a world record.

To illustrate the various causes of defects, numerous other examples could be easily cited.

In sum, it's as impossible to manufacture a roulette wheel without defects as to operate one without its developing flaws through ordinary wear and tear, and fortunately for the biased-wheel player, normal maintenance—cleaning and oiling ball bearings—doesn't correct all of the flaws.

Every time a professional, high-rolling biased-wheel player wins some spectacular sum at a casino somewhere around the world—for as we've seen, biased-wheel play is a worldwide activity—and the casino's loss can't be blamed on lax maintenance, manufacturers confide to momentarily anxious customers that the defect has been remedied through a novel, protective design change.

And then the whole cycle begins all over again.

Chapter 19

Recognizing a Biased Wheel

Practical Steps for Detection of Bias

How Long Does It Take to Clock a Wheel?

How long does a professional biased-wheel player need to detect whether a wheel is random or biased? Here are two important, authentic examples.

For our first example we recall that my pit-boss friend on the Las Vegas Strip declared that a Venezuelan advance man claimed that his biased-wheel team needed eight hours to clock a wheel to detect bias, which in Las Vegas, at 110 spins an hour, would be $(8)(110) = 880$ spins.

For our second example let's take the $500,000 win of the Billy Walters syndicate at the Claridge Casino in Atlantic City in July 1989. We recall (from Chapter 10) that his syndicate had six clockers clocking eight wheels for eight days. How long did it take them to detect bias in the two wheels which the team's four actual players then exploited? Of the eight-day period, the clockers spent four days detecting bias in each wheel; but because the clockers, obviously enough, had to eat and sleep, it's difficult to translate each four-day period into the actual number of work hours or spins. My own estimate is that the Walters clockers needed from five to eight hours per wheel, which in Atlantic City or Las Vegas would be from $(110)(5) = 550$ to $(110)(8) = 880$ spins. Thus let's call it from 500 to 800 spins.

A problem with how long it takes to detect a biased wheel is that we don't know the *degree* of bias which a biased-wheel player may impose on the data of his cumulative spins.

Suppose a biased-wheel player decides ahead of time that he's going to play *only* a *strong* biased number. We recall from Chapter 16 that I arbitrarily defined this as a number whose advantage to the player ranges from 20%, with p = 1/30, to 44%, with p = 1/25 (see Table 6, p. 79). As I mentioned, this percentage range is perhaps the requirement of some professional biased-wheel players, who may consider, given their very high wagers, an advantage of less than 20% a financial waste of time.

It should be pointed out that, with the same high bets, a *smaller* percentage return would require a *longer* stay at the gaming table and a *higher* risk of ruin before the goal would be accomplished.

Drawing on Allan Wilson's method of roughly estimating the advantage of the Jones Boys in Las Vegas as ranging between 4 % and 8% (see Chapter 6), I estimate the bias advantage of the Billy Walters syndicate for both the 1986 and 1989 Atlantic City wins as *strong*—as at least 20% on both occasions, with p = 1/30 or larger.

Accordingly, we may tentatively conclude from the foregoing reasoning that, should a biased-wheel player require a *strong* bias of 20% or more, he will need from 500 to 800 spins to check out a wheel.

Practical Steps for Detection of Bias

Given the foregoing, if we sit down and clock a wheel, what will tell us whether, in our cumulative sample, our lead number is merely a *random* winner or a truly *biased* number?

Here is a formula to calculate this: $(n/37) + (2.5)\sqrt{npq}$, which reduces to $(n/37) + .4\sqrt{n}$, where n signifies the number of spins in the sample.

The formula gives an estimate of the *theoretical total maximum number* of occurrences if the lead number is *random*. Thus, in our sample, if the *actual* lead total is *larger* than the calculated theoretical total, we should consider the number on the wheel a potentially biased number and play it. I call this a *play-plus* number (see Table 28, p. 191).

In the above formula the constant 2.5 yields a confidence limit of about 80%. This means that, in using the formula, 80% of the time we will be correct in assuming that our actual lead number is biased if it's larger than the calculated play-plus number; but also, unfortunately, 20% of the time the actual number will turn out to be a temporarily

TABLE 26

Lindau Casino, Germany, 1975

January	1 Actual spins	2 Actual Leader Occurs	3 Theory
1	218	11	12
2	222	**13**	12
3	202	9	11
4	211	**13**	12
5	225	11	12
6	245	12	13
7	189	10	11
8	268	14	14
9	244	12	13
10	212	11	12
11	259	11	14
12	304	14	15
13	172	9	10
14	279	14	14
Average:	232	12	12.5

$(p = 1/37)$

Note: By using the constant .4 (yielding a confidence limit of 80%) the average of column 3 is 12.5; by using .5 (yielding one of 95%) the average becomes 14.

upward-fluctuating random number only *masquerading* as a biased number—on which presumably we would waste our time, energy, and money. On the other hand, if for the constant 2.5 we substitute the smaller 2.0, we will be right only 50% of the time and wrong 50%. If we substitute 3.0, we will be right as much as 95% of the time and wrong only 5%. Then why not use 3.0? Isn't it more profitable to be right the largest possible percentage of the time? Not necessarily, because there is a price we pay. In selecting a constant there is always a *trade-off*. The drawback of using 3.0, for example, is that although the formula then correctly indicates practically 100% of all the very strongly biased numbers—the very best ones among those we're hunting—the price we pay is that it excludes from consideration the many *strongly* as well as *weakly* biased numbers also. I myself would rather delude myself into playing some worthless random leaders in order to catch the more moderately biased numbers. Hence I prefer the constant 2.5, which means $.4\sqrt{n}$.

On the other hand, it is important to point out that the exceedingly competent Belgian gambler and mathematician Pierre Basieux prefers the more conservative $(n/37) + 3.0\sqrt{npq}$, which reduces to $(n/37) + .5\sqrt{n}$. See Chapter 9.

Here are two tables showing that, out of 14 consecutive days in each casino, only (coincidentally) two days in each were potentially playable. (I picked both samples at random.)

Table 26 (p. 189) represents the daily totals for the Lindau Casino, Germany, in January 1975. Column 2 lists the actual daily total of the lead winner, and Column 3 gives its theoretical daily total (calculated via the formula, using $.4\sqrt{n}$).

Let's always remember the simple playing rule: whenever the *actual* total of the lead number is *larger* than theory predicts, we may play the number as potentially biased.

As we observe, at the Lindau Casino only on January 2 and 4 is the actual total larger than theory, being 13 to 12 in both cases. (On the 12 other days, as the actual total is either equal to or smaller than the theoretical total, we wouldn't play those days.) As 13 is only triflingly larger than 12, however, I myself wouldn't play them anyway.

The purpose of the formula is to separate the random sheep from the biased goats. We don't want to play random numbers at all, for we don't want to waste time or money.

Table 27 opposite represents the daily totals for the Royal Inn Casino (now the Paddlewheel) in Las Vegas in January 1979. As American roulette dealers spin their wheels on average twice as frequently as European croupiers (110 spins vs. 55 spins in an hour), the daily total of spins in column 1 here is roughly double that of the Lindau Casino, being on average 420 to 232.

As we observe, at the Royal Inn Casino, again on only two days is the actual total larger than theory: on October 4 it's 22 to 20, and on October 7 it's 25 to 22, so these are the only two potential playing days. But again, I consider the difference of both too trifling to play. In other words, I think these are random, not *strong* biased numbers.

Do we have to do an algebraic calculation every time we go to the casino hunting biased numbers? Of course not. In Table 28 opposite I have applied the formula to typical totals of spins. Opposite *play plus* are the theoretical totals of the lead winning, random number pertaining to these totals. Following the rule, if we have a sample whose actual

TABLE 27

Royal Inn Casino, Las Vegas, 1979

		1	2 Actual Leader	3
October		Actual Spins	Occurs	Theory
1		452	19	21
2		479	21	22
3		380	17	18
4		444	**22**	20
5		443	18	20
6		382	17	18
7		479	**25**	22
8		310	15	15
9		426	19	20
10		344	15	17
11		420	18	19
12		458	20	21
13		500	19	22
14		<u>343</u>	<u>13</u>	<u>17</u>
Average:		420	18.4	19.4

$(p = 1/38)$

Note: By using the constant .4 (yielding a confidence limit of 80%) the average of column 3 is 19.4; by using .5 (yielding one of 95%) the average becomes 21.4.

TABLE 28

spins:	50	100	150	200	250	300
play plus:	4	7	9	11	13	15
spins:	350	400	450	**500**	550	600
play plus:	17	19	21	23	25	26
spins:	650	700	750	**800**	850	900
play plus:	28	30	32	33	35	37
spins:	950	1,000	1,500	2,000	2,500	3,000
play plus:	38	40	57	72	88	104
spins:	3,500	4,000	4,500	5,000		
play plus:	119	134	149	164		

Note: Although these play-plus figures were calculated for a 37-slot wheel, they are reliable in practice for a 38-slot wheel.

winning total is *larger* than the theoretical total, then we play the roulette number the actual total represents.

Using Table 28 (p. 191) is very easy, and let's pretend that we've just sat down to play the 1,000-spin sample of W. Duppa-Crotch (Table 2, p. 46), for we know ahead of time that its lead number (which was number 1) was *strongly* biased, coming up a whopping actual total of 48 times in the 1,000 spins, in which only 27 occurrences would be average.

Again, the purpose of theory is to prevent us from wasting time on roulette wheels producing only random winners. Table 28 (p. 191) assists us in telling the random sheep from the biased goats.

Table 29 (p. 193) lists the appropriate figures illustrating how soon we may begin to detect the biased number lurking in Duppa-Crotch's sample.

By 200 spins the total number of occurrences of the lead random number should be theoretically no more than 11 (see Table 28 for 200 spins), but here it's actually 13. As we recall from the Lindau sample, however, in so few spins a difference of only 1 or 2 is probably insignificant. (In the Lindau sample it was twice 13 actual to 12 theory in 222 and 211 spins.) So we don't play the lead number but continue only to clock. (Of course, while clocking, we bet some insignificant amount to keep our seat. I prefer to bet on two dozens or two columns.)

By 400 spins theory predicts 19 maximum occurrences if the number is random (see Table 28 for 400 spins), but actual here gives 23. In only 400 spins a difference of 23 − 19 = 4 should alert us, but it's optional whether we begin to play or not. By jumping in and playing lead winners at this point we'll catch more random numbers and lose, and catch more biased numbers and win. As I consider that at this early level such wins and losses cancel each other out, I would prefer not to play so soon. But again I stress that this is optional.

Let's jump ahead to 800 spins. By 800 spins theory predicts only 33 occurrences if the lead number is random (see Table 28 for 800 spins), but actual here gives us 40, for a large difference of 40 − 33 = 7. We should now be definitely alerted to the lead number's *probably being biased*, and so we should definitely begin to play, following the rule: whenever the actual number (here 40) is *larger* than theory (here 33), we should begin playing.

Here is an important point. At the beginning of this chapter I cited both the Venezuelan and Billy Walters teams as in fact requiring only from 500 to 800 spins to detect whether a particular wheel is *strongly* biased or not. *Thus at around 800 spins they begin to gamble.* Accordingly I

TABLE 29

From the W. Duppa-Crotch sample of 1,000 Monte Carlo spins (see Table 2, p. 46); the lead number is *strongly* biased, occurring 48 times in 1,000 spins.

Spins:	200	400	600	800	1,000
Actual Occurrences:	13	23	**32**	**40**	**48**
Theory if Random:	11	19	26	33	40

don't consider it at all coincidental that, by referring to Table 28 (p. 191), we discovered that at 800 spins we too should begin to gamble on the number produced so frequently in the Duppa-Crotch sample. After all, if a theory is accurate, it should indicate the same starting point for everyone.

Here is a tip which helps to cut down on one's gambling expenses clocking random wheels. Instead of betting every spin of the wheel, wager only every second or third spin, the way many ambivalent, superstitious system players do. Thus instead of having to bet 110 spins an hour we bet only a third of them, all the while noting on our scorecard all 110 results.

And lastly by 1,000 spins theory predicts only 40 occurrences if the lead number is random (see Table 28 for 1,000 spins), but actual here gives us an incredible 48 occurrences, for a large difference (given the relatively small number of spins) of $48 - 40 = 8$. Thus as the bias continues, we go right on continuing to play this *strongly* biased number... and inevitably win. That's the wonderful thing about a biased number.

We now see how easy Table 28 (p. 191) is to use in practice. Given that at least 800 spins are necessary for a *strong* biased number to show itself, we needn't bother to refer to the theoretical figures until after clocking, say, 500 spins. Then we look to see if our roulette wheel has produced a winner occurring... in 500 spins, more than 23 times; in 600 spins, more than 26 times; in 700 spins, more than 30 times; in 800 spins, more than 33 times... and so on for any number of spins.

Thus when clocking, there are only four figures we really need to remember: 23-26-30-33 for 500-600-700-800 spins. (And in a pinch just add 3 to each play-plus number for each 100 spins, beginning with 23.)

And of these four figures the key combination to remember, of course, is simply:

$$800/33$$

Players desiring a greater assurance that a number is truly biased will have, of course, to clock a wheel beyond 800 spins to many thousands in the conservative manner of Pierre Basieux (see Chapter 9 as well as the Appendix).

The foregoing example, using the Duppa-Crotch sample of 1,000 spins, shows how simple and easy are the practical steps for the detection of a biased wheel or the early rejection of a random one. But this applies, of course, only if we're playing a game of *more* than 800 spins. (For illustrative purposes the difference between a game of 800 and 1,000 spins is insignificant.)

What happens if we begin playing the biased-wheel system seriously *before* the arbitrary benchmark of 800 spins, i.e., from the very first spin of the wheel when we sit down? Then all we're doing is chasing a will-o'-the-wisp, and if we win, it's only through luck, and if we lose, only through ill luck. That's the essence of randomness. We must remember that in playing the biased-wheel system we're hunting for and playing a *particular biased wheel: we're not playing the game of roulette.* But suppose we're stubborn and want to try out the system anyway, beginning with that very first spin? What happens? We're expecting too much too soon, and the Monte Carlo and Bad-Durkheim games that follow illustrate exactly what happens. (What follows may be as easily applied to the two-week Wiesbaden sample of Table 24, pp. 164-165.)

While clocking a sample at a particular wheel, to keep one's seat one may play any simple betting system of one's choice, perhaps choosing arbitrarily two single numbers, separated on the layout, or a section, easily within reach, of three or six numbers. Any favorite, inexpensive betting system is appropriate here.

As I've mentioned, I myself wager simultaneously on two dozens (or columns)—more specifically, on the two that *have most recently occurred*—among other reasons so that I may quickly get onto any biased number and stay on it with one of my two chips, while the other chip covers one of the two other dozens (or columns). (And I like to sit at the end of the table to avoid the crowd and the recurrent arguments over chip ownership.) The worst permutation or losing run for this *last-two-occurring* dozens or columns system is when they come up in the order or cyclical series of 1-2-3-1-2-3-1-2-3...etc., in which at every spin we unfortunately lose both chips. But zeros aside, with p = 2/3 and q = 1/3, and payoff of 1/2 to 1, this is fortunately a rare occurrence. (The probability of an immediate losing run is for one spin .33, for 2 spins .33 × .33 = .11, for 3 spins .33 × .33 × .33 = .04, and so on. As I explained concerning Tables 8, p. 115, and 9, p. 116, for the general frequency losing run the formula is pq^r. For a winning run it is qp^r.)

We recall our discussion in the last pages of Chapter 16 in which we employed the two-week Wiesbaden sample of Table 24 (pp. 164-165) to illustrate my optimal betting procedure of hopping back and forth from one number to another as the *cumulative* lead changes. What we're trying to do, of course, is get onto any biased number as soon as possible. Our motto is that, as we have no foresight and hindsight is useless, we must constantly change horses (numbers) in midstream (as the game progresses).

Table 30 (p. 196) illustrates this optimal betting procedure. The sample (picked at random) lists the *cumulative* daily totals on one wheel for the first week in March 1973, at the Monte Carlo Casino. Each day exactly 148 spins were played (4 × 37 = 148). Thus the total for the whole week was 7 × 148 = 1036 spins.

Hindsight shows us that number 15 was the big winner for the week: on Day 7 its cumulative total reached 44 occurrences, for a favorable frequency of 44/1036 = 1/23.545...or 1/24. (As the sample is cumulative, the *noncumulative* total of occurrences for each of the 37 numbers on a *daily* basis is shown, of course, for only Day 1. To get the noncumulative total for any number, if we use number 15 for illustration, here's how we proceed. Day 1: 6 occurrences [given in Table 30, p. 196, without computation]. Day 2: 19 − 6 = 13 occurrences. Day 3: 22 − 19 = 3 occurrences. And so on for all 7 days. Listed in Table 31, p. 197, these daily, noncumulative results for number 15 are: 6, 13, 3, 11, 4, 6, 1...whose total by Day 7 is the 44 cumulative occurrences.) Using Table 30 (p. 196), here's how we play the biased-wheel system in fewer than 800 spins. (Actually it's the same way we would play it in any number of spins, including more than 800.) To render my explanation rapid and succinct I'll pretend that we don't jump back and forth, as the cumulative lead changes from number to number, *during* each day (which is how the system should be played) but that we wait until the *end* of every day before changing to a new lead number (to be bet on the next day). This, of course, in no way affects the validity of the system.

TABLE 30

One week *cumulatively* by day. Monte Carlo, March, 1973

Day:	1	2	3	4	5	6	7			1	2	3	4	5	6	7
0	8	12	15	20	26	31	35		19	3	6	10	14	16	19	22
1	3	4	7	9	10	13	15		20	3	9	11	14	17	22	24
2	6	8	9	14	21	25	31		21	3	9	16	18	22	23	30
3	4	7	10	17	25	28	31		22	4	5	13	15	19	22	27
4	3	5	8	13	18	23	32		23	3	8	14	19	24	26	26
5	6	11	15	22	29	34	38		24	2	8	14	17	20	24	30
6	4	6	13	17	22	26	27		25	3	8	13	18	24	30	36
7	3	5	6	10	17	20	23		26	7	19	24	26	28	35	35
8	3	10	15	16	21	24	29		27	4	4	11	12	13	17	22
9	4	10	13	16	17	22	24		28	4	7	10	15	17	25	29
10	5	6	10	11	16	17	25		29	2	2	5	8	12	14	18
11	6	9	15	16	18	21	24		30	5	7	10	19	24	28	32
12	6	13	19	20	24	31	36		31	4	7	14	18	23	27	36
13	3	7	11	15	22	27	31		32	3	5	8	11	13	15	16
14	2	6	10	14	18	22	25		33	3	5	6	10	13	16	22
15	**6**	**19**	**22**	**33**	**37**	**43**	**44**		34	4	10	13	17	18	23	25
16	2	7	10	12	16	23	26		35	6	11	13	17	21	23	26
17	4	7	11	18	23	28	27		36	3	4	7	11	17	19	26
18	4	10	13	21	23	27	31									

Note: Total spins each day were 148; hence total spins for the week were 7 × 148 = 1,036.

Day 1. During these first 148 spins we just clock the wheel. By the end of the day we see that zero is in the lead. The Day-1 column indicates that it occurred eight times.

Day 2. Hence we spend the whole 148 spins of the second day just betting 1 unit on zero. Each day the theoretical average number of occurrences of any number is 148/37 = 4. As zero occurred 12 − 8 = 4 times, we did no better than average. But that's not what interests us. Of the 37 numbers, which one is now in the cumulative lead? Looking down the Day-2 column, we see that numbers 15 and 26 tie for the lead, as both occurred 19 times.

Day 3. We flip a coin and, as it's first on the list, go with number 15. Hence we spend the whole 148 spins of the third day betting 1 unit on number 15, the lead number. But continuing to clock the wheel, we see from the Day-3 column that number 26, whose cumulative total is 24 occurrences, did slightly better than number 15, whose cumulative total is 22. So number 26 becomes the new leader.

Day 4. Betting on number 26 for the fourth 148 spins (we're now up to a cumulative total of 4 × 148 = 592 spins), we see by the end of the day, from the Day-4 column, that the cumulative lead has switched from the present number 26 to number 15, whose cumulative total has jumped to a big 33 occurrences (for on Day 4 number 15 occurred a very unusual 33 − 22 = 11 times).

Days 5, 6, and 7. For the rest of the week we do no more switching from leader to leader but happily keep betting 1 unit on number 15 day after day, because as indicated by the three columns for Days 5 to 7, on these last three days its cumulative total (being 37, 43, and 44) is way ahead of that of any other number, making it the continuing leader for the whole game. By Day 7 number 15 has occurred 44 times in the 7 × 148 = 1036 spins, yielding, as I mentioned before, a favorable frequency

TABLE 31

Number 15 **Non Cumulatively** by day. Monte Carlo, March, 1973

Day	Daily Spins	Daily Occurrences	Frequency
1	148	6	1/25
2	"	**13**	**1/11**
3	"	3	1/49
4	"	**11**	**1/14**
5	"	4	1/37 (average)
6	"	6	1/25
7	"	1	1/148
8	"	1	1/148
9	"	6	1/25
10	"	7	1/21
11	"	2	1/74
12	"	4	1/37 (average)
13	"	4	1/37 (average)
14	"	3	1/49

Note: Theoretical average daily occurrence is always 148/37 = 4. From March 15 to 31 the actual daily occurrences of number 15 were: 4, 3, 1, 6, 2, 4, 3, 3, 2, 4, 6, 1, 3, 4, 4, 5, and 2.

of 44/1036 = 1/23.545...or 1/24. We bear in mind that 1/37 is the frequency of average occurrence.

About this fraction 1/24. Whenever we play the biased-wheel system in games *fewer* than 800 spins, it's helpful as well as fun to keep our eye out for any very favorable frequency *larger* than 1/24, because by coincidence that of our benchmark combination 800/33 (see Table 28, p. 191) is 33/800 = 1/24.242...or 1/24. Hence any frequency which is larger, i.e., whose *denominator* is in the *teens* or *low twenties*, i.e., 1/11, 1/12, 1/13...1/20, 1/21, 1/22, 1/23, or 1/24—as in this Monte Carlo game at 1/24—may be blossoming into a biased number. Thus we recall that the very biased number in the Duppa-Crotch sample occurred 48 times in 1,000 spins, for a favorable frequency of 48/1000 = 1/20.83...or 1/21. And the denominators of both 1/24 and 1/21 are in the low twenties. (For games of more than 800 spins, denominators will gradually increase, *viz.*, 1/25, 1/26, 1/27, etc., if we do the divisions using the figures in Table 28, p. 191. (For examples, see Table 5 [p. 75], column 5.) Whether the two numbers represented by these frequencies are definitely biased or not would require our clocking each wheel, of course, for more than 800 (or 1,000) spins.

As we see, the optimal system of jumping from one lead number to another is a childishly simple betting procedure, but it's essential to understand it within the context of an actual game of from 1 to 800 (more accurately, 1,036) spins.

Table 31 (p. 197) is the same 1,036-spin game at Monte Carlo but shows only the *noncumulative* daily results for the week's outstanding leader, number 15, which, as we learned, by Day 7 occurred a total of 44 times. Any *cumulative* table, like that of Table 30 (p. 196), is naturally based on a simple one of daily occurrences like that of Table 31.

Looking down the column of daily occurrences of number 15, we see that the reason for its being the outstanding weekly leader at 44 occurrences is because of *only two* unusually favorable days. These were Days 2 and 4, when number 15 occurred respectively a very frequent 13 and 11 times, yielding very favorable frequencies as large as 13/148 = 1/11 and 11/148 = 1/14, whose denominators are in the low teens. As we know, the theoretical daily average for any number would be 148/37 = 4 occurrences, and a glance down this column indicates the banality of every other single day in not only the first two weeks but during the whole month. On Day 10 the daily total struggles up to 7 occurrences— the best for the second week. And from Day 15 to 31 the results continue in the same abysmal way—only twice do the daily totals get up to even 6 occurrences from the average of 4.

Is there any way we can predict, from a *previous* day's total, whether the *next* day will be either a big winner or loser? In other words, are there detectable *trends*? Alas, without foresight, none whatsoever.

But let's give the method a try. Has a total of, say, 6 the mysterious property of always preceding a big winning day? In favor of this notion we note that the total of 6 on Day 1 precedes the big win of 13 occurrences on Day 2, and the total of 6 on Day 9 again precedes the 7 occurrences on Day 10. (Remember, 4 is average.) But, alas, in disfavor we must point out that the total of 6 on Day 6 precedes the very low total of 1 on Day 7, and from Days 15 to 31 the only two appearances of the total of 6 are followed by more abysmal totals of 2 and 1.

So in a game of *fewer* than 800 spins there can be no detectable trends, because the fluctuations of a random and biased number are too close to be distinguishable. And in a game of *more* than 800 spins there are likewise never any trends either *unless* there actually be a biased number (or numbers) in the sample. As I mentioned near the close of Chapter 11, there are never any predictable trends in random roulette, because events in random roulette are a chain of *disconnected* links. (And in our discussion here, let's define each day's total as an event.)

Given this, we may now answer the crucial question concerning Table 31 (p. 197). Given that a win of eight or nine occurrences would be a normal upward fluctuation for the lead number in 148 spins (for $8/148 = 1/19$, and $9/148 = 1/16$), on Days 2 and 4 do the extraordinary wins of 13 and 11 occurrences (yielding $13/148 = 1/11$, and $11/148 = 1/14$) indicate that number 15 is possibly biased? There is only one answer to this: unless we clock *more* than 800 spins, we simply can't tell. Until then, as we go along, wagering our 1 unit on the leader of the moment, we must accept the extraordinary winners of Days 2 and 4 in the same philosophical spirt as the terrible losers of Days 7 and 8, when number 15 occurred on both days only once in 148 spins, for a depressing frequency of $1/148$.

Just the same, let's examine further this matter of trends, i.e., of whether a previous day's total may be used successfully to predict the next day's total, because the belief in trends is perhaps the preeminent delusion of roulette players. Table 32 (p. 200) (again picked at random) gives us some edifying results for a single wheel for December 1-14, 1990, at Bad Durkheim, Germany.

TABLE 32

Bad Durkheim, December, 1990

Day	1 Daily Spins	2 Lead Number	3 Occurred	4 Frequency	5 Number 18 Occurred	6 Frequency
1	344	19	14	1/25	10	1/34
2	290	12	11	1/26	8	1/36
3	307	9	15	1/21	8	1/38
4	274	30	13	1/21	9	1/30
5	327	9	15	1/22	11	1/30
6	311	15	13	1/24	11	1/28
7	288	**18**	16	1/18	16	1/18
8	395	**18**	17	1/23	17	1/23
9	285	**18**	12	1/24	12	1/24
10	344	19	17	1/20	2	1/172
11	381	36	18	1/21	12	1/32
12	340	9	13	1/26	3	1/113
13	435	19	18	1/23	11	1/40
14	332	16	18	1/18	7	1/47
Average:	332		15	1/22	10	1/48

First, a little theory. In connection with Tables 17 (p. 132) and 18 (p. 133) we discussed the relative *improbability* of a single number's occurring twice or thrice in a row. If we walk up to a table and put down a bet, we have a probability of $p = 1/37$ or 2.70% or about 3% of winning this predesignated wager on the next spin, and one of $q = 36/37$ or about 97% of losing it. Thus at roulette we'll be right on average once every 37 spins.

By the same token, if we predesignate or define our bet as the *lead* number for one whole *day* (or for a session of any length, be it 148, 800, 1,000, etc., spins), we have one chance in 37 of predicting it, and we'll be right on average consequently only once every 37 days.

Thus the probability that today's lead number will be the same as yesterday's (i.e., occur *twice* in a row) is $(37/37)(1/37) = 1/37$, and similarly that today's lead number will be not only the same as yesterday's but also that of the day before (i.e., occur *thrice* in a row) is only $(37/37)(1/37)(1/37) = 1/1369$. And this means an occurrence only once every 1,369 days or $1369/365 = 3.75$ years, extremely infrequent.

Trying to exploit the foregoing facts for a betting purpose reveals how foolish we would be to confound an ordinary frequency, like the repetition of a lead number, with some nonexistent trend manifesting bias.

First of all, as the lead number repeats *three* days in a row only once every 3.75 years, it's obvious that this frequency is absurdly impractical for anyone's betting purpose.

But how about when the leader occurs *twice* in a row? That happens once every 37 days, and we win only once. But here is the point: What is the difference between that and our sitting down and simply betting on any arbitrary number (not the previous day's leader) day after day for 37 days? Answer: none whatsoever, for again we'll win just once.

And that's my point. Past events never promote trends that help us tomorrow. If number 18 occurred yesterday, say, either not at all, or the average number of times, or was even the leader for the day, that has absolutely *no causal bearing* on whether it comes up with any of these frequencies tomorrow.

I have gone into these matters because I don't want a reader to delude himself into thinking we may detect some form of a trend of a biased number in *fewer* than 800 spins. If we won in either the Monte Carlo or Bad Durkheim games, it was just luck; and if we lost, it was just ill luck.

But *after* 800 spins may be a different matter. Given a sufficient number of spins to detect bias (and see the Appendix about *weak* numbers), the biased-wheel system—as all the narratives in the first part of this book so vividly attest—may be exploited with phenomenal success.

Summary

Go to an area where there are plenty of roulette wheels, like Las Vegas or the French Riviera. (For a list of such areas see Miscellanea.)

If possible, always select a casino whose roulette wheels are of the high-fret variety. (Remember that many casinos have both.)

While playing any ordinary, low-stakes game of your choice, clock the wheel in the conventional fashion of system players, using an ordinary pencil and scorecard provided by the casino.

On the basis of the figures in Table 28 (p. 191), move to another table as soon as you're convinced—optionally around the 800th spin—that you're playing only a random wheel.

Never be discouraged by the prevalence of random wheels or surprised by the discovery of a biased one. Remember, if you persist in betting, on a random wheel you can't win, and on a biased wheel you can't lose.

Good luck!

Appendix

In Chapter 16 I stated that the statistical betting problem is how to distinguish between a random winner and a biased winner. I arbitrarily separated biased numbers into three groups or ranges: a *weak* biased number is one with p = 1/35.5 to 1/31; a *strong* biased number is one with p = 1/30 to 1/25; and a *very strong* biased number is one with p = 1/24 or larger.

First, using a sample of 14 days from the El Cortez Casino in Las Vegas, a sample into which I injected the artificially created *very strong* number 0/00 (p = 1/19) among the ongoing cumulative totals of the regular random 38 numbers, we found no trouble in distinguishing the biased number 0/00 from the random winners, because as it was *very strong*, it soon bobbed up to the top, where it fluctuated relentlessly between ranks 1 and 2.

Second, using a sample of 1-15 (etc.) days from the Wiesbaden Casino, I cited Table 25 (p. 170), and, with the middle range of *strong* numbers in mind, indicated the difficulty of distinguishing between a random and a biased winner *unless we increase the number of spins*. Naturally we never want to increase the number of spins: who either wants to or may stay on in *one* casino collecting data for 4, 7, 15, or many more days? Undoubtedly the professionals can do this: for the rest of us, such lengthy clocking periods are unfeasible.

Third, to illustrate the very serious and even more frustrating problem arising from *weak* biased numbers, I cite herewith Table 33 (p. 204) (compare with Table 25, p. 170), into which I injected the artificial, imaginary *weak* number *xx* (p = 1/32), whose probability of success directly reflects the frequency of actual runs of 4 (or more) reds (qp^4 = 1/32) in a sample of 5,860 spins from the Royal Inn Casino in Las Vegas for October 1-14, 1979.

TABLE 33

Royal Inn Casino 1979, Oct. 1–14: Cumulative Top 10 winning numbers plus imaginary number **xx**, whose p = 1/32. Total spins: 5,860.

Days:	1	1–2	1–3	1–4	1–5	1–6	1–7
	26	20	8	8	1	20	1
	20	8	20	20	8	**xx**	**xx**
	3	29	29	29	20	1	2
	32	31	31	1	**xx**	8	0
	24	26	00	**xx**	3	30	20
	18	28	26	3	31	17	12
	21	**xx**	**xx**	31	29	29	30
	34	3	3	33	30	0	31
	xx	2	28	00	0	00	8
	31	22	2	0	00	3	17
	8	24	32	2	21	21	32

Days:	1–8	1–9	1–10	1–11	1–12	1–13	1–14
	1	1	1	1	1	0	1
	xx	**xx**	0	0	0	1	**xx**
	20	11	**xx**	**xx**	**xx**	**xx**	0
	2	0	11	11	11	11	20
	0	2	20	12	31	20	11
	12	20	32	31	20	30	5
	11	32	31	20	5	12	32
	32	12	12	32	12	31	18
	8	31	2	4	30	2	30
	30	17	4	9	4	5	31
	00	30	23	17	2	24	12

As we note in Table 33, the *weak* number *xx* has no trouble in rising on Day 1 from rank 9 to fluctuate among the top 3 ranks, beginning on Day 6, and continuing accordingly through Day 14.

Let's assume that in this sample all other numbers, with p = 1/38, are random and therefore might suddenly or slowly decrease in frequency of occurrence. Obviously we don't want to wager on these random numbers and be drawn down to the depths with them.

Simply because *I put it* there, we know that number *xx*, at p = 1/32, is a sure, veritable, biased winner. But here is the great betting problem: if we didn't know that number *xx* is a *weak* biased number, how could we statistically distinguish it from the fickle, random winners themselves?

There is, for example, number 20, which invariably fluctuates (except on Day 11, when it is rank 6) among the top 5 ranks. Doesn't it have every appearance of being a biased winner? Then there is number 1, which, beginning on Day 7, fluctuates between only the very top 2 ranks. Doesn't it too seem like a biased winner? And lastly, just as we happily watch the true biased number *xx* rise to the top ranks, how can we say that the random number 0 isn't likewise a biased number at around p = 1/32?

These three random numbers, which *mimic bias*, so to speak, illustrate the very serious, frustrating, practical statistical problem of selection in biased-wheel play in the range of *weak* biased numbers.

Unless we inconvenience ourselves by staying a long time in the casino to *increase* the sample of spins, how may we distinguish statistically a true *weak* biased number from the false random winners that eventually fluctuate all over the place and through which we'll lose? This question I have put to two professors of mathematics, experts in roulette theory and play, whom I quote elsewhere in this book, and they both declare sadly that they have thus far no statistical method to offer as a practical solution. For the greater success of biased-wheel play, let's hope that some day a solution may be found.

Miscellanea

Here is a list of the approximate total number of legal roulette wheels in various areas.

Las Vegas (downtown):	35	Dominican Republic:	56
Las Vegas (strip):	135	Guadeloupe:	7
Reno/Lake Tahoe:	85	Haiti:	7
Elsewhere:	45	Martinique:	9
Nevada total:	300	Puerto Rico:	49
Atlantic City:	155	St. Kitts:	2
Mississippi River boats:	8	St. Maarten:	25
Cruise ships (from American ports):	98	St. Vincent:	2
Connecticut State Indian Reservation:	8	Turks & Caicos:	2
		Caribbean total:	257
New York State Indian Reservation:	7	Costa Rica:	11
United States total:	576	Honduras:	10
		Nicaragua:	2
Canada:	30	Panama:	29
Antigua:	12	Central America total:	52
Aruba:	36	Argentina:	243
Bahamas:	29	Chile:	36
Bonaire:	4	Colombia:	26
Curaçao:	17	Ecuador:	57

Paraguay:	15	Greece:	50
Surinam:	6	Hungary:	13
Uruguay:	<u>67</u>	Italy:	90
South America total:	450	Luxembourg:	5
London:	87	Malta:	9
Elsewhere:	<u>213</u>	Monaco:	40
England total:	300	The Netherlands:	80
Austria:	75	Poland:	15
		Portugal:	35
Belgium:	50	Spain:	150
Czechoslovakia:	15	Sweden:	20
Denmark:	10	Turkey:	70
Finland:	50		
France:	500	Yugoslavia:	<u>80</u>
		Europe total:	1,503
Germany:	140		
Gibraltar:	6	Grand total:	3,138

Miscellanea

In my opinion every roulette gambler and scholar should have at least one sample of *actual* roulette spins recorded under the auspices of a legitimate casino, because such samples in handy book form may serve to illustrate and answer a gambler's questions about random fluctuations—answers otherwise obtainable only through tedious mathematical calculations.

At present such samples (called *permanences* in Europe) may be obtained from:

(1) Insider-Press, Postfach 1752, 6380 Bad Homburg, Germany. The advantage of these clearly printed samples is that, on each page, besides the *daily* consecutive roulette numbers the editor *totals* the results for single, three, six, twelve (dozens, columns), eighteen (red, even, etc.) numbers, allowing one to play at a glance a whole day at roulette.

(2) GBC Press, Box 4115, Las Vegas, Nevada 89127. This book company publishes three computer-simulated samples (suitable for most

purposes), two compiled by Allan Ackerman and one by Huey Mahl (see Bibliography). Although one sample, for 25,000 spins, lists consecutive roulette numbers, another sample consecutive reds and blacks, and the third consecutive dozens and columns, all totaling must be arduously done by the reader.

Bibliography

Articles (signed)

Barnhart, Russell T. "The Banker's 'Secret' Strategy at Baccara-en-Banque," *Win Magazine*, November/December (1990), p. 54.

————. "Can Trente-et-Quarante Be Beaten?", *Gambling Times*, December (1983), p. 74

————. "Gambling in Revolutionary Paris—The Palais Royal: 1789-1838," presented at the Eighth International Conference on Risk and Gambling, London (August, 1990); published in *Journal of Gambling Studies*, vol. 8, no. 2, Summer (1992) and in the book, *Gambling and Public Policy: International Perspectives*, edited by Eadington, William R., and Cornelius, Judy A. (Reno, 1991)

————. "How Voltaire Beat the Lottery," *Gambling Times*, October (1986), p. 42

————. "The Invention of Roulette," *Proceedings of the Seventh International Conference on Gambling and Risk Taking*, edited by Eadington, William R., vol. 1 (1988), pp. 294-331

de Lisle, Charley. "We Beat the Wheel," *Gambling Times*, April (1979), p. 38. (On wheel watching and electronics)

Dormoy, Emile. "Théorie Mathématique des Jeux de Hasard," *Journal des Actuaires Français*, vol. 1 (1872), pp. 120-46, 232-57; vol. 2 (1873), pp. 38-57; vol. 3 (1874), pp. 432-61. (On mathematics of baccara, standard deviation, roulette, and minor games)

Downton, F., and Holder, R. L. "Banker's Games and the Gaming Act of 1968," *Journal of the Royal Statistical Society*, Series A, vol. 135, no. 3 (1972), pp. 336-64. (On main table games; pp. 338-39, tables on roulette)

Downton, F. "Rational Roulette," *Bulletin of the Australian Mathematical Society*, vol. 26, no. 3 (1982), pp. 339-420. (On staking systems to exploit biased numbers)

Dubins, Lester E. "On Roulette When the Holes [Slots] Are of Various Sizes," *Israel Journal of Mathematics*, vol. 11 (1972a), pp. 153-58.

Duppa-Crotch, W. "A Thousand Games [Spins] at Monte Carlo," *The English Illustrated Magazine*, vol. 8, July (1891), pp. 723-26. (A roulette sample with one very biased number)

Ethier, Stewart N. "Testing for Favorable Numbers on a Roulette Wheel," *Journal of the American Statistical Association*, vol. 77, no. 379 (1982), pp. 660-65. (To date, the definitive article)

Grossman, Wilfried, et al, editors. *Mathematical Statistics and Applications, Proceedings of the 4th Pannonian Symposium on Mathematical Statistics, Bad Tatzmannsdorf, Austria, 4-10 September, 1983*, Volume B (Dordrecht, Boston, Lancaster, Tokyo, 1985) (On fluctuations of roulette numbers)

Iverson, Gudman R., *et. al.* "Bias And Runs In Dice Throwing And Recording: A Few Million Throws," *Psychometrika*, vol. 36, no. 1 (1971), pp. 1-19. (On theory of runs, short and long)

Kimmel, Stephen "Roulette and Randomness," *Gambling Times*, December (1979), p. 49. (On dealer's signature)

Sala, George A. "Gambling Sketches," *London Society*, vol. 9 (1866), pp. 491-500. (On gaming scene at Homburg)

Schlesinger, Donald E. "The Ups and Downs of Your Bankroll," *Blackjack Forum* (Oakland), vol. 5, no. 2 (1985), pp. 8-17. (On standard deviation in a favorable game)

————. "A Day in the Life of a Table Hopper," *Blackjack Forum* (Oakland), vol. 4, no. 4 (1984), pp. 5-10. (On the difficulties in the life of a successful semi-professional gambler. Also in the same issue, by Case, Samuel, "Any Way the Ball Bounces," pp. 17-20, an article on wheel watching and electronics)

Schneider, Manfred. "Ein Authentischer Bericht über das Kesselgucker-Spiel," *Roulette* (Bad Homburg), no. 54/2 (1989), p. 44, and no. 55/3 (1989), pp. 28-9. (Two articles on an unfortunately unsuccessful, non-electronic, wheel-watching venture)

Scott, Laurance. "Nevada Roulette," *Blackjack Forum* (Oakland), vol. 11, no. 3 (1991), pp. 10-13. (On a successful wheel-watching trip to Reno, he claims skillful, practiced dealers directed a significant percentage of balls into those sections containing his lowest or no bets [this without substantiation], secretly switched balls, altered ball/wheel speeds, and worse; finally rudely barred him)

————. "How to Beat Roulette," *Win Magazine*, November & December (1991). (Two articles on wheel watching.)

Sinnema, Lyda. "Innovations in European Roulette," *Gambling Times*, August (1984), p. 24. (On Mauksch, George S., and electronic countermeasures against biased roulette wheels used in some European casinos.

For more detailed information see Mauksch, George S., "Information Systems for Casinos," *Proceedings of the Seventh International Conference on Gambling and Risk Taking*, edited by Eadington, William R., vol. 2 [1988], pp. 314-29)

————. "Innovations in Roulette Wheels," *Gambling Times*, December (1984), p. 26. (On the new-fret, low-profile wheel introduced by John Huxley, Ltd.)

Smith, Gerald J. "Optimal Strategy at Roulette," *Zeitschrift für Wahrscheinlichkeitstheorie und verwandt Gebiete*, vol. 8 (1967), pp. 91-100

Snyder, Arnold. "A Roulette System That Flies," *Blackjack Forum*, September (1990), pp. 18-22. (Review of Laurance Scott's 124-page book and two-hour video on a non-electronic wheel-watching system)

Thomsen, Ian. "The Gang That Beat Las Vegas," *The National Sports Daily*, June 6, 7, and 8 (1990), pp. 36-40, 30-34, and 30-33. (On Billy Walters and others in a non-roulette, interstate, sports-betting imbroglio)

Thorp, Edward O. "Optimal Gambling Systems for Favorable Games," *Review of the International Statistical Institute* (sometimes filed under *Institut International de Statistique, Revue*, La Haye), vol. 37, no. 3 (1969), pp. 273-93.

Wong, Stanford (pseudo.). "Finding a Tilted Roulette Wheel," *The Player* (Atlantic City), October (1990), p. 10.

Articles (unsigned)

Casino Chronicle, edited by Borowsky, Benjamin (Cherry Hill), September 22, 1986, p. 2. (On the win of $3,800,000 in June, 1986, by Billy Walters in Atlantic City)

Der Spiegel, August 7, 1989, no. 32, pp. 50-6: "Roulettbetrug:..." (On can croupier control ball, on players cheating at roulette by using a laser gun with Freon, and on Vladimir Granec)

Gaming Confidential, edited by Munari, Gino (Las Vegas), vol. 2, no. 9 (1987), pp. 5-7: "The Biased Roulette Wheel." (On some physical causes of biased wheels)

Las Vegas Evening-Review Journal, Friday, April 16, 1948, through Tuesday, May 18, 1948, passim. (On the win of $15,000 by Albert R. Hibbs and Dr. Roy Walford in Las Vegas.)

Le Monde, February 11-12, 1979. (On arrest of cheating roulette-wheel mechanic at Monte Carlo)

Life, December 8, 1947, p. 46. (On the win of $6,500 by Albert R. Hibbs and Roy Walford in Reno.)

Nature, vol. 78, June 18, 1908, p. 147: "Roulette at Monte Carlo." (On annual profits at, and estimating the roulette hold PC of, the Monte Carlo Casino.)

Newark Star Ledger, Tuesday, July 15, 1986, p. 22. (On the win of $3,800,000 by Billy Walters and his partner in June 1986 in Atlantic City.)

New York *Daily News*, Monday, January 27, 1969, p. 4, and Friday, February 7, 1969, p. 3 (On the several large wins of Dr. Richard W. Jarecki at San Remo)

Nice-Matin, August 10, 1978: February 13, 1979; October 30, 1981; August 10, 1983; March 13, 1986; December 23, 1986; June (passim), 1987. (On Vladimir Granec and his associates.)

Omni, vol. 10, September, 1988, p. 68: "Edward O. Thorp Interview." (Includes data on his roulette and other gaming ventures.)

Reno Evening Gazette, Thursday, November 20, 1947, p. 1. (On the win of $6,500 by Albert R. Hibbs and Roy Walford in Reno.)

Reno Evening Gazette, April 20, p. 7; May 3, p. 5, May 7, p. 3; May 11, p. 3; May 12, p. 4, and May 15, p. 1, 1948. (On the win of $15,000 by Albert R. Hibbs and Dr. Roy Walford in Las Vegas)

Rouge et Noir News, edited by Tyminski, Walter (Midlothian, Va.), January 31, 1985, p. 12, and November 6, 1989 (vol. 21, no. 3), pp. 8-10. (On the win of $3,800,000 in June, 1986, and $500,000 in July, 1989, in Atlantic City by Billy Walters, et al.)

Roulette, edited by Wagentrotz, Jürgen (Bad Homburg), nr. 32/4/1983, pp. 58-60, and nr. 44/4/1986, p. 40. (On Vladimir Granec.)

San Francisco Chronicle, Thursday, November 20, 1947, p. 1, and Sunday, November 23, 1947, p. 8. (On the win of $6,500 by Albert R. Hibbs and Roy Walford in Reno.)

The Daily Telegraph (London), February 9, 1979. (On arrest of cheating roulette-wheel mechanic at Monte Carlo.)

The New York Times, Sunday, January 26, 1969, p. 3. (On the several large wins of Dr. Richard W. Jarecki at San Remo.)

The New York Times, January 17, 1946, p. B8. (On the riot at Mar del Plata between the roulette players and the Argentine police.)

The Sunday Express (London), August 27, 1972 (On Dr. Richard W. Jarecki being barred in London as he had been in Las Vegas.)

Time, February 12, 1951, p. 34: "Argentina Bank Breakers." (On the

Mar del Plata roulette syndicate [Helmut-Berlin] that won 6 million pesos [$420,000].)

Vanity Fair (London), 1895 (quoted in the New York *Sun*, Sunday, July 5, 1895, p. 6). (On the anonymous English gambler's complaints about Monte Carlo's roulette countermeasures; article includes the seven-day sample of 4,012 roulette numbers)

Variety, vol. 306, April (1982), p. 1. (On the State of Nevada Gaming Control Board's statistics for 1981 hold PCs for the main table games, including roulette, which yielded 27%)

Books

Ackerman, Allan. *Roulette by the Dozens* (Las Vegas, 1978) (A computer simulated roulette sample of 25,000 spins.)

_____. *Roulette Rouge et Noir* (Las Vegas, 1978) (A computer simulated roulette sample of 25,000 spins on red and black.)

Arnold, Peter. *The Encyclopedia of Gambling* (Secaucus, 1977)

Bachelier, Louis. *Le Jeu, la Chance, et le Hasard* (Paris, 1914)

_____. *Traité sur le Calcul des Probabilités* (Paris, 1912)

Bain, Joseph M., and Dror, Eli, editors. *Casinos, The International Casino Guide* (Port Washington, 1991)

Barnhart, Russell T. *Banker's Strategy at Baccara Chemin-de-fer, Baccara-en-banque, and Nevada Baccarat* (Las Vegas, 1980)

_____. *Casino Gambling, Why You Win, Why You Lose* (New York, 1978/London, 1979)

_____. *Gamblers of Yesteryear* (Las Vegas, 1983)

Barstow, Frank. *Beat the Casino* (Santa Monica, 1979)

Basieux, Pierre. *Roulette, Die Zähmung des Zufalls* (Munich, 1987/1988/1992)

_____. *Roulette Im Zoom* (Munich, 1989)

Bass, Thomas A. *The Eudaemonic Pie* (Boston, 1985)

Beresford, S. R. *Beresford's Monte Carlo* (Nice, 1926)

Bertrand, Joseph. *Calcul des Probabilités* (Paris, 1889/1907/New York, 1972)

Bethell, Victor. *Monte Carlo Anecdotes and Systems of Play* (London, 1901/1927)

Billiken (pseudo.). *The Sealed Book of Roulette and Trente-et-Quarante* (London, 1924)

Birague, Charles de. *La Roulette et le Trente-et-Quarante* (Paris, 1862)

Blancin, Paul. *Les Joueurs et les Cercles, avec des Notices sur Monte-Carlo, Aix-les-Bains* (Paris, 1885)

Boll, Marcel. *Les Certitudes du Hasard* (Paris, 1951)

————. *La Chance et les Jeux de Hasard* (Paris, 1936)

————. *La Roulette* (Monte Carlo, 1944)

Borel, Emile. *Elements of the Theory of Probability* (Englewood Cliffs, 1965)

————. *Le Jeu, La Chance, et Les Théories Scientifiques Modernes* (Paris, 1941)

————. *Probabilities & Life* (New York, 1962)

Borthiry, Enrique David. *El Alemán Que Venció a La Ruleta* (Mar del Plata, 1979)

Boursin, Jean-Louis. *Les Structures du Hasard* (Paris, 1966)

Burnside, William. *Theory of Probability* (Cambridge, 1928/New York, 1959)

Byrne, Edmund F. *Probability and Opinion* (The Hague, 1968)

Comtat, Jean. *Passe, Pair...et Gagne!* (Paris, 1988)

Coolidge, Julian L. *An Introduction to Mathematical Probability* (Oxford, 1925)

Delannoy, Pierre, and Pichol, Michel. *La Triche et les Tricheurs* (Paris, 1983)

————. *La Saga des Casinos* (Paris, 1986)

De Morgan, Augustus. *Essay on Probabilities* (London, 1838)

Derennes, Charles. *La Fortune et le Jeu* (Paris, 1926)

Epstein, Richard A. *The Theory of Gambling and Statistical Logic* (New York, 1967/1977)

Fabricand, Burton P. *The Science of Winning* (New York, 1979/1983)

Feller, William. *An Introduction to Probability Theory and Its Applications* (New York, 1950/1957/1968)

Figgis, E. Lenox. *Gamblers Handbook* (Northbrook, 1976)

Frischauer, Willi. *The Grand Hotels of Europe* (New York, 1965)

Gall, Martin [pseudo. of Arnous de Rivière, Jules]. *La Roulette et Le Trente-et-Quarante* (Paris, 1883)

Goldberg, Samuel. *Probability, An Introduction* (Englewood Cliffs, 1960/New York, 1986)

Gollehon, John. *Casino Games* (Grand Rapids, 1988)

Gonzalez, Michel. *Je Parie Que Je Gagne* (Paris, 1980)

Goodman, Mike. *How to Win at Cards, Dice, Races, Roulette* (Los Angeles, 1963/1983)

Graves, Charles. *The Big Gamble, The Story of Monte Carlo* (London, 1951)

————. *The Price of Pleasure* (London, 1935)

Griffin, Peter A. *Extra Stuff. Gambling Ramblings* (Las Vegas, 1991)

Hopkins, Marsh. *Chance and Error* (London, 1923)

Jacob, Maurice. *Etude des Appareils du Jeu de Roulette de Monaco* (Paris, 1883)

Keynes, John M. *A Treatise on Probability* (London, 1921)

Kingston, Charles. *The Romance of Monte Carlo* (London, 1925)

Koken, C. *Roulette: Computersimulation & Wahrscheinlichkeitsanalyse von Spiel und Strategien* (Munich, 1987)

Lang, Scott (pseudo.). *Beat Roulette With a New Patented Discovery* (Bedford, 1983)

Leigh, Norman. *Thirteen Against the Bank* (New York, 1976) (London, 1991)

Le Queux, William. *Secrets of Monte Carlo* (New York, 1900)

Levinson, Horace C. *Chance, Luck and Statistics* (New York, 1939/1963)

Littlewood, Ian. *A Paris Literary Companion* (New York, 1988)

McGervey, John D., *Probabilities in Everyday Life* (New York, 1986/1989)

Mahl, Huey. *Roulette by the Numbers* (Las Vegas, 1978) (A computer simulated roulette sample.)

Mosteller, Frederick. *Fifty Challenging Problems in Probability with Solutions* (Reading, 1965)

O'Neil-Dunne, Patrick. *Roulette for the Millions* (Chicago, 1971)

Packel, Edward. *The Mathematics of Games and Gambling* (New York, 1981)

Perla, Mariano. *Cálculo y Azar en la Ruleta* (Buenos Aires, 1953)

Player, A. T. (pseudo.). *Roulette and Trente-et-Quarante* (Menton, 1925)

Polovtsoff, Pierre. *Monte Carlo Casino* (London, 1937)

Proctor, Richard A. *Chance and Luck* (London, 1891)

Richards, Steve. *Luck, Chance & Coincidence* (Wellingborough, 1985)

Richardson, P. W. *Systems and Chances* (London, 1929)

Rosset, Francis. *Monte-Carlo de Charless III à Rainier III* (Monte Carlo, 1985)

Rossi, Sergio. *Roulette, Tavola di Probabilità di Guadagno sui Numeri Pieni* (Genoa, 1982)

Sagan, Hans. *Beat the Odds* (Rochelle Park, 1980)

Scarne, John. *Scarne's Guide to Casino Gambling* (New York, 1978)

Scott, Laurance. *How to Beat Roulette* (Dona Ana, 1989/1990)

Scrutator (pseudo.). *The Odds at Monte Carlo* (London, 1924)

Shelley, Ron. *A Roulette Wheel Study* (Atlantic City, 1987; distributed by GBC Press, Las Vegas, Nevada)

Silberer, Victor. *The Games of Roulette and Trente-et-Quarante as Played at Monte Carlo* (London, 1910)

Spanier, David. *The Pocket Guide to Gambling* (New York, 1980)

Stuart, Lyle. *Casino Gambling for the Winner* (Secaucus, 1978/New York, 1987)

Szabo, Alois. *The Pitfalls of Gambling and How to Avoid Them* (Paris, 1954)

Terheggen, E. H. M. *La Ruleta, Teoría y Práctica* (Barcelona, 1979)

Thackeray, William M. *Letters and Private Papers* (Cambridge, Mass., 1945-46), 4 vols.

Thorp, Edward O. *Elementary Probability* (New York, 1966)

———. *The Mathematics of Gambling* (Secaucus, 1984)

Vessillier, Gaston. *Chances Simples à la Roulette* (Paris, 1924)

Villiod, Eugene. *Crooks, Con Men, and Cheats* (Paris, 1905/Las Vegas, 1980)

———. *How They Cheat You at Cards, or Mr. Rakeoff in the Provinces* (Paris, 1909/Las Vegas, 1979)

———. *The Stealing Machine* (Paris, 1906/Las Vegas, 1976)

Vinson, Barney. *Las Vegas Behind the Tables* (Grand Rapids, 1988)

Weaver, Warren. *Lady Luck* (New York, 1963/1983)

Whitworth, William A. *Choice and Chance* (London, 1901/New York, 1951/1965)

Wiley, Dean. *Money Management in the Casino* (Las Vegas, 1978/1981)

———. *Understanding Gambling Systems* (Las Vegas, 1975)

Wilson, Allan N. *The Casino Gambler's Guide* (New York, 1965/1970)

Woitschach, Max. *Logik des Fortschritts* (Stuttgart, 1977)

Woon, Basil. *From Deauville to Monte Carlo* (New York, 1929)